The Nez Percés

THE
Nez Percés

TRIBESMEN OF THE COLUMBIA PLATEAU

Francis Haines

UNIVERSITY OF OKLAHOMA PRESS: NORMAN

BY FRANCIS HAINES

The Nez Percés (Norman, 1955)
Oregon in the U.S.A. (Seattle, Washington, 1954)
The Appaloosa Horse (Lewiston, Idaho, 1950)
The Story of Idaho (Boise, Idaho, 1942)
Red Eagles of the Northwest (Portland, Oregon, 1939)

Library of Congress Catalog Card Number: 55–9626

Copyright 1955 by the University of Oklahoma Press, Publishing Division of the University. Manufactured in the U.S.A. First Edition, 1955; second printing, 1972.

To my wife, Plesah

Preface to the Second Printing

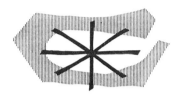

THIS account of the Nez Percés treats them primarily as human beings and avoids, as far as possible, the stereotypes of Indians prevalent in some works. Here are the many problems of a primitive people confronted by a rapidly changing environment. They found it necessary to adjust themselves and their entire social structure to new conditions under the rule of a people alien in race, language, and culture.

As in any other community, among the Nez Percés could be found a great variety of men and women, good, bad, and indifferent, but each with a distinctive personality, and each reacting as an individual in any given situation. With this reality firmly in mind, I have traced the development of the tribe over a period of ninety eventful years, from their first meeting with the whites until the breakup of the tribe.

The initial inspiration for this work came from a childhood spent in the Montana range country, where Chief Joseph of the Nez Percés is a great legendary figure. A study of the history of the Nez Percé tribe was part of the work for my doctorate, completed under the guidance of Professor Herbert E. Bolton of the University of California. Later my thesis received a new title and new chapter headings, and in 1939 it was published as *Red Eagles of the Northwest*.

The Nez Percés

That book, which went out of print during World War II, was the basis for this one.

In the seventeen years following the writing of the thesis, additional study and research on this topic included extensive field trips in the Wallowa and Clearwater areas and traversing the Nez Percé war trail of 1877 from its start in Wallowa Valley to the site of its bitter finish thirteen hundred miles away at the Bear Paw battlefield in northern Montana. In addition, I prepared a detailed tribal history to be used in the Nez Percé land claims and gold claims cases against the federal government. Throughout this entire period, close acquaintance with several members of the tribe supplied me with important supplementary material. This additional research has caused a modification of many of the earlier findings and has added important new ones.

The active, friendly interest of the Nez Percé tribal council was of real help, as were the friendship and assistance of the following tribal members: Mr. and Mrs. Dan Arthur, Mr. and Mrs. Joseph Blackeagle, Mrs. Elizabeth Wilson and her son, Eugene Wilson, Harry Wheeler, and Mrs. Sam Watters. They guided me through the Nez Percé lands, pointed out the significant places, identified Indian foods, told me their folk tales, and displayed many cultural items saved from the old days.

Francis Haines

Sun City, Arizona
June 1, 1971

Contents

xi

Illustrations and Maps

Illustrations

The Nez Percés

Maps

humane conduct of the Nez Percés, coupl
of underdog, won them a great deal o
white men before they were finally co
by sheer weight of numbers. Ov
legends, including that of th
genius of the first water.

This, then, is the st
of the western plat

Introduction: The Nez Percés

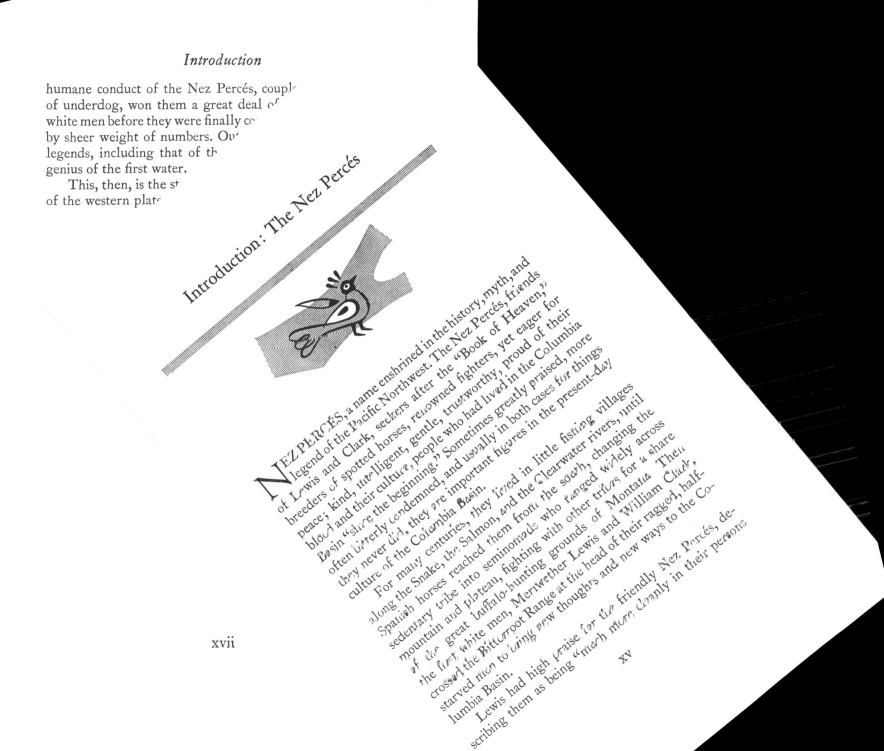

NEZ PERCÉS, a name enshrined in the history, myth, and legend of the Pacific Northwest. The Nez Percés, friends of Lewis and Clark, seekers after the "Book of Heaven," breeders of spotted horses, renowned fighters, yet eager for peace; kind, intelligent, gentle, trustworthy, proud of their blood and their culture, people who had lived in the Columbia Basin "since the beginning." Sometimes greatly praised, more often utterly condemned, and usually in both cases for things they never did, they are important figures in the present-day culture of the Columbia Basin.

For many centuries, they lived in little fishing villages along the Snake, the Salmon, and the Clearwater rivers, until Spanish horses reached them from the south, changing the sedentary tribe into seminomads who ranged widely across mountain and plateau, fighting with other tribes for a share of the great buffalo-hunting grounds of Montana. Then the first white men, Meriwether Lewis and William Clark, crossed the Bitterroot Range at the head of their ragged, half-starved men to bring new thoughts and new ways to the Columbia Basin.

Lewis had high praise for the friendly Nez Percés, describing them as being "much more cleanly in their persons year...

Nez P...
tribe app...
religious pr...
try beyond th...
missionaries an...
nighted savages. ...
missionary movemen...
of the Pacific Northwe...
answering the call in that...
credit one another in the ey...
observe: "We may quarrel ab...
earth, but we never quarrel s...
learn that."

The steady influx of white settler...
vations, and agents who managed to div...
payments to their own pockets. Then rich...
lands lured adventurous, greedy prospecto...
the thousands, who took most of the country...
violate" reservation guaranteed by the United S...
ment, crowding the Nez Percés into a small fracti...
former vast domain.

Finally, white encroachment and Indian resistance...
bloody war, with a small band of fighting men trying to w...
stand the might of the United States. The skill, bravery, an...

The Nez Percés

1: Nez Percé Land

BETWEEN the Cascade Range and the Rocky Mountain system stretches a vast plateau region, gently rolling, arid, almost treeless, cut by deep canyons and ravines; a plateau formed by the surface of an ancient lava flow, which, in ages past, filled the valleys and covered the hills of the former land surface, lapping high on the flanks of the mountain barriers to the east and west. Winds from the Pacific drop most of their moisture in crossing the great ramparts of the Cascades before they pass on, dry and warm, across this inland region. The scantiness of the rainfall resulting from these conditions is evident in the sparse vegetation, the alkaline soil, the intermittent streams, and the lack of erosion. The huge canyons carved through the lava beds are the work of rivers draining the high, snow-covered mountains on either side.

The ragged crest of the Bitterroot Range, the western advance guard of the Rockies, forms the eastern rim of this great basin, stretching from northwest to southeast in a vast sweep, until just beyond the Ross Hole country it joins with the Continental Divide. From this point of junction, the Divide swings south and east in a long loop to Yellowstone National Park, while a massive spur branches off to the west and southwest, extending across Idaho and far into Oregon;

3

a huge, dark, timbered peninsula jutting into the gray and tan of the lava flow. A hundred miles or so to the north of this great spur, a smaller ridge extends west from the Bitterroots across the panhandle of Idaho until it finally merges with the plateau in eastern Washington.

In the deep pocket thus formed between the parent Bitterroots and the two westward-sweeping spurs lies the country of the Nez Percé or Shahaptian people, the Chopunnish of Lewis and Clark. This country contains part of the Snake and Salmon valleys, and all of the Clearwater drainage.

The Snake River, rising on the slopes of the Continental Divide in northwestern Wyoming, swings across the entire width of southern Idaho, eating its way deeper into the basaltic rock which forms its banks and bed. Then it turns to the north in a great sweep, cutting through the mountain spur in a narrow, mile-deep canyon; its wild, foaming rapids and treacherous whirlpools swirling between sheer cliffs. This is the famous Hell's Canyon, a joy to the adventurous boatman. At the lower end of the great canyon, the Snake is joined by the turbulent Salmon, and forty miles farther on by the Clearwater. Then it turns west, leaving the Nez Percé country through the great western gate between the converging arms of the mountain spurs.

The Salmon River rises in the mountain mass of central Idaho, its main branches joining under the shoulder of the Continental Divide just south of the Ross Hole country and the great spur. The augmented stream turns west through the heart of the mountain mass for more than a hundred miles, its deep, rough canyon earning for it the fanciful title, "The River of No Return." In the early days, the wild waters were shunned by Indian and trapper alike, but in recent years many daring parties have made the dangerous run from Salmon City to Riggins just for adventure.

To the north of the Salmon River Canyon lies the Clearwater drainage, sheltered by the encircling mountains. Here, on the westward slopes of the Bitterroots, the heavy rainfall has carved a maze of high ridges and narrow, crooked canyons, filled from foot to crest with a dense growth of evergreen forest, while the creek bottoms are a tangled mass of swamp alder, willow, and cedar. The many mountain torrents unite to form the main stream of the Clearwater, and the canyon maze becomes one great trench through the plateau to the west of the mountains. Along this deep, narrow valley are many rapids and a few box canyons, but here and there it broadens, with small alluvial flats in the river bends where tall pines grow. The many side ravines are overgrown with thickets of syringa, scrub willow, haw, wild rose, chokecherry, and serviceberry, interspersed with cottonwood, fir, and pine.

On both sides of the Clearwater Valley, the plateau is a succession of gently sloping grassy knolls and hollows, dotted with groves of towering pine. The sheltered northern slopes are covered with a dense growth of smaller evergreens.

From the first breath of spring until midsummer, the Nez Percé country is a blaze of color. Blue windflowers, purple shooting stars, yellow bells, blue bells, blue and purple pentstemon, blue and yellow lupine, yellow sunflowers, and Indian paintbrush in various hues follow one another in wild profusion. Mingled with the flowers are many important food plants, the feathery leaved cowish (cous or kouse), the pink bitterroot, and, above all, the camas, covering the open meadows with blue carpets until at a distance they resemble little lakes.

The climate of this isolated region is much milder than that of the Great Plains or the mountain valleys among the Rockies. The high barrier of the Bitterroots shuts out the dreaded northern blizzards with their biting winds, driving snows, and sub-zero temperatures. At the same time, it traps the winds from the Pacific, robbing them of their moisture to be deposited in huge drifts of snow to furnish water for the streams through the dry summer months. The deep valleys, sheltered from the winds, hoard the scanty heat of the winter sun, tempering the climate through the cold months, but this same hoarding of heat through cloudless summer days makes the lowland uncomfortably warm. Then the higher meadows and the mountain slopes are ideal for outdoor life, a convenient refuge from the sweltering heat of the valley.

The Bitterroot Range is also an effective barrier against human enemies from the east. The entire horseshoe curve of the protecting mountains can be crossed in but four places, and, even there, narrow, hazardous trails wind for many miles along the crests of rocky ridges.

The northernmost trail, starting from the forks of the Clearwater, follows a high, timbered ridge for about a hundred miles to Lolo Pass, made famous by Lewis and Clark, and thence winds down the canyon of Lolo Creek to the Bitterroot Valley. Far to the south, on the rough divide between the Clearwater and the Salmon, the Nez Percé Trail keeps to the high, rocky ground except where it dips deep to cross the Selway Fork. Here it branches, the southern prong crossing to the Salmon Valley above the canyon, the northern prong crossing the mountains and going down the Nez Percé Fork of the Bitterroot River.

From the Nez Percé country, a well-traveled trail led south up the Little Salmon River to the mountain meadows near its source, where the Indians liked to camp each August. From the meadows, a war trail climbed the low ridge to the west and followed down the Weiser River and so to the Boise country. A second trail south ran west of the Snake Canyon, up the Grande Ronde River, and on into the big valley until it cut the main trail from the upper Snake country to the lower Columbia, a trail that later formed a part of the transcontinental highway for white immigration to the Oregon country.

Nez Percé Land

Only to the west is there no mountain barrier. Between the rim of the Snake Canyon and the mountain spurs to the north and south lie belts of gently rolling land, each crossed by one of the main trails to the Nez Percé country. The trail south of the canyon followed the foothills of the Blue Mountains to the valley of the Walla Walla River, where lived the two friendly tribes, the Wallawalla and the Cayuse. The trail led on west, down the Walla Walla and the Columbia to The Dalles.

The northern trail swung west just enough to miss the mountain spur, then wound past Steptoe Butte to the falls of the Spokane River, through the land of the friendly Palouse and Spokan tribes. Thus the only real danger from enemies was to the east and south, across trails blocked by snow half of each year.

An abundance of elk, deer, mountain sheep, and bear roamed the hills. Grouse were plentiful on the uplands and waterfowl flocked to the streams. The annual run of salmon furnished fish, properly preserved, for the entire year. The grasses of the plateau supported herds of antelope. Root crops furnished security against famine if game should be scarce. It was a land well suited to the needs of man, red or white.

7

2: The Days of Long Ago

WHEN the world was new, before the first men appeared, there lived in the Clearwater country a huge monster whose gross body completely filled the beautiful Kamiah Valley. To satisfy his hunger, he devoured all the animals for miles around until Coyote finally jumped down his throat and cut up his heart with an agate knife. Coyote then cut the body into small pieces, from which he made the many different tribes of Indians and sent them across the mountains and plains to their future homes. When Coyote had finished his task, Fox looked at the beautiful Kamiah Valley and regretted that there was nothing left from which to make a tribe for such a fine country. Coyote did not despair. He took a few drops of the heart's best blood that still clung to his fingers and from them made the last and noblest of the tribes, the Nez Percé, in their own language the Nimapu, the Real People. To them Coyote gave the Kamiah Valley for a permanent home. In proof of their story, the Nez Percés can still show the heart and liver of the monster, two mounds of basalt across the Clearwater River from the village of Kamiah.[1] This creation story indicates that the ancestors of the Nez Percés reached the Clearwater country so many centuries ago that all remembrance of the migration has been lost.

[1] Kate McBeth, *Nez Percés Since Lewis and Clark*, 257–59.

8

The Days of Long Ago

Artifacts from the area support this conclusion. Placer diggings, plowed fields, and sand bars along the streams have yielded stone implements of various kinds. Mortars, pestles, wedges, and hammers, all fashioned from the hard river rocks, indicate a long period of occupation by a sedentary people. Knives, awls, drills, and spear and arrow points of agate, jasper, and obsidian show a steady improvement in flaking technique, a sign of occupation by a single culture group. This is in sharp contrast to the artifacts from the Owyhee region in southwestern Idaho, where six distinct cultures, with sharp breaks between, indicate migratory peoples.

A village site in the old days was always on the riverbank and near a good fishing place, usually at the mouth of a small stream. The sandy alluvial fan washed down by the stream furnished a well-drained, fairly level plot for the large lodges.

On such a site, a family would settle and start a lodge, digging away the dirt to a depth of two or three feet, some twelve by sixteen feet in area. The excavated dirt was piled in a sort of wall around the edges. Heavy driftwood logs, carried down by the spring floods, were used as posts along each side and down the middle to support the A-shaped roof. Cross timbers were lashed to these uprights to support the rafters. The roof was then covered with large mats made by sewing together stalks of cattail or teasel. Smoke from the central cooking fire escaped through vents along the ridge pole.

As the family prospered and grew, the lodge was extended, with a new cooking fire for each new family, until it was a hundred feet or more long. From the outside, the lodges looked low and crowded, their slunting roofs reaching to the piled dirt on either side, but the system of excavating gave plenty of headroom within. Several doors along each side gave easy access to the central aisle and to the cooking fires. A large lodge might contain thirty families, with double that number of fighting men. One or two such lodges, with the accompany-

9

ing auxiliary structures, would suffice for an entire village. Near the community lodge was the combined sleeping chamber and sudatory for the older boys and young men. This was a large underground affair, its flat roof of split timber covered with a heavy layer of rye grass on which dirt was piled to a depth of several inches. Here, on a bed of dried grass, the young men slept warm and snug with little covering even in the bitter winter weather. Each morning it was the duty of some of the group to heat stones in an outdoor fire and pile them on the floor of the sudatory. With the entrance carefully closed by robes, water poured on the hot stones filled the room with steam. After the inmates had sweated copiously for a time in the steam bath, they would dash from the doorway to plunge headlong into the icy waters of the stream with the skylarking and horseplay to be expected from such a crowd.

Other members of the tribe took their baths in small sod-covered huts built near the water. These frequent baths were for the double purpose of cleansing and purifying the bather, the latter being more important to the Indian. Such purifying baths were considered a necessary part of the preparation for any dangerous or important undertaking, or as a means of counteracting the evil consequences of some past mistake. Even when the band moved to the plateau in the summer to pick berries, brush-framed, skin-covered lodges were usually constructed at the overnight camps for these important rites.

Another underground lodge, more commodious than the sleeping chamber for the young men, was maintained for the women and the adolescent girls. In this lodge each woman passed her menstrual periods, in it each girl lived at the onset of puberty, and in it the children were born. No man was allowed to approach this lodge at any time for any purpose. Articles for the inmates were delivered by women, but messages might be shouted from a safe distance.

All of these lodges were constructed by the united efforts

of the entire band and belonged to the village, although the grass mats used to cover the lodges may have been owned by the separate families. These mats were carried to the camas grounds in the summer, where they were used to cover temporary shelters. Meanwhile, the permanent lodges stood open to the wind and sun, the rafters piled on scaffolding for safe keeping. In this way, the Nez Percés kept their homes much cleaner than did the Indians of the lower Columbia.

In the Nez Percé country, spring comes first to the bold southern slopes of the hills fringing the deep valleys. Here the jutting ledges of rock catch and hold the heat of the noonday sun, quickly melting the snow and warming the sandy soil. Here on the warm sunny slopes the cowish plant flourished, sturdy and vigorous, even before the snows had melted from the sheltered coves and hollows. To these cowish patches the Indians flocked, craving fresh vegetables after their winter diet of dried camas and dried salmon. Large quantities of the succulent roots, steamed or boiled into mush, furnished the central dish of the spring feast, the Time of First Eating. From then on, until the salmon appeared, cowish roots were the staple food, earning for the Nez Percés the name "kouse eaters." Cowish, properly cooked in the form of bread or biscuit, would keep for months. In this form, it tasted so much like stale biscuit that it was called "biscuit root" by early white travelers in the Northwest.

On the upland plateau, many poorly drained spots held several inches of water collected from the melting snows and spring rains. Here, in the deep black soil, grew the famous blue camas, the hyacinth-like wild lily of the Northwest. The bulbous roots of the camas put out their leaves in the early spring, the green tips rising so thickly they obscure the surface of the water. A few weeks later, in early June, a tall, graceful stem rises, with a cluster of blue blossoms. This soon dies and withers, but the leaves, still green and vigorous, set about storing a reserve of starch in the bulbous roots for next year. Then the summer sun dries the surface moisture, the leaves wither too, and the camas meadows are ready for the crowds of harvesters assembled from the many small villages in the deep, neighboring valleys.

The temporary mat-covered shelters were pitched on the higher ground in the groves of stately pines, while the women busied themselves gathering a winter supply of camas bulbs. The men hunted or gambled, while the children played all sorts of games around the camp. The digging tool was a sharp curved stick about three feet long, with a handle of wood or elkhorn tied to the upper end. This was thrust into the ground near the bulb and twisted to break away the sod. The bulb then was lifted out and later was cleaned of its black outer husk, ready to be piled on a bed of grass spread over the hot stones in the fire pit. Twenty-five or thirty bushels at a time were cooked, covered with more grass. Water poured on the hot stones produced steam, which was held in by a layer of dirt covering the grass, and a fire on the dirt kept the whole mass hot until the following day, when it was taken out to be dried in the sun, or to be made into small loaves which were steamed again before being dried. The long period of cooking broke down much of the starch content of the camas to sugar, producing a food resembling the sweet potato in flavor.

Through May and early June, the rivers of Nez Percé land ran bank full, their torrents fed by the melting snows of the high country. As the wild floods subsided under the glare of the summer sun, Indians from their stations along the banks watched for the coming of the silver horde, the great salmon migration that would supply the villages with 80 to 90 per cent of their entire food needs for the year, according to some estimates. When, at the height of the run, every rapid was alive with flashing bodies, and every pool and backwater was filled with the resting fish, the men labored from dawn to dusk with spear, net, and trap, heaping the beaches high with fat fish for the women to clean, split, and place on the drying frames or over the smoking pits. With their stores of dried salmon and dried roots, the Nez Percés seldom suffered from famine as did many of the tribes.

Elk and mountain sheep, slain with slender, agate-tipped arrows, supplied meat for feasts, robes for couches, skins for garments, and horns for craftsmen. Shirts, leggings, moccasins, shields, and body armor for the men were made of elk skin. Wedges for splitting wood, handles for digging sticks, and some of the bows were fabricated from elk horns. The soft, light sheepskin was favored for the ankle-length dresses of the women, for coverings for the cradleboards, and for babies' wraps. From the sheep horns were fashioned the cups, bowls, spoons, and most of the famous Nez Percé bows, most highly prized of any in the Northwest.

Indian hemp, growing in patches along the streams, furnished the raw material for the flat twined wallets, another valued article of Nez Percé handicraft. These wallets, now known as cornhusk bags, were woven in all sizes, from a small purse to a large sack. The better weavers decorated their work with an overlay or false embroidery of bear grass and produced bags that would hold water. Such a bag would survive a generation of camp use, holding roots, dried meats, trinkets, toilet necessities, and the like. After missionaries introduced corn culture to the Nez Percé, cornhusks were used for the overlay instead of bear grass because they were easier to secure and were a more pliable material. Later still, white man's twine replaced the Indian hemp cord in most bags, with a great loss of durability.

Baskets tightly woven of cedar root were used for picking and storing berries. These sometimes had a decorative overlay, but the Nez Percés did not excel in basketwork as they did in the twined wallets.

The Nez Percés

From early June until late fall, wild berries of various kinds furnished tasty additions to the regular diet. Of these, the serviceberry and huckleberry were the most important, being plentiful and easy to pick. The surplus berries were pressed into cakes and dried for winter use, when they were used to flavor the cowish or camas mush. In later times, these cakes became a staple article for intertribal trade.

In time of famine, the people searched the thickets for rose haws and gathered festoons of moss from the trees. Sometimes they peeled the succulent inner bark from the trees. But even in time of famine they did not use dogs for food, as many other tribes did.

Among the Nez Percés, securing food was a family problem, and all game belonged to the hunter who killed it, except in the case of a community surround of rabbits, antelope, or deer, or a group hunt for a grizzly bear. This powerful, dangerous animal was too much for the ordinary hunter armed with a spear or a bow and arrow and was hunted only by a large group. Once in a while, a hunter of exceptional luck and ability might gain lasting glory by killing one singlehanded. A necklace of the claws and a robe of the skin were his honored badges to be worn on special occasions, to the envy of his fellows.

Possibly because bears were usually killed by a group of hunters, the meat of such a kill formed the chief dish for a community feast. It was cooked by being steamed on hot rocks, with pine boughs instead of grass being used as a covering. Four hours of such steaming was enough for even the toughest of old bears, while the resin from the boughs gave the meat a distinctive flavour, unpleasant to most white men.

Although the Nez Percés are usually considered a tribe, sometimes even being called a nation, they had no definite tribal organization until this was urged on them by the white men. Up to that time, they were a group of people with a common language and a common culture who lived in some seventy small independent communities in the same area.

Their name is French and was given to these people by the French-Canadian trappers who visited them for the first time in 1812. There are two explanation for this name Nez Percé, or "Pierced Nose." The first is that the French-Canadians saw a few women in the Nez Percé villages who wore nose ornaments of shell. Such ornaments were common on the lower Columbia, and these women probably came from there.

The second explanation is based on the sign language of the Plains Indians. One of their signs for the Nez Percé was made by passing the extended index finger of the right hand from right to left close to the nose. The French-Canadians assumed that this sign meant a pierced nose. Some of the Indians explain that the sign means a person who would not flinch from an arrow shot right by his nose, hence a brave man.

In his story of Captain Bonneville, Washington Irving explained that the name was usually pronounced "Nepercy" by the mountain men. The common practice in the Pacific Northwest is to pronounce the "Nez" as though it were English and the "Percé" to rhyme with nurse. The acute accent mark on the final "e" is often dropped.

The various Nez Percé villages were usually friendly to one another, quarrels being infrequent and mild. The villages were bound together by ties of blood, since the young people were encouraged to marry outside the village group, which was so often the family group.

Of the ten to fifty men of all ages in each village, three or four of the older and more respected would constitute the village council, an informal group. One of the council would be called chief, or head of the village, and he would be a relative by blood of most of the people. When he died, his son

15

might become chief, but this did not always happen. After the white men came, they often thought of the oldest son of the dead chief as the present chief and called him by that title.

It was the duty of the chief to patch up family quarrels and to settle any disputes. Sometimes he was asked to administer mild punishment to unruly children, for the ordinary Nez Percé parent seldom punished his children in any way. There were few recognized laws, and no law-enforcement machinery of any kind. The few rules were enforced by social pressure and public opinion.

When large groups gathered at the fishing sites or, more usually, at the camas meadows, the leading men from each village would hold informal council meetings to talk over common problems. Even when this council reached a decision, no one was obliged to conform to it. There would be social pressure on him, of course, but that was all. He could not be coerced.

None of the village chiefs had any obligation to become a war leader because of his position as chief. A young man who distinguished himself in war would have more volunteers to follow him on each succeeding raid, until he gained a high rating as a fighting man. If his record proved exceptional, he might even be considered a war chief who had earned the support of all the men of the tribe, but there are only two or three such instances known in Nez Percé history. Usually the various war parties were led by one of the ranking warriors, who also had the right to invite himself to a meal in any lodge because of his exploits.

Each village was considered the owner of all the land near the village, including the fishing place, in all but a few instances. Three or four of the best fishing places were open to all with invitation, as were the camas meadows. The Nez Percés welcomed members of the Palouse, Yakima, and Wallawalla tribes to their camas grounds and intermarried freely with them. Since these were all of the Shahaptian stock, with a common culture and a common language, it is probable that such visitors were regarded more as being from another village rather than from another tribe. Perhaps the tribal concept did not become prominent until the Nez Percés became seminomads.

The tribal religion was a simple form of nature worship with few superstitions or tabus. The personal code of ethics was high. The medicine men were not very numerous or powerful and used their powers mostly to treat the sick. This was a hazardous occupation, for the death of a patient might be followed immediately by the death of the attending doctor at the hands of a close relative of the corpse.[2]

The only traditional enemies of the early period were the Coeur d'Alênes, of Salishan stock, to the north, and the Shoshoni to the south. With these tribes, the Nez Percés carried on desultory wars, small raids taking place from time to time.

Although horses originated in North America, the last of these prehistoric animals disappeared from the continent some 15,000 years ago. Meanwhile, horses had crossed the land bridge to Asia and spread over the grasslands of Asia and Europe. They were domesticated and ridden by the native tribes of Central Asia, probably along the Oxus River, more than 5,000 years ago, for mounted horsemen from that area invaded the Tigris and Euphrates valleys near Babylon about 3500 B.C. Domesticated horses spread westward across Europe and North Africa until they reached the Spaniards, who reintroduced them into North America as a part of their conquest. Gradually several Indian tribes became accustomed to the strange animals by watching how the Spaniards used them. Usually an Indian tribe could learn to use horses in about 15 or 20 years if they had neighbors who used them.

[2] The ethnological material in this chapter is based on Herbert J. Spinden, *The Nez Percé Indians*, and on some field work of my own.

17

The Nez Percés

This process was speeded up by the Pueblo Revolt of 1680, when the Indians of New Mexico killed off or drove out all of the Spanish settlers and captured vast herds of sheep, cattle, and horses. To the Pueblo Indians, horses were of doubtful value. They ate grass that could be used for sheep, they destroyed crops in the unfenced fields unless they were herded constantly. As a result, the Indians traded most of their horses to the nomadic tribes to the north and east, who passed them along, often unwillingly, to tribes beyond.

The northward-moving horses reached the Shoshoni in southeastern Idaho about 1690, some ten years after the revolt. In this natural horse country, the herds increased rapidly, to the benefit of the Shoshoni and their neighbors both to the northwest and northeast. These tribes, the Crows, Blackfeet, Flatheads, and Nez Percés, sometimes bought, but more often stole Shoshoni horses for their own use.[3]

Many times, the Nez Percés showed their intelligence and adaptability by borrowing new weapons, new tools, and new customs from friend and foe alike. It did not take them long to decide to get some horses from the Shoshoni. Since horses could be of little value to people living in sedentary fishing villages, it is hard to conceive of the Nez Percés' wanting them, but want them they did, possibly more for prestige than for use. At any rate, several villages combined their resources and gathered up a large amount of trade goods, including strings of dentalia then used as money in the Northwest. Several Nez Percés took this wealth south along the old war trail to buy the horses.

On their return, they distributed the horses among the various villages participating in the venture. To a village at the mouth of Asotin Creek went the prize of the lot, a white mare heavy with foal. The Indians of the valley, attracted by

[3] Francis Haines, "The Northward Spread of Horses to the Plains Indians," *American Anthropologist*, Vol. XL, No. 3 (July, 1938), 429–37.

the strange animal, spent hours at a time watching it graze on the hills. As news of the mare spread up and down the river, people came for miles to observe the wonder with their own eyes, returning home with details for their own villages. Tradition has it that this white mare and the colt born to her were the foundation stock for all the Nez Percé herds of later times.[4] While many details of this tradition may be true, it is probable that this is the story of the first white horse, rather than of the first horse, and the white mare was regarded with some of the superstitious awe surrounding albino buffalo and deer which the Indians found from time to time.

Most Indian tribes used their horses as pack animals for some time before they tried to ride them. The Nez Percés say that they broke their first horses by loading them with skin pouches filled with stones to accustom the animals to carrying loads. Since they had been using dogs as beasts of burden for many years, it was a simple matter for them to substitute horses for the same kind of work. But learning to ride was a more difficult task, especially since they had no close neighbors to observe. Even the Assiniboins, living next to the mounted Blackfeet, used pack horses for many years before they became accustomed to riding.

In traditions of the Columbia Basin are preserved two accounts of how tribes learned to ride. The Sanpoils, neighbors of the Spokans, watched them for about a hundred years before they secured their first horses in 1840. When the Sanpoils first practiced riding, one man would lead the horse while the rider tried to balance himself with two long sticks, one in either hand, reaching to the ground.[5] One band of Coeur d'Alênes had their first lesson from a visiting Flathead warrior. They were much bolder than the Sanpoils, riding without

4 Herbert J. Spinden, "Nez Percé Tales," *Journal of American Folk-lore,* Vol. XXI (1908), 158.

5 James A. Teit, *Salishan Tribes of the Western Plateau,* 249–50.

the use of sticks, with no one leading the horse. Only one of the Coeur d'Alênes was able to maintain his seat when the horse trotted, and so earned much approval from his comrades.[6]

The unrecorded story of the Nez Percés is probably somewhat like these two. While there is no indication that they had a teacher, like the Coeur d'Alênes, they were more daring by nature than the Sanpoils. In a generation or so, the tribe became noted for its horsemanship. Meriwether Lewis, in 1806, commented on their ability to handle their mounts and to ride at full speed across rough country.

The acquisition of the horse had a far-reaching effect on the culture of the various western tribes, in some cases modifying the basic culture; in others, changing it radically. Any of the buffalo-hunting tribes would be a good example of the first. Long before the coming of the horse, these tribes were dependent on the buffalo herds for most of their food, tools, and weapons, and for all their robes, clothing, and tipi coverings. The necessity of following the herds on their migrations across the Plains restricted the Indians to few possessions and to small tipis easy to carry. The resulting culture in these tribes was so alike from tribe to tribe, and so different from other tribes in other areas, that this is often called the Plains, or buffalo, culture, with boundaries the same as the limits of the large buffalo herds. The influence of this Plains culture was felt to some extent in the plateau area to the west, where scattered herds of buffalo furnished important supplementary supplies for the tribes there, but were not their primary means of subsistence.

Areas suitable for buffalo were also well adapted for horses. To the Plains Indian, dependent as he was on the moving herds for his very existence, the horse was a most valuable servant which fitted into the old way of life with little basic change. The great influence of the horse was to raise considerably the Indian's standard of living, hence the changes were

[6] *Ibid.*, 109.

mostly of degree, not of kind. The Indian still followed the migrating buffalo herds, but now he could do so with less effort and could kill more of them with less danger to himself. He was still a nomadic creature, transporting all his belongings as he moved, but with the horse he could secure more wealth and could carry it from place to place. He continued to raid his enemies, but with greater frequency, greater boldness, and over greater distances. The horse fitted into his scheme of existence so easily and completely that he might be called a horse Indian as appropriately as he was called a buffalo-hunting Indian.

In similar fashion, the plateau tribes were able to adapt the horse to their use by slight changes in their fundamental scheme of living, the most noticeable change being their increased use of the buffalo. This was true of the Shoshoni living along the valley of the Snake River in southeastern Idaho and across the Continental Divide in Montana on the headwaters of the Missouri, for buffalo moved west to this area in large numbers about the time these tribes secured horses.

The sedentary Nez Percés, living in their little fishing villages far from the buffalo country, found horses to be a luxury item. A horse was of little use in salmon fishing or camas gathering. Some of the Indians did spear salmon from horseback in shallow water, but this was not a common practice. Horses could be used, a few days each year, in carrying people to the camas meadows and home again with their crop. They could be ridden on deer or antelope hunts or for visiting from one village to another. Such small advantages, of themselves, would not have encouraged horse keeping or horse raising under difficult conditions, but the Nez Percé land proved to be a fine natural horse country. The foothills and upland plateaus supplied well-watered grazing lands during the summer months, while the deep, protected valleys furnished food and shelter through the mild winters, and stock could live well on the open range the entire year. Natural enemies, such as wolves and pumas, were few. Natural barriers prevented the herds from straying and protected them from enemy raiders. This favorable environment, with some intelligent management, produced great numbers of horses of superior speed and endurance. By the nineteenth century, the Nez Percé horses were famous throughout the western country and east to the Dakotas.

The superior Nez Percé horse was the result of the practice of selective breeding. The poorer stallions were castrated, and the low-grade animals were traded off to neighboring tribes in large numbers.[7] Also, from time to time, choice breeding stock was imported from New Mexico or Chihuahua, with the Shoshoni, Utes, and Navajos acting as unwilling intermediaries. During the first half of the nineteenth century, some stock was brought from California, often by trade. This combination of favorable environment and intelligent management produced good-sized, well-built stock much different from the undersized ponies of the Northern Plains.

The Nez Percés are the only tribe of Indians on record who practiced selective breeding of livestock without being taught it by a civilized neighbor. It is possible that some Indian trained on the Spanish ranches near Santa Fé traveled to the Nez Percé country and taught them the technique. It is improbable that they could have developed such a method by their own efforts in less than a century. At any rate, when the first white men visited the Nez Percés in 1805, they found the Indians quite skillful at gelding animals, to the great benefit of their herds. In addition to raising superior horses, they raised them in large numbers. Individual herds of from 100 to 500 head were common, and Meriwether Lewis mentions one man who owned 1,500.

[7] Reuben Gold Thwaites (ed.), *The Original Journals of the Lewis and Clark Expedition, 1804–1806*, V, 36, 39, 58–59.

The Days of Long Ago

All of the horse-using Indians prized gaudy mounts. Usually they took a white or a light-colored horse and decorated it lavishly with paints of various colors. While the Nez Percés painted their horses too, they had what is probably the gaudiest horse nature has thus far produced. These horses have been described rather aptly as two-toned sport models with polka dots, and the Indians loved them.

By the use of their selective-breeding technique, the Nez Percés were able to raise hundreds of the spotted horses from a few animals. These were used chiefly for war and for parades. The early fur traders called these spotted horses Nez Percé horses, but they are commonly known today as Appaloosas. The origin of the breed is lost in antiquity. Cave artists in southern France painted spotted horses very like the modern animals. Herodotus, writing in 480 B.C., reported that these spotted horses came from Turkestan, in the valley of the Oxus River, and assumed that readers in Greece and Asia Minor would recognize the horse by its name, the sacred horse of Nesaea. King Xerxes of Persia had a number of these prized horses when he invaded Greece. The Appaloosa held a high rank in the legends of Persia. Rakush, the great war horse of the Persian hero Rustam, was supposed to have been the first of the breed.

Appaloosas were taken to China from Turkestan by a general of the Han emperor Wu Ti in 101 B.C. The military expedition to Ferghana, where the horses were raised, cost the emperor the lives of 40,000 men and 100,000 horses. These new steeds were so superior to any the Chinese had ever known that they were named the "Heavenly Horses," and were honored by the artists and poets of the court.

A few Appaloosas reached the state of Chihuahua, in northern Mexico, late in the seventeenth century, probably from the Spanish Netherlands, since they were unknown in North Africa or Spain. It was from the ranches of Chihuahua that the Nez Percés, along with other tribes, secured their Appaloosas. It is interesting to note that the Appaloosa of today matches, in color, pattern, and build, the "Heavenly Horses" depicted by the Chinese artist centuries ago and the Persian horse Rakush as described by the poet Firdausi.

The name "Appaloosa" is derived from the Palouse River in eastern Washington, the center of the spotted-horse country a century ago. Palouse may be a variant spelling of *pelouse*, a French term for green, grassy meadows, such as were found along the river by the French-Canadian fur traders. It may be from a Nez Percé word, *peluse*, meaning "something sticking up out of the water." At the mouth of the Palouse River, in the main current of the Snake, is a great rock ledge, the "something" that sticks up out of the water here to give the place name. The transition from *pelouse* to Palouse, to Palousey, to Apalousey, and finally to Appaloosa is easy to follow. The last form has been adopted as the official name of this breed of horses, but is quite commonly pronounced as though it still ended with a "y."

The superiority of the Nez Percé horses over those of other tribes was noted and recorded by many of the early travelers in the Northwest, and this superiority continued until the influx of farm horses after 1860 practically ruined the range stock. The neighboring Cayuses also raised large numbers of horses of good grade, making these two tribes quite wealthy in comparison with the other tribes of the Northwest, and offering them many opportunities to engage in intertribal trade at The Dalles of the Columbia and across the mountains to the east.

Once the Nez Percés became accustomed to longer trips, they crossed the main range of the Rockies to the Helena Valley, where they began to hunt buffalo. Almost at once, they were attacked and driven back by the numerous, powerful Blackfeet, who had secured an ample supply of guns from British traders coming in from Hudson Bay. With their superior weapons, they opened a campaign to drive the Shoshoni and the western tribes back across the mountains. This enmity on the part of the Blackfeet allowed the Nez Percés to do very little buffalo hunting and interfered with their trade with the other Plains tribes.

According to Nez Percé tradition, a large party of Shoshoni raided the Middle Fork of the Clearwater between Kooskia and Kamiah in the summer of 1803. At that time, most of the tribe was camped in the camas meadows at Weippe, but the raiders surprised a family fishing along the river and killed all of them except one boy, who managed to escape and so carried news of the attack to the main Nez Percé camp. At once the men organized a large war party to drive off the Shoshoni, who were not expecting such a strong, prompt counterattack. After a short pursuit, the Shoshoni were trapped in a pocket in the cliff on the west bank of Cottonwood Creek some four miles above its mouth and were wiped out after several hours of bitter fighting.

It was the custom of the Nez Percés to offer peace to an enemy after such a victory. In the summer of 1805, when the tribal leaders met at Kamiah, Tin-nach-e-mul-tolt, or Broken Arm, their great war chief, proposed that the tribe send a delegation of three men to carry a peace offer to the Shoshoni. His suggestion was adopted, a delegation was chosen, and the ambassadors left for the Boise country over the old north-south trail.

Another important matter discussed by the council that year was the ever-present problem of defense against the encroaching Blackfeet. Their war parties, numbering as many as 1,000 and armed with guns, were pushing farther to the south and west each year until even the Bitterroot Valley was a place of danger. The Nez Percés needed guns to meet this menace.

Far to the east, in the Dakotas, the Mandans and Hidatsa

had been buying from French and British traders for many years. More recently, some of the enterprising Indians of those tribes had engaged in trade of their own, buying from the British and reselling to the western tribes who had no access to the white traders. Each year a number of Crows came from along the Yellowstone River with their horses and hides, paying double prices for every article they bought.[8] The Nez Percés decided to send three of their daring young men to the Dakotas to buy guns for the tribe.

The young men followed the well-known trails across the Bitterroots and the Rockies, up the East Gallatin and down the Yellowstone to join with the Crows on their annual trip. They bought six guns from the eastern Indians, probably using horses in the trade. When they returned to Kamiah in safety, they startled the home folks with a strange story of a band of pale-skinned, bearded men from the east who were on their way to the western ocean. These men had spent the winter at the Mandan villages and had left there by boat up the Missouri. To the Indian tribes along the way they brought messages and presents from the Great White Father, who asked that all the tribes live at peace with one another under his protection, enjoying the benefits of trade with one another and with the white people. These men had worked marvelous cures on the sick and ailing, and possessed many strange objects with magic powers. The Mandans held them in great respect and advised that they be treated well by the western tribes. These white men were expected to pass through the Nez Percé country that fall.[9]

A great council was held at Kamiah in September to discuss the news brought by the young men. A few of the tribe suggested that the strangers be ambushed and slain, so their

[8] Elliott Coues (ed.), *New Light on the Early History of the Greater Northwest: The Henry–Thompson Journals*, I, 354, 361, 398, 403.
[9] Thwaites (ed.), *Journals of Lewis and Clark*, V, 19, 23.

goods might be taken for the use of the tribe. Among the Nez Percé women at the time was one, Wat-ku-ese, who had been a captive of the Minetarees (Hidatsa) and had met white people at Red River Settlement who treated her well. When she finally escaped and returned to her own people, she was given the name Wat-ku-ese, "one who has returned from a far place." Many times she had told her story of the kindly white men, calling them So-yap-po, "the crowned ones," on account of their hats, or Allimah, "from near the water." She was sure that the white men approaching the Nez Percé country must be of the same kindly white people and should be well treated by the Nez Percés. William Clark reported in his journal that he met this woman and that the Nez Percés were friendly to his party from the first, so she may have paved the way to friendship and understanding between her people and the whites.[10]

While the young men were away seeking guns, the three men of the peace delegation to the Shoshoni were killed through either treachery or error. The same council that discussed the white men decided that the fighting men need not be held at home to guard against friendly visitors, so Broken Arm, the great war chief of the tribe, took the war trail south at the head of his fighting men on September 17, 1805.[11]

[10] McBeth, *Nez Percés Since Lewis and Clark*, 24–26.
[11] Thwaites (ed.), *Journals of Lewis and Clark*, III, 77–78.

3: So-yap-po: The Crowned Ones

IT was the time of the fall harvest of camas bulbs on the Weippe meadows, and here the families gathered while the fighting men were away. The women worked steadily, gathering and cooking the bulbs, while the few men idled around camp, hunting a little and gambling a good deal. The small boys had a most enjoyable time, roaming about in small bands, playing war games, or hunting the mighty rabbit and the elusive chipmunk. Three of the bold ones, scouting to the east of the camp one afternoon, were surprised by seven bearded strangers who rode from a clump of pines along the Lolo Trail. The boys scattered like quail and hid in the tall grass, but one of the men dismounted, handed his gun to a companion, and advanced smilingly toward their hiding place, making the well-known peace sign in token of his friendliness. He soon found two of the boys, spoke pleasantly to them in a strange tongue, and sent them on to camp to announce the arrival of the party, each messenger proudly wearing a strip of beautiful red cloth tied in a band around his head.

Some of the men rode out at once to meet the visitors, conversing with them by using the sign language of the western Plains. Once amicable relations had been established, the Indians escorted the weary, half-starved men to the village, fed them well on camas and salmon, and gave them a quantity of food for the rest of their party, still some miles to the rear.

This party of explorers were the first group of white men on record to reach the Columbia Basin. They were led by Meriwether Lewis and William Clark and were of great interest to the Nez Percés, who had never seen anyone like them. Clark's red hair, York's black skin, the spyglass, the compass, the magnet, the burning glass, all added to the attraction.

Lewis and Clark soon left the Weippe meadows and went down the hill to the banks of the Clearwater River. Here they camped for several days, resting from the hardships of the mountain crossing and constructing dugout canoes for the rest of the trip to the western ocean, for the Nez Percés had explained by signs and a crude map drawn on elkskin with charcoal that there was but one portage ahead of them. When the canoes were ready, the horses belonging to the party were branded and turned over to one of the lesser chiefs, Twisted Hair, who promised to keep them until the travelers returned in the spring. The saddles and some of the supplies were cached along the riverbank, medals were presented to the chiefs, together with a small flag for Broken Arm on his return from war, and the whites floated off down the river, leaving the tribe with plenty to talk about during the long winter evenings around the lodge fires.[1]

Soon after the white men left, Broken Arm returned at the head of his triumphant forces, with forty-two Shoshoni scalps as the first payment for the three peace envoys killed. Only three Nez Percés had been lost in the fighting, making this a notable victory.[2] Broken Arm accepted with pleasure the medal and flag left for him by the whites and showed considerable interest in every detail of their dress and equipment. Perhaps he considered it would be to the advantage of the

[1] Thwaites (ed.), *Journals of Lewis and Clark*, III, 77–98.
[2] *Ibid.*, V, 24.

tribe to secure a formal alliance with the white men when they returned the next spring.

Meanwhile, Twisted Hair had rather neglected his duties in caring for the horses left with him. Some of the young men had ridden them during the fall hunt, and six of the horses had developed large sores on their backs. Broken Arm far overstepped tribal custom by taking all the horses from Twisted Hair and putting them with his own herd to keep them safe.[3]

Toward the end of April, 1806, word reached the Nez Percés that the white men had started up the Columbia on their way east. They traded off their canoes at the mouth of the Walla Walla River, planning to travel by land across to the Missouri. Shortly after they took to the trail, they were met by Chief Big Horn from the Grande Ronde River. He had guided Lewis and Clark down the river the previous fall as far as The Dalles, securing friendly receptions for them at the various Indian villages along the way. Now he came to help them on the return trail.

The winter of 1805–1806 was one of great severity in the Columbia Basin. The snows came early and stayed late, piling up in huge drifts on the higher elevations. Supplies stored for an ordinary winter were all gone before the late spring brought out the cowish. The Nez Percés were reduced to short rations, and used quantities of boiled moss to eke out their scanty supplies. They needed an early run of salmon, but the late spring and the extra runoff from the melting snows delayed the fish beyond their usual schedule. The severe winter played havoc with the game, too, killing many of the deer and antelope.

Under such circumstances, it was difficult for the Nez Percés to supply their visitors with more than a bare subsistence ration. The roots kept them from starving, but did not satisfy the hunger of men used to plenty of meat in their diet.

[3] *Ibid.,* V, 6–7.

They bought a few dogs from the Indians, who were rather disgusted that anyone would eat such food. Chief Big Horn did what he could to meet the emergency, but there were too many of them for his meager resources. Broken Arm heard of the problem and sent his son with four other men to deliver a supply of roots at the mouth of Lapwai Creek and to guide them across the hills to Kamiah, but the relief party missed the travelers in a heavy spring snowstorm.

When the explorers stopped at Twisted Hair's village for their horses, they learned of the difficulties of the previous fall. Even though Twisted Hair did not like to have the young men ride the horses, under tribal custom he could do no more than show his disapproval, which was not enough, since he was not an important man in the tribe. It took a great war chief like Broken Arm to handle such an occasion. Twisted Hair tried to convince the whites of his good intentions. Under his direction, his men had carried to safety the cache of saddles exposed by the spring rains and had taken care of other articles cached or lost on the westward trip, to the surprised appreciation of Captain Lewis.

Up to this point, the relationship of the explorers to the Nez Percés had been rather friendly, but no more so than it had been with several other tribes. It was the marked kindness of Broken Arm which smoothed out the difficulties between the two groups and cemented the lasting friendship that attracted so much interest in later years. Until Lewis and Clark arrived at Kamiah village, their accounts of the Nez Percés showed little of the appreciation so obvious in their journals a few days later, after Broken Arm had used his prestige to have formal guest status extended to the entire party.[4]

All sorts of people were welcomed to the Nez Percé country and, if they behaved themselves well, were allowed to join the tribe. This custom included people from enemy groups,

4 *Ibid.*, V, 23.

even war captives, which helps to explain the presence of a Shoshoni man at the mouth of Lapwai Creek. Through this fortunate circumstance, the two groups were able to communicate with each other across the barrier of alien tongues, but only in a slow, roundabout fashion.

Although this man was from a different band than Sacagawea, the Bird Woman, the two could talk readily to each other, and each could talk to his own companions. This Shoshoni remained with the party for some time as interpreter and came to regard himself as quite an important person, but the whites could always deflate his ego sufficiently merely by ignoring him for a few hours.[5]

Lewis carried instructions from President Jefferson to hold a formal council with each village or tribe along the route when it was possible. Here he could give the Indians instructions from the President and learn from them a great deal about their country and their neighbors. At Kamiah such a council was held with Chief Broken Arm as host. After the formalities of opening the council had been observed, Captain Lewis began his speech by saying one sentence in English. One of his men translated it into French for Toussaint Charbonneau, Sacagawea's husband, who put it into Hidatsa for Sacagawea, who changed it to Shoshoni for the interpreter, who repeated it in Shahaptian, the language of the Nez Percés. One of the tribe, possessed of a loud clear voice, repeated it to the entire assembly. After Lewis had finished and Broken Arm had responded, the same process was reversed.[6] Under these conditions, sentences were kept short and simple. Flights of oratory were out of the question, even when sign language could be used to help clarify the meaning. It would be interesting to know just what the Nez Percés thought Captain Lewis said, in comparison to what he did say.

At this council, Lewis told the Indians that all their land

[5] *Ibid.*, IV, 359; V, 9.
[6] *Ibid.*, V, 19.

had been annexed by the United States. He explained to them the advantages of their having a good trading post nearby and asked them to live at peace with all their neighbors. He invited the tribe to send two or three of their men east with him to Washington, so they could observe for themselves the country of the white men.

The Nez Percés found these suggestions quite to their liking. They explained how they lived at peace with all their neighbors except the Shoshoni to the south. They had tried to make a peace with them, too, but their envoys had been killed. They suggested that the whites would have to arrange some sort of peace between the western tribes and the Blackfeet and Hidatsa across the mountains or there would be fighting every time the western tribes went to a trading post on the Missouri. They were not sure that they wanted to send men to Washington, but they would make a decision before the expedition left.

After all this discussion on both sides, the council voted to accept the peace and friendship of the whites and to extend to them the status of guests. The action of the council was then announced to the whole gathering, and all who approved were invited to eat from the bowls of steaming mush, made by boiling together camas bulbs, cowish roots, and dried berries. Anyone voting against the action was expected to go hungry, but this time all the men came forward to eat. As they gathered around the food, the women wailed and mussed their hair in token of their fears of such change.[7] Perhaps their actions were a necessary formality rather than an expression of real concern.

Although the Lolo Trail was usually open to travel by the end of May, in 1806 the snows still blocked the way until the end of June. The explorers, with their work completed among the Nez Percés, were anxious to be on their way. They now had plenty of camas and cowish for their daily needs and were

[7] *Ibid.*, V, 23.

able to store some away for their trip across the mountains. This they secured by giving each man a little packet of trade goods and scattering them over the whole area to do their buying. In this trading, the Nez Percés were much more interested in useful articles such as knives, awls, and needles, than in the gaudy trinkets, except that they had a great fondness for blue beads.

Hunting was poor that spring after the severe winter, and the hunters could not keep the camp supplied with meat, so a few of the poorer horses were killed for food. While the Nez Percés did not kill horses for their meat, even in time of famine, they had no scruples about eating horse meat, as did their Shoshoni neighbors, who ate almost everything else in the animal kingdom.

The root diet, so satisfactory to the Indians, played queer pranks with the digestive systems of the whites. Some relief was gained by using a root which Sacagawea dug for them, but the entire party dreamed of the days of plenty which would be theirs when they reached the elk and buffalo ranges and could feast on juicy roasted ribs or broiled tongue, or possibly a raw liver, still warm, with a few drops of gall for seasoning.

William Clark was the doctor for the party and had a small chest of the common medicines and drugs to treat the sick. Once the Indians learned of this, their sick and ailing came each morning to Clark's lodge for treatment. While the average health of the tribe was high, for those days, many of them had sore eyes, possibly from the smoke and dust. Clark, with his kit of simple remedies, his practical experience, and his cheerful smile, was of real service to most of his patients. He worked some quick cures by lancing boils, dressing sores, and the like. For the sore eyes he used a mild eyewash. On the more difficult cases, he used a good deal of faith healing, always being careful to give no medicine or treatment that might injure the patient.

So-yap-po: *The Crowned Ones*

The sympathy shown the weak and distressed and the care this tribe gave to helpless invalids are strikingly illustrated by the case of one chief brought in for treatment. He had been paralyzed for years, even being unable to wash his face and hands. When this chief and his relatives heard of Clark's skill, they sought his aid. The paralyzed man was brought in and examined, but Clark could find no apparent reason for his condition. He gave the man a few pills and explained he could do nothing more, but the chief was brought back each day, hoping for some miracle.

Finally Clark decided to try a severe sweat bath, with the patient supported in the bath by his father during the treatment. After the man had been thoroughly sweated, he was rubbed down and given a sedative to relieve the pain caused by such drastic treatment. Much to the surprise of Clark and the joy of the patient, a decided improvement resulted. Day by day the patient improved until he could again wash and feed himself. Before Clark left, the man could walk a little, although he was still weak from his long period of inactivity.[8]

Even with such a cure to their credit, it is a tribute to the character and personality of these two leaders, ragged and penniless, destitute and half-starved, that they supervised their men so that no unpleasant incident marred their friendship with the Nez Percés and that they so impressed this tribe that their names are household words a century and a half later. On the other hand, consider the character of the Nez Percés that they should have been so praised for their honesty, cleanliness, intelligence, and high social standards. The peace made at the great council on the banks of the Clearwater endured for seventy years, even when the Indians were under serious provocations at the hands of intruding white men.

In Nez Percé history, this visit of Lewis and Clark became the important event, dividing the old days from the new.

[8] *Ibid.*, V, 22, 62, 66, 72, 78, 82, 88–89.

The Nez Percés

Before that time, they were a sedentary, isolated tribe of fishing Indians, living in their small, permanent villages. Then, stimulated by the strangers and emboldened by the possession of guns, they mounted their horses and flocked to the buffalo country in great numbers, changing in a few years to a seminomadic people ranging from central Montana and western Wyoming to The Dalles and the Yakima Valley. They combined forces with the Flatheads to hold in check the dreaded Blackfeet, and thus made good their claim to a share of the buffalo country. The rapidity of this change is startling. In 1806, Lewis and Clark found them living in large community lodges constructed of heavy timbers and grass mats. Only one small band had occasionally hunted the buffalo. Six years later, a large village at the mouth of the Clearwater was using skin tipis, and about half the tribe were going to the buffalo country from time to time.

Right: *The Grand Canyon of the Snake River forms the boundary between Oregon and Idaho.*

Overleaf: *Wallowa Lake, in the Wallowa Mountains of northeastern Oregon, is in the area once claimed by Old and Young Joseph's band of Nez Percés.*

Appaloosa stallion.

Appaloosa mares in the Nez Percé range country.

Woman's saddle and trappings, Kamiah, about 1891.

4: New Ways

WHEN the Nez Percés traveled across the mountains to the east, they carried with them many articles of trade goods which they exchanged with the buffalo tribes for Plains products. From their own country came dried berries and cakes of camas and cowish; horns of the mountain sheep, and the bowls, ladles, and spoons made from them; baskets of cedar root, flat wallets of Indian hemp, eagle feathers, arrows, and the famous Nez Percé bows, each valued at the price of a good horse. In addition, they had salmon oil and dried salmon, pounded to powder, both packed in salmon skins; Indian hemp and twine; dentalia and other sea shells, all obtained at The Dalles. From the Plains tribes, they secured buffalo products—bone beads, horn spoons, pemmican, wallets and parfleches of rawhide, and buffalo robes, finely tanned and ornamented with quill work, the handiwork of the Crow women. Another article they wanted was the Sioux war bonnet with its long double tail of eagle feathers, an article useless except to a horseman, and unknown west of the mountains in earlier times.

Peacefully inclined bands, interested mostly in hunting and trading, usually headed for one of the recognized trading areas, but two roving bands, even war parties, could scarcely meet on the Plains without pausing for the purpose of swapping trinkets, wearing apparel, and horses before they got around to the chief sport, fighting. A truce established on such an occasion was binding until the two parties had passed from each other's sight, but no longer. Men who had smoked with each other and traded goods were now bent on killing one another by trickery if possible.

The intelligent Nez Percés had always been great borrowers. Now they had the whole Plains culture complex spread out before them and they borrowed profusely. One of them is reported to have skulked for days around a Crow encampment just to learn some of their dances. Later they borrowed dances from other tribes, until now it would be a rash man who could observe the Nez Percé dances and say that any one item was from their own culture.

The Nez Percés borrowed the Eagle feather headdress, the Plains-type pipe, the handy little war club, and horse trappings galore. They used the travois in the buffalo country, even though the Lolo Trail was too rough for them to take their tipi poles across the mountains. They adopted the Indian suitcase, the parfleche, from the Crows, and, although the parfleche is rather easy to make, once you have the pattern, the Nez Percés still get theirs from the Crows. They say, in explanation, "We make cornhusk bags. The Crows make parfleches. We trade."

The "stick game," played by passing a small bit of stick or bone from hand to hand, until the opponent guesses where it is, the sacrifice of a horse at the grave of the dead, and many other practices were borrowed with the material culture, until a casual observer might easily mistake the Nez Percés for a Plains tribe, but underneath remained a solid core of the old ways.

The practice of buffalo hunting had a profound effect on the Nez Percé social grouping. Each fall a hunting party would be made up of families from various villages. They would cross the mountains for a stay of from one to five years. Their old ties with their villages were weakened. Now they looked to the hunters and fighters of their band for leadership, since village chiefs had no authority away from the villages, even if they went along.

When the families traveled, they needed tipis to live in, so the old community houses were soon discarded. Even the Indians who did not go to the buffalo country traded for tipis. Nothing was owned in common anymore except the fishing place and the camas grounds.

In the buffalo country, the bands ranged from the Sun River to the Yellowstone, and east to the bend of the Mussel-shell. Among the tribes they met there, the Blackfeet were their bitter enemies until 1855. The Nez Percés skirmished from time to time with the Crows, but there is an old tradition of friendship between the two tribes. In later years, the Nez Percés sometimes fought the Sioux and the Assiniboins farther to the east. They usually had the Flatheads and the Lemhi Shoshoni for allies in their warfare against the Plains tribes.

And yet with all this change, many hundreds of the Nez Percés never went to the buffalo country. They lived on the old village sites and fished for salmon. They dug the cowish and camas. They picked the berries and hunted the deer and elk. They held fast to much of the old culture until the white men came with the gold rush.

5: Fur Posts Change the Picture

ONCE the Lewis and Clark expedition had blazed the trail, fur traders soon made their appearance in the Columbia Basin, Canadians among the Flatheads and Americans from St. Louis in the Bitterroot Valley and on the Three Forks of the Missouri. Then John Jacob Astor's enterprise established a post at the mouth of the Columbia, and his employees soon reached the Nez Percé country.

In late December, 1811, eleven ragged, starving white men reached the tribal villages on the Salmon River below the mouth of the Little Salmon.[1] They were a portion of the Wilson Price Hunt party that had left St. Louis in 1810 and had finally met with disaster at Caldron Linn (now Milner Rapids), where the Snake River plunges into the tortuous canyon carved through the lava beds of southern Idaho. Here the party, forced to abandon their boats, divided into several small groups so that they might have a better chance of living off the country as they continued their way to Astoria. Most of their goods were cached nearby, to be recovered later.

Eleven of the men, led by Donald McKenzie, headed north, hoping to cross the mountains and strike the trail used by Lewis and Clark. After two months of incredible hardship

[1] Washington Irving, *Astoria*, 210.

46

and suffering, they managed to traverse the country appropriately named the Seven Devils, a rough mountain wilderness buried under several feet of snow, where a single mountain sheep supplied enough meat to save the party from starvation. They were greatly pleased to reach the lower country, where the absence of snow facilitated travel and the sight of range horses indicated the presence of Indian villages.

The Nez Percé villages welcomed the wayfarers, supplied them with food and clothing, and sold them canoes for the rest of the trip, which was completed with little difficulty. That spring, when the partners of the Pacific Fur Company met at Astoria to discuss plans for the coming winter, they were interested in the accounts of the Nez Percés given by Lewis and Clark and by McKenzie, with the result that they decided to send McKenzie with a large supply of goods to winter with the tribe. At the same meeting, they laid plans for a post near Spokane Falls under the management of John Clarke to compete with the Northwest Company post built there two years before under the direction of David Thompson. The two parties traveled together up the Columbia and the Snake in canoes until they reached the mouth of the Palouse River. Here Clarke made arrangements to leave his canoes in charge of the local chief. He packed his goods across country on horses purchased from the Indians, while McKenzie went on up the Snake, looking for a good campsite near the mouth of the Clearwater.

Clarke did not get on well with the Palouse tribe. The Indians were unable or unwilling to recognize his superiority or to kowtow to the great trader in their midst. It angered Clarke that the Indians did not rush to sell him all the horses he wanted at the prices he chose to pay. Members of his party shared his anger since they could not buy riding horses and had to trudge across the country to the Spokane River. Clarke also considered it a personal insult that a few articles had been

47

stolen from the camp during the time. After several days of increasing friction, he managed to buy enough pack animals for his goods and proceeded to his winter quarters, but the feeling of resentment built up on both sides smouldered through the winter.

McKenzie located his winter camp on the north bank of the Clearwater River a few hundred yards above its confluence with the Snake.[2] Here on the great trading trail, with bands of Indians constantly passing back and forth, he expected a prosperous season. He called a council of the leading men and explained that the trade goods on display would be given in exchange for furs, particularly beaver, but in some way his presentation of the subject had been faulty, or the account does not give all the details, for the Nez Percés showed no desire to trade and from that day on showed an increasing hostility toward the whites. From the Indian point of view, the proposal was a blow to their pride. These spirited warriors dominated the entire region from the Cascades to the Rockies and their influence was great even in the buffalo country to the east. They dictated the intertribal policies at the great council of the tribes held each spring in the Yakima Valley; they led the allied war parties against the common foes; they guarded the mountain passes to the east and south. Their horses supplied them with all the best in Indian trade at no special effort on their part. One can imagine, then, their indignation toward a stranger who asked that they do woman's work for a few gaudy trinkets which did not appeal to them. They could secure guns, ammunition, knives, and blankets in exchange for some of their surplus horses without stooping to do such labor.

Too late McKenzie realized his mistake. Although there was little chance of trade with the tribe, he hoped to salvage something from the wreck of his plans by sending out parties

---

[2] Francis Haines, "McKenzie's Winter Camp, 1812–13," *Oregon Historical Quarterly*, Vol. XXXVII, No. 4 (December, 1936), 329–33.

of his own men equipped for trapping, but the Indians refused them the right to trap, or even to hunt, and sent them back to camp minus their equipment. McKenzie then decided to move to some better location farther up the river, but he disliked making such a drastic change without consulting his superiors. In December, 1812, he set out for the Spokane post to discuss plans with Clarke. During his stay there, he learned of the war between the United States and Great Britain from a Northwest Company man, McTavish, who had just come across the mountains with supplies and reinforcements for Thompson. McTavish reported that a British warship was expected at the mouth of the Columbia to capture Astoria. McKenzie decided to carry this important news to Astoria at once to prevent a surprise attack. He returned to his post on the Clearwater, cached his supplies, and hastened down the river with all his men.

Now the Nez Percés had no more compunction about stealing from strangers than did most other tribes. Although they had been rather friendly toward Lewis and Clark from the first, the latter lost several small articles to petty thieves before they were received as guests of the tribe in a formal ceremony. After the ceremony, it was no longer permissible under the tribal code to steal from the guests, and some of the articles stolen the previous fall were returned, even though it cost one of the chiefs a horse to get back a tomahawk pipe so he could return it to the whites.

Since McKenzie and his men had not been given guest status and had insulted the men with a request that they do trapping, it was permissible to rifle their caches. No sooner had the canoes of the traders disappeared down the river than the men dug up the goods and divided them. When McKenzie returned a month later to retrieve his goods and to purchase horses for Clarke to pack out his furs in the spring, he found an empty hole where his cache had been. The Scotchman was not the type to submit tamely to such a loss and appealed to the chiefs to give him back his goods, but they disclaimed all responsibility in the matter.

Failing by peaceful means, McKenzie decided on drastic action. He led his men, fully armed, into the Indian village early one morning, taking them by surprise. The men kept the Indians at a distance with drawn bayonets while McKenzie and a comrade entered the nearest lodge, cutting and ripping open everything that might possibly contain any of the stolen property. The angry Indians, pressing against the ring of armed guards, hardly knew what to do. While they could wipe out the whites in a pitched battle, they would lose heavily and their families would suffer. A dependence on this factor had led McKenzie to his seemingly hazardous course of action.

After five or six lodges had been searched in the manner mentioned, the chiefs called for a parley. Sufficient goods had been found to prove the guilt of their band, so they proposed a discussion on a nearby hill, but McKenzie knew that once he left the camp his chance was gone, so he refused to move. The chiefs finally agreed to return his property in order to get rid of him, surrendering about a third of their loot.

Following this incident, the hostility of the Indians soon reduced the fur men to short rations. Their camp, located by a busy trail, was a poor locality for game. The Indians in the village depended mostly on dried camas and dried salmon for their needs, supplemented by some fresh meat from the mountains to the south. The traders preferred fresh meat and had no supplies of dried food stored for a siege. They had planned to secure part of their meat by hunting and to purchase the rest of it in the form of low-grade horses from the Indians. This plan worked quite well until the dispute, but now the Nez Percés, anxious to be rid of their uninvited guests, decided to starve them into leaving by refusing to sell them any more horses.

Fur Posts Change the Picture

Soon the situation became serious. McKenzie did not want to return to Astoria, for there were no surplus supplies there. Besides, Clarke was depending on him for pack animals to move his furs from Spokane Falls to his canoes at the mouth of the Palouse. He decided to sit tight and await developments, but he did not propose to starve while he waited. He sent his hunters to stalk the horse herds of the Indians, shooting the fatter ones for camp use. To pay for the animals killed in this way, a bundle of trade goods was left on a pole by the discarded head of each horse, to be claimed by the owner, who could recognize his property by the ear markings. The Indians were annoyed. Not only had they been outwitted, but the better horses were being killed. Strangely enough, they did not use a patrol to keep the horse herds out of reach. Instead, plans were made for an attack on McKenzie's camp.

McKenzie suspected trouble was brewing when two or three Nez Percés brought in horses to trade for ammunition, refusing any other goods. To prevent a surprise attack, he moved his camp to an island in the river, where he stayed in a state of siege, raiding the horse herds from time to time for meat. Seemingly, his daring and ingenuity gradually won the admiration of the tribe, for they finally called a truce and agreed to supply him with any number of horses at the usual price. McKenzie then bought eighty animals for Clarke's pack string, in addition to those he used for his camp, and parted from the Nez Percés with friendly feelings on both sides.

McKenzie's work with the Nez Percés was entirely ruined by Clarke's overbearing behavior at the Palouse village that spring. Clarke was pleased to find that the Palouse chief had taken good care of the canoes left in his charge and, to show his appreciation, decided to give him a very special treat in addition to the agreed payment.

To distinguish himself from the common crowd, Clarke always carried a pair of beautiful silver goblets for his after-dinner wine. He now brought them out, talked at great length of their beauty, rarity, and costliness, and finally allowed the chief to take a sip of wine from one of them before locking them in his special chest. Much to his consternation, one of the goblets was missing in the morning. In a great rage at such an insult, Clarke swore that the thief would hang. The village must ferret out and deliver up the offender at once. After a short time, the chief returned the unharmed goblet to Clarke and, at Clarke's request, pointed out the culprit standing unabashed in the crowd. Overruling the protests of the Indians and his own men, Clarke had the thief hanged immediately on gallows hastily constructed from tipi poles.

Luckily for Clarke, his victim had a poor reputation in his own village and had no relatives to avenge him. As the Indians continued to protest this gross violation of hospitality, the trader made his escape at once, embarking his furs and his precious self in the canoes and hurrying down the Snake to the rendezvous at the mouth of the Walla Walla. Here he was surprised to find his deed condemned heartily by the entire gathering, either because it violated their sense of decency or because they feared it would harm the fur trade. While such an act might have cowed a degenerate people, in this instance it inflamed the whole area against the company's traders, undoing in a few minutes all of McKenzie's work and leaving a hostility toward the whites which lasted for many years.[3]

After this affair, the Nez Percés and their allies held aloof from the traders except for an occasional trip to Spokane for guns and ammunition. Almost every boat brigade up or down the Columbia had to run the gauntlet of threatening throngs of mounted braves crowding the banks of the river, but each time open warfare seemed imminent it was avoided by some

[3] Alexander Ross, *Adventures of the First Settlers on the Oregon or Columbia River* (Vol. VII in Reuben Gold Thwaites [ed.], *Early Western Travels*), 212–14.

fortunate turn of affairs, or by the prompt and decisive action of some leader on either side. The best known of such incidents is that of Alexander Ross and his knife at the great Yakima council, where his self-control and ready wit turned 3,000 warriors from hostile to neutral in a moment.[4] On another occasion, an impassioned speech by the Cayuse chief, Morning Star, prevented a bloody fight, his eloquent description of the advantages of trade with the whites changing the tide of sentiment at the opportune moment.[5]

In 1813, the Pacific Fur Company had sold its property to the Northwest Company, and three years later Donald McKenzie accepted a high position with his former company's rival. In 1818 he decided to abandon the Spokane Falls post, at that time the headquarters for the entire inland region, and to build a new post, to be constructed near the junction of the Snake and Columbia rivers, which would facilitate the transportation of goods and furs and the purchase of the many horses needed each year. From the new post, he planned to tap the rich fur country of the upper Snake Valley, forestalling American enterprise in that area. After much opposition from other members of the company at Astoria, now called Fort George, he finally started up the river with his men and supplies to inaugurate the new venture.[6]

News of his coming spread quickly, arousing the latent hostility of all surrounding tribes. They assembled in thousands at the proposed site, offering every sort of opposition short of open conflict. Permission for the whites to hunt and fish was refused in order to force them to purchase all their food from the Indians at exorbitant prices. In vain, McKenzie sought to meet with the chiefs in a great council to discuss terms. The hordes surrounded the small, poorly fortified

[4] Alexander Ross, *The Fur Hunters of the Far West*, I, 25-27.

[5] Ross Cox, *Adventures on the Columbia River*, II, 20-25

[6] Ross, *Fur Hunters*, I, 172.

camp of the whites, pitched on a sand bar, its inmates oppressed by dirt and flies, subjected to all sorts of petty insults and annoyances. Under the iron control of McKenzie, they waited with what patience they could muster, knowing the Indians would subside if no new provocation arose. Finally, the chiefs agreed to a council and presented their demands. They first asked an annual rent for the fort site, payment for all timber used, the right to supply all provisions for the establishment, and a gift for each warrior present.

McKenzie could not have met the last demand even by using his entire stock of goods, nor could he see any chance for profit to his company under the proposed terms, so he boldly refused. He pointed out the advantage of such a post to the tribes, particularly in trading horses, and asked that he be given a free site, free timber, and unlimited rights to hunt and fish. Gradually his patience and tact won them over, and they finally consented to his terms, largely because of their admiration for the big man.

With the basic points settled, McKenzie was ready to offer added suggestions. His new fort would be of little value unless he could trade with the Shoshoni, traditional enemies of both the Nez Percés and the Cayuses, who would oppose any plan to furnish their foes with a source of arms and ammunition. McKenzie approached his goal in roundabout fashion. He proposed a general peace among all the tribes of the Northwest, stressing the advantages of such a plan. The Nez Percés then told how their peace delegation to the Shoshoni thirteen years before had all been killed, proving that such efforts were sure to fail. McKenzie replied with the advice left them by their good friends, Lewis and Clark, that all the tribes should live in peace. His carefully laid plans were thwarted by the arrival of a successful war party with Shoshoni scalps and prisoners.

After a victory celebration lasting several days, the council met again and agreed to make a lasting peace treaty if the Shoshoni would, but they felt that those people could not be trusted even then. At a later conference on the upper Snake River, the Shoshoni took the same attitude regarding the Nez Percés, saying a man could as well hope to stop the flow of the Snake in flood with his fingers as he could hope to bind the Nez Percés by a treaty.[7]

An Indian custom common to this area added greatly to the trials of the traders. Each tribe was held responsible for all deeds committed in its territory, even if the offender belonged to another tribe. Likewise, war parties were considered freed from all tribal restrictions when in the boundaries of another tribe. Thus a solemn and binding treaty with the Nez Percés was good only while the trader was in their territory, where he was under the protection of the tribe and guarded against all foes. But if the same Nez Percés who guarded the trader while he was in their country should meet him in Shoshoni territory a few days later, they were free to attack him, since the crime would be charged to the Shoshoni, in whose country the attack took place. A party of Nez Percés, following this custom, attacked one of McKenzie's pack trains in Shoshoni territory in the summer of 1819, killing two of the men.[8] The tribe never felt any guilt over the affair and did not count it as chargeable against themselves in later years.

McKenzie's post, called Fort Nez Percé by Alexander Ross, but more commonly known as Fort Walla Walla, proved quite profitable to the Nez Percés and Cayuses during the next several years. The traders bought about 250 horses a year for food and another 100 for pack animals. In payment, the tribes secured guns and ammunition to use against the Blackfeet. Every effort was made by the whites to keep on good terms with these two tribes, even though they had few furs for the

[7] *Ibid.*, I, 180–83.
[8] *Ibid.*, I, 221.

traders. In 1825, the chief factor of the Hudson's Bay Company, which had taken over the Northwest Company in 1823, ordered the Snake River expedition to be outfitted at Flathead House in Montana and to leave the Snake country through southern Oregon, heading for Fort George on the lower Columbia, making a huge circuit of the Nez Percé country to avoid possible friction.[9]

Cayuses were the chief source of trouble for the traders at Fort Walla Walla. Their warriors, reinforced by restless young men from the Nez Percé bands, made frequent raids across the Blue Mountains against the Shoshoni. They resented the trade of the fur men with that tribe because several of their number had been killed by the new guns in the hands of their enemies. When the traders tried to patch up the quarrel, they found it to be of long standing, caused, according to the Cayuse version, by the Shoshoni's forbidding them to hunt deer in the Blue Mountains. Since the Cayuse tribe had come from the southwest in comparatively recent times, it is possible that they had encroached on ancient Shoshoni hunting grounds, but they retaliated by blocking the Shoshoni from the salmon fisheries and trading places on the Columbia, particularly at The Dalles. This enmity between the tribes was maintained unabated until the virtual destruction of the Cayuse tribe by disease and war during the period from 1845 to 1855.

By the constant exercise of boldness, tact, skill, and honesty, the various traders at Fort Walla Walla made their post the center of a large peaceful area. Some of the traders were held in high esteem by the various tribes, who were gradually influenced to favor white customs and practices, most of them possibly an improvement on the Indian way of living. The district appeared ready for missionary work under a competent man. Some of the traders even began to teach the rudiments of Christianity, with very interesting results.

[9] Frederick Merk (ed.), *Fur Trade and Empire*, 55.

6: The Macedonian Cry

O F supreme importance in the spiritual life of each Nez
Percé was his wy-ya-kin, a personal attending spiritual
helper that first appeared to him during a period of fasting
and vigil undertaken when he was about ten years old. The
spiritual guardian appeared in the form of some animal, and
as the belief in the guardian was strong, so would the person
be strong; as its instructions were obeyed, so would he be
fortunate during his life. Weakness, sickness, or bad luck were
attributed to the disregarding in some way of the spiritual
guide. A token of the animal in the medicine bag and a close
observance of the tabus connected with it furnished the person with his medicine for all emergencies. As his medicine was
weak or strong, so would his accomplishments be small or great.

Before the coming of the white men, the Nez Percés had
believed that they had strong medicine because of their ability
to dominate the region. Hence they had little incentive for
further search or inquiry into the spiritual practices of their
neighbors, particularly since a casual inspection had revealed
no great difference from their own.

With the coming of the white men, this sense of superiority
was rudely disturbed. The strangers conducted themselves
like members of a dominant race, confident in their own

prowess. They were stronger than the Indian and more skill-ful in many ways. Their weapons were endowed with miracu-lous powers, much superior to anything owned by the red man. Although a Nez Percé could buy guns and knives, the mys-tery of their construction and the great power of the burning powder were beyond his comprehension. The burning glass would work for red man as well as white, but the red man could not fashion such an object. Steel tools, infinitely supe-rior to those made from the best flint or obsidian, were of a material found only in the country of the whites. Various other articles of trade were equally strange, equally wonder-ful, and equally beyond the Indian's skill. Surely people pos-sessing such powers must be aided by a medicine greater than any the red man had ever known.

Almost as mysterious was the ability of the white man to send messages several hundred miles by his "talking paper." The written word seemed endowed with miraculous powers that it could thus convey information. Although the art of writing was more comprehensive than the power of the gun, the burning glass, or the steel, it was still in the realm of spirit magic, and written messages were treated accordingly. Donald McKenzie was quick to turn this respect to his own advantage. He instituted a postal service in the Northwest, using Indian runners to carry the messages from one village to another. It was a point of honor as well as profit for a village to furnish a runner to carry the packet on to the next village, for each runner sold the message for more than it had cost him, until the final messenger gave up his precious packet at the end of the route, receiving all the pay for the task.[1] Thus, in a coun-try where a white man could pass safely only with a heavily armed escort, his messages were under the special care of the very natives who would have cheerfully welcomed the op-portunity to rob or murder the writer.

[1] Ross, *Fur Hunters*, I, 156–57.

The Macedonian Cry

In addition to their contact with written messages, the Indians knew something of the books possessed by some of the traders, the most common being the Bible. From the books, the white man would sometimes read great stories for his Indian friends, conveying to some extent the idea that the Bible was connected with the white man's religion. This associated in the Indian's mind the magic of writing and the ability to control the great spiritual forces that were needed for duplicating the achievements of the whites. Perhaps the possession of the book and the ability to read it might give the Indian the white man's power, enabling him to hold his own against the invaders.

Had the Indian associated only with the traders, such a misconception would probably have been kept unchanged, since the white men who could talk to the various tribes would be those least likely to instruct anyone in religious matters. Possibly their first definite information came from a group of eastern Indians, either Iroquois or Hurons,[2] who had been brought from the St. Lawrence Valley as servants of the Northwest Company about 1818. They proved to be unsatisfactory workers, and were classed by Ross as sullen, indolent, fickle, cowardly, and treacherous.[3] When sent out trapping, they traded all their equipment for wives, food, or trinkets as soon as they were away from their superiors. Naturally, such conduct, repeated time after time, was very annoying to the officials responsible for the profits of the western area. Their displeasure caused the Indians to desert in order to escape punishment, most of them finally joining the Flatheads, who adopted them into the tribe. The new environment seemed better suited to their natures, and they rose to responsible positions in their new surroundings.

[2] Father Mengarini ("The Rocky Mountains," *Woodstock Letters*, Vol. XVII, No. 3, 308–309) calls them Hurons. They were probably a mixture of the Hurons and Christian Iroquois from Caughawaga Mission near Montreal.

[3] Ross, *Fur Hunters*, I, 195.

59

Encouraged by the interest of the Flatheads, the Iroquois explained as best they could what they had learned in the East, stressing the colorful processions, the festivals, and the pomp and ceremony all so dear to the red men. Probably they also told of the schools conducted by the nuns, where some of the Indian boys and girls were taught to read and write. They still remembered several of the church songs which they sang to lighten the labor of paddling on long journeys and a few of the moral precepts in which they had been drilled. Their discussion of these topics convinced some of the Flatheads that missionaries would be a benefit to their tribe.

While the Flatheads were learning something of religion from the Iroquois, someone, probably at Fort Walla Walla, was giving elementary instruction in morals to the Nez Percés. This work has been attributed to Pierre Pambrun, in charge of the post from the spring of 1832 until his death eight years later, but at least a part of the work must have been done before Pambrun's arrival. Mountain men meeting the Nez Percés in the upper Snake Valley were amazed to observe that they recited simple prayers and observed the Sabbath.[4]

The interest of the several tribes in religion was noticed by Sir George Simpson on his inspection trip in 1825. At a great council held by him at Spokane House in April, 1825, the chiefs of the Spokans, Flatheads, and Kutenai joined in asking that someone be sent to instruct their people in the white man's religion and the white man's ways. Simpson was so impressed that he wrote to the directors of the Hudson's Bay Company advising that at least one mission be established. He recommended three possible sites and estimated the effectiveness of each compared to its cost. He also took two boys, Spokane Garry and Kootenai Pelly, sons of chiefs, with him to the Red River Settlement for instruction in the school

[4] Cornelius James Brosnan, *Jason Lee, Prophet of New Oregon,* 36.

there.[5] Ross says that later several more were taken, including Ellis of the Nez Percés. The boys were about eleven years old at the time. It was hoped that they would return in a few years to act as leaders of their people.

On his journey west in 1828, Simpson carried letters from the two boys to their parents.[6] Kootenai Pelly died soon after writing his letter, but Spokane Garry returned to his people two years later. The other boys who were sent east probably went some time later than 1825 and did not return until about 1835. This left Spokane Garry the only educated Indian in the entire region for some time. He created quite a sensation among the red men by his ability to read and write. The Indians flocked around to hear him read from the Bible. Some of them attended classes in the large school house erected by the Spokans, and many learned to plant small gardens in which potatoes were the chief crop.

It must have been galling to the pride of the Flathead and Nez Percé chiefs when the lowly Spokans acquired such prestige through the return of their educated member, and now were so important in the intertribal councils. Civic and personal pride demanded that something be done at once to restore the Nez Percés to their former position of leadership.

Here then were the factors necessary to start the Nez Percés on their quest for teachers. They were not divinely inspired toward Christianity, nor were they seeking for a higher moral standard. They wanted better "medicine" to increase their prestige and power. They did not seek reading and writing as tools but as magic formulas to aid their "medicine." Hence it is absurd to argue whether they were seeking Catholic or Protestant teachers, or whether they really asked

[5] Merk (ed.), *Fur Trade and Empire*, 55.

[6] Archibald McDonald, *Peace River, a Canoe Voyage from Hudson's Bay to the Pacific by the Late Sir George Simpson in 1828*, 34.

for the white man's "Book of Heaven." They were looking for new incantations to use on this earth, not information on a possible world to come.

It was natural that the Nez Percés turned to the United States instead of Canada for their teachers, even though one of their boys was then in the Canadian school. For twenty-five years, Lewis and Clark had been considered the greatest of the white men. Every incident of their visits had been incorporated into the tales told around the evening fires. Reports of Clark's work as the United States Commissioner of Indian Affairs at St. Louis had probably reached them through the traders who came to the Rockies each year from that town. It is entirely probable that the trip they were to make was as much to see Clark as to ask for teachers. Such was the state of affairs among the Nez Percés in the eventful year of 1831.

A high spot of the summer hunt in the buffalo country was the great intertribal camp, during this period usually located somewhere in the Sun River Valley west of the Great Falls of the Missouri. Here could be found fine grazing for the horse herds and a plentiful supply of mountain water, quite different in flavor and effect from that of the Missouri or the prairie creeks. The riverbanks supplied driftwood for camp fuel. Willow thickets and cottonwood groves furnished sticks and brush for myriad camp uses. Above the rimrock to the south, rolling grasslands pastured thousands of buffalo which could be driven over the cliffs. Great heaps of bones still mark the death leap. Even today flint skinning knives and arrowheads can be found which were lost in the excitement of a big kill.

After months of wandering about the Plains in small bands, the Nez Percés and Flatheads would gather here for a week or two of feasting, visiting, trading, and celebration. While the young folks flirted and the braves gambled, the wise men of the tribes would gather around the council fire on the warm summer nights to discuss topics of common interest and to decide the proper action for common problems, the stars over the clustered tipis gleaming brightly and the mournful howls of the coyotes quavering in the still air.

To such an encampment in the summer of 1831 came three Nez Percés from Kamiah village on the Clearwater. Four had set out for St. Louis, facing nearly 2,000 miles of unknown trail beyond their own eastern range, but one old man had turned back on the Lolo Trail, fearing that he would be a hindrance to the others.[7] Of the three who continued, we are sure only of the chief, Black Eagle. When the Flatheads heard of their quest, three of that tribe, headed by Man-of-the-morning, joined them, and another Nez Percé decided to go along with the group for the adventure promised. This last was either No-horns-on-his-head or Rabbit-skin-leggings, the other being in the original group from Kamiah. The name of the fourth Nez Percé has been forgotten.

Lucien Fontenelle, of the American Fur Company, carried the party down the Missouri that fall when he took his furs to market.[8] Day after day, the heavily laden craft floated on the muddy river, past groves of cottonwood and willow, sandbars and mud flats. The air grew hot and close. Alkali water combined with the enervating heat to lower the vitality of the mountain Indians. By the time they reached Council Bluffs, the two unnamed Flatheads and the fourth Nez Percé turned back. Black Eagle and Man-of-the-morning pushed resolutely on with the two young men, reaching St. Louis about October 1, 1831. Here they were warmly welcomed by General Clark, who was pleased with the opportunity of returning some of the kindness shown him on the western trip twenty-five years before. To him the Indians explained as best they could the purpose of their visit.

[7] McBeth, *Nez Percés Since Lewis and Clark*, 29–32.

[8] "The Whitman Journal," *Oregon Historical Quarterly*, Vol. XXVIII, No. 2 (July, 1937) 256.

The Nez Percés

Since there have been so many conflicting stories told concerning the requests made by the delegation, possibly it would be best to consider the attending circumstances. As Clark always needed an interpreter to talk with any of the Nez Percés during his stay with the tribe, it is highly improbable that he could have remembered more than a word or two of their language after so many years. A search of St. Louis failed to find anyone who could understand either the Nez Percés or the Flatheads. All communications must have been carried on through the medium of the sign language of the western Plains, a language well known to both of the tribes. Although this sign language was highly developed and well adapted for ordinary Indian communications, it was decidedly lacking in terms for the abstract ideas which the delegation wished to discuss. All the accounts agree that the Indians were interested in the white man's religion and were anxious that a teacher be sent to them. It is also quite possible that they tried to ask for a Bible, for the one owned by Spokane Garry had fascinated them. Since they had no chance to learn the difference between the various Christian churches, it is doubtful that they specified a teacher of any particular denomination.

The situation was clearly one of a group of strange Indians asking, in sign language, that the people of St. Louis give them something connected with religion and education, but not being able to make themselves clearly understood because of language limitations. As none of the people who conversed with them could tell exactly what the Indians were after, their conflicting versions are quite unimportant. The Indians wanted to secure some kind of "big medicine." By sign language, they could not have specified any desire for either Catholics or Protestants, as they had no sign for either at that time. The widely circulated "Indian lament" attributed to them is an outright fake.

While the delegation rested at St. Louis, hoping for some-

No-Horns-on-His-Head, a member of the Nez Percé-Flathead dele-
gation to St. Louis in 1831. Catlin painted him in a Sioux shirt in 1832.
(From a painting by George Catlin, courtesy Smithsonian Institution)

Rabbit-Skin-Leggings, also a member of the Nez Percé-Flathead delegation to St. Louis in 1831. Catlin says he painted him in Sioux costume, 1832. (From a painting by George Catlin, courtesy Smithsonian Institution)

body who could speak their language, Black Eagle died of disease. He was buried by the Catholic church on October 31, 1831. Man-of-the-morning soon followed him, being buried by the same church on November 17, 1831. The two young men dropped from sight for a time. Bishop Rosati, writing on December 31, 1831,[9] stated that they had returned to their own country, but they could not have gone far because they were on the steamer *Yellowstone,* an American Fur Company boat, when it left St. Louis March 26, 1832. On the trip up the river, the boat was delayed at Fort Pierre from May 31 to June 5.[10] It was here, probably, that the two Nez Percés were feasted by the Sioux and presented with complete costumes of Sioux finery. In their gay new attire, they attracted the notice of the artist George Catlin, who had come to the West to paint western scenery and western Indians. He made a portrait of each man labeled with his name, without knowing of their mission to St. Louis. Catlin wrote that No-horns-on-his-head died from disease shortly after the *Yellowstone* reached Fort Union.[11]

The lone survivor, Rabbit-skin-leggings, crossed the Montana plains to join a portion of his tribe at a camp in the buffalo country. There he made his report, telling of the deaths of his comrades and of his failure to bring back any teachers. Later that fall, he was killed in a fight with the Blackfeet on the headwaters of the Salmon River.[12] Thus the mission brought toil, privation, and death to all its members and ended, seemingly, in complete failure. Yet, in five years, the missionary zeal inspired by the story of these Indians had planted

[9] "Bishop Rosati's Letter to Belgium, December 31, 1831," *American Catholic Historical Society of Philadelphia Yearbook, 1888,* Vol. II, 188.

[10] Hiram Martin Chittenden, *The American Fur Trade of the Far West,* II, 952.

[11] George Catlin, *Letters and Notes on the Manners, Customs, and Condition of the North American Indians,* II, 109.

[12] F. M. Drury, *Henry Harmon Spalding,* 84.

stations on the Willamette, the Walla Walla, and the Clearwater rivers, to be followed shortly by others in the Bitterroot Valley and at Spokane Falls. The strange quirk of fate that produced such a result is worthy of notice.

During Andrew Jackson's administration, a determined effort was made to move all the tribes of Indians from their reservations in the various states so the land might be sold to settlers and land speculators. The Indians were to be moved to areas west of the Mississippi then regarded as worthless for farming and forever beyond the cupidity of the whites.

One of the Huron tribes, known to the American frontiersmen as the Wyandots, had a reservation near Sandusky, Ohio. With many settlers moving to that section in the early thirties, a special effort was made to move the Wyandots west of the Mississippi, somewhere in the Missouri Valley, as quickly as possible, but the Indians wanted to see the new land before they signed away their homes. In the fall of 1831 a delegation from the tribe was sent west with William Walker, an intelligent, well-educated part-Indian, as their interpreter and supervisor. Walker was interested in Indian missions and wrote occasionally to mission supporters in the East.[13]

When the Wyandot delegation reached St. Louis, Walker paid an official visit to William Clark, the Indian commissioner, to have his credentials verified and to secure additional credentials to use up the Missouri. During his stay in St. Louis, possibly from Clark, Walker heard of the Nez Percé visit. He was impressed with this opportunity for opening a new mission field and made some additional inquiries in the matter.

Walker returned to Sandusky with his mission completed, and about a year later, January 19, 1833, he wrote to one of his eastern correspondents. This man, G. P. Disoway, a New York merchant, had shown an active interest in Indian missions and in the proposed removal of the Wyandots. With his

---

[13] Chittenden, *American Fur Trade*, II, 896.

imagination fired by Walker's account of the Nez Percés, he embellished the letter with some added material on both the Wyandots and the Nez Percés and published the entire account, together with a drawing of his own, in the *Christian Advocate* and the *Zion's Herald* of March 1, 1833.[14]

If Walker had met the Nez Percés and had described them accurately, it is possible that his letter would have aroused little interest and might not even have been printed. In the several months intervening between Walker's visit to St. Louis and the writing of the letter, the story had grown, as stories sometimes do, and it would seem that Walker heard a garbled version in the first place. This is evident from the description of the Indians, as Walker passed it on, as small and delicate, with delicate bones and grotesquely flattened heads, a description which might fit the Pacific Coast Chinooks, but certainly did not apply to the sturdy, barrel-chested Nez Percés.[15]

While Indian mission work had been growing for twenty years, it was becoming increasingly difficult to secure new material on the eastern tribes that would attract public attention and open pocketbooks. Walker's letter, touching a new note, and the accompanying sketch, drawn largely from Disoway's imagination, fanned the enthusiasm of the church people to a fever heat. Many were willing to contribute toward the salvation of poor heathens with misshapen heads. Young men by the score, impelled by a love for travel and adventure as well as by a desire to serve their fellow men, offered their services as missionaries. Can it be that the Indians were considered more worthy of salvation because they asked for missionaries, or did their supposedly outlandish appearance and barbarous customs arouse the interest? Would the good people of the East have been as zealous in helping if they had known that

[14] *Ibid.*, II, 894–901.
[15] Francis Haines, "The Nez Percé Delegation to St. Louis in 1831," *Pacific Historical Review*, Vol. VI, No. 1 (March, 1937), 1.

an intelligent, advanced tribe sent the call? There is more than a suspicion that the Northwest is indebted for its first missionaries to Walker's erroneous account of the heathens with flattened heads. However, the contributions poured in from all sides, a search was made for suitable workers, and each denomination, purely in an excess of Christian zeal, strove mightily to pre-empt the desirable field, fearing lest someone else might get the spiritual credit for saving the tribe. Hampered by vast distances, poor communications, and lack of knowledge of the western country, the first missionaries were rather slow in reaching the scene of their labors.

7 : The First Missionaries

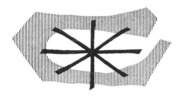

ONE popular wintering place of the Nez Percé bands in the buffalo country was the upper valley of the Salmon or just across the Continental Divide in the Beaverhead country. Here the timbered mountains furnished shelter from the winter storms and game was plentiful. In the spring, before the snow had left the high trails leading to the home villages, these bands often went south into the Snake Valley and on to the annual rendezvous of the fur traders, with whom they conducted their yearly trading rather than waiting to visit Fort Walla Walla later in the summer. With their wants thus supplied for another year, they might wait until fall to go home, or they might stay another year or two.

July marked the height of the activities at the Green River rendezvous, for it was then that the wagon trains of goods came in from Missouri, having been on the road since May. Here the mountain men gathered to turn in their year's catch, renew their outfits, and squander their money on wild drinking parties or Indian wives. Thousands of Indians from many tribes came in, under a strict truce, to trade furs and other goods for arms and trinkets. After a few weeks of feverish activity, the traders would load their furs on the wagons and return to St. Louis, the mountain men would load their pack animals for another winter in the wilds, and the Indians would scatter to the hunting grounds for a supply of meat before the snows came.

While the whites in St. Louis misunderstood the Nez Percé delegation in the fall of 1831, it appears that the delegation also misunderstood the whites. At any rate, the Nez Percés hoped and rather expected that a teacher would come to them with the wagon train in 1833, and a band of them planned to be on hand to welcome the expected visitor, although it is probable that most of them would have gone to the rendezvous anyway.

Nez Percés on the march usually traveled a leisurely ten to fifteen miles a day, remaining in camp each Sunday for simple religious ceremonies and spending an extra day now and then at a favorable spot, particularly after a forced march of thirty or forty miles across a waterless stretch. In this way, they did not wear out themselves or their horses on a long trip. While their moving was carried on without apparent plan or supervision, the results were satisfactory.

Preparations for breaking camp began early. The first rays of the morning sun, dispelling the dawn chill of the high country, would find a confusion of men, women, children, horses, and dogs milling about the cooking fires and the half-dismantled lodges. Snorting, skittish horses sidled away from the packers. Dogs skulked underfoot, alert to steal a morsel of food from a pack, a cooking kettle, or the hand of a careless child. One unaccustomed to such a scene might well suppose that half a day of such effort would find the work no further along, but in a short time a family, its preparations completed, would urge its string of laden animals up the trail. Camp equipment was usually strapped on the older, more sedate animals, often with a small child tied securely on the load, a whip in his hand. The horses of the women were usually more spirited, with the favored wives and daughters of the wealthy

Indians astride fine animals. With the help of the children, the women drove the pack train, and some of them had the prized duty of leading one of the precious buffalo horses or a spotted war horse.

Close on the heels of the first group would come the rest of the camp, straggling across the slopes in small irregular bands, and in half an hour nothing would be left of the busy camp but a few smouldering embers of the cooking fires, still circled by groups of blanketed braves, each holding his trail horse for the day, all easy-gaited, mediocre animals of non-descript colors. Finally they too would mount and ride forth in a body, usually to gain the head of the column in search of game. The large herd of extra horses for remount duty and trading purposes, which often wandered from the line of march in search of better pasture, was under the care of the young men and the older boys.

During the morning, the band moved steadily along the chosen route, making no general halt until the new camping place was reached. Individuals might drop behind to adjust a pack or the like, and small parties of the women often stopped to pick berries or to gather other food items. Warm and tired in the bright sunshine, the small children would fall asleep on their mounts, their little heads bobbing helplessly to the motion of the horses. By noon or shortly after, the new camp-site would be reached and the confusion of the morning repeated. The women hurried to and fro, unpacking horses, sorting packs, setting up lodges, gathering wood, carrying water, mending camp gear, and cooking food. In an hour, the camp would be set up, with all the tipis in place, only its cleanliness indicating its newness. The men, having rested and smoked on some convenient knoll, would then ride in, sending their horses to join the main herd, but keeping the buffalo horses and war horses close to camp under special guard. If there seemed to be real danger of enemies, these horses were tethered alongside the tipis and fed with grass which the little girls laboriously picked by hand or cut with a hoe made of a shoulder blade of some animal. The main horse herd was guarded day and night, being bedded down near the camp under ordinary occasions or picketed among the tipis if danger threatened. Hunters and scouts ranged the hills in search of game and the sign of an enemy. This daily pageant, so colorful to the stranger, soon became monotonous through daily repetition, and was enlivened only by storms or clashes with hostile bands.

One busy camp in the Snake country was located near a bed of white clay. Here clothes and robes were cleaned by being smeared with a creamy paste of clay and water. When this dried, the clay brushed off readily, leaving the garment soft and clean.[1] These cleaned clothes were then saved to be donned, with added finery, behind the last ridge or swell separating the Nez Percés from the rendezvous. Once they were dressed in holiday attire, the warriors dashed toward the camp in battle array, shouting, firing their guns, and waving their weapons as they displayed the fine points of their gaudily decorated steeds. After a few minutes of such maneuvers, the entire band rode in to receive a warm welcome from the traders, who liked to do business with them. Then too, the clean, well-mannered Nez Percés were favorites with the mountain men, their women having a reputation for beauty, modesty, industry, and fidelity that became almost proverbial in a few years.

At the rendezvous in 1833, the Nez Percés were disappointed to find no news of their expected teacher. They did not know that a man appointed for the work by the kindly Bishop Rosati had died on the lower Missouri before he could

[1] Samuel Parker, *Journal of an Exploring Tour Beyond the Rocky Mountains under the Direction of the A.B.C.F.M. Performed in the Years 1835, '36 and '37*, 100.

even complete his plans for the trip. The next year, 1834, the Indians were pleased to find a missionary with the wagon train. Jason Lee had come west in answer to the call set forth in the Walker letter, expecting to open a station at once in anticipation of the promised help that would follow soon. For some reason, his enthusiasm for working among the Nez Percés and Flatheads waned as he neared their country. Possibly he was disappointed to find such sturdy, intelligent, self-reliant people instead of the fragile people with misshapen heads as shown in Disoway's drawing. At any rate, he decided to pass by the Clearwater country and the Kamiah Nez Percés, who had sent the call, in order to settle in the Willamette Valley near the sea and other white people. In his report to the Board of Missions, he indicated that a post among the Nez Percés would be too far from the Pacific Coast, too near the Blackfeet, and in a too thinly settled country. So Lee rode by the 3,000 Nez Percés, waiting with outstretched hands, to work among the remnants of the Willamette tribes who had expressed no interest in missions.

The summer of 1835 brought new encouragement to the waiting Nez Percés. With the caravan from the East came two men interested in surveying the country for suitable mission sites. When the leader of the two, Samuel Parker, realized how interested the Nez Percés were in teachers, he decided to make every effort to hasten the establishment of a mission among them. He decided to go on alone with the Indians while his companion, Marcus Whitman, returned at once with the caravan so he might bring the permanent workers out the next spring, thus saving a whole year. Whitman objected to leaving the older man in the wilds with no white companion, but Parker maintained that with God's protection he was safe in any case, and that without it even Whitman would be of little aid. Unable to refute this argument, Whitman turned back. Parker promised to meet him at the rendezvous in 1836 with a detailed report on the country and its inhabitants. On his trip east, Whitman took two Nez Percé boys, one of whom could speak a little English. He was expected to instruct Whitman in Shahaptian, and he and his comrade were to help arouse enthusiasm and to raise funds at church meetings during the winter. The two boys, renamed Richard and John for the convenience of the whites, spent the winter in upper New York State attending school, well cared for by the village people.[2]

Parker traversed great stretches of the Northwest under the protection of the Nez Percés. The Indians pampered him with special foods and attention, some of it surely at his own suggestion, for he had a reputation of hinting rather broadly for any object that caught his fancy. He held frequent services with the aid of an overworked, underpaid interpreter for large, attentive audiences. From his own account, Parker seemed more interested in explaining intricate points of church doctrine than in giving his auditors a workable conception of applied Christianity. Some of his acts on this journey appear unnecessarily harsh and arbitrary. For instance, when he attended the funeral of a little fever victim, he angrily destroyed the small cross placed by the sorrowing parents at the head of the grave, ordering them to substitute a stone marker.[3] In this trying situation, the Indians accepted Parker's actions rather calmly, displaying better manners and self-control than their visitor, who seems boorish by comparison.

For some unexplained reason, Parker did not return to meet Whitman as he had promised. Instead, he went on down the Columbia to Fort George, where he took a ship for home by way of the Hawaiian Islands. His letter to Whitman, carried by the Nez Percés, had information of little value.

In anticipation of the return of Whitman, a much larger

[2] Drury, *Spalding*, 103.
[3] Parker, *Journal*, 275–76.

group of Nez Percés arrived at the rendezvous in 1836. When the messenger rode in to announce the approach of the wagon train, a large band of warriors and mountain men hurried eastward to welcome the new comers, the Nez Percés interested in the teachers, the mountain men thrilled at a chance to see a white woman once more. One of these Indians was later baptized as Joseph, sometimes known as Old Joseph of the Wallowa, half-brother of Five Crows, a Cayuse chief, and father of Chief Joseph. Joseph had been an interested listener when Parker gave his talks and was eager to help with the work of starting a mission. One of the missionary women, Mrs. Henry Spalding, described the meeting of the wagon train and the party from the rendezvous:

JULY 4, 1836—Crossed a ridge of land today called the Divide, which separates the waters which flow into the Atlantic from those which flow into the Pacific, and camped for the night on the headwaters of the Colorado. The brave Nez Percés who have been awaiting our arrival at the rendezvous for several days, on hearing we were near, came down to meet us, and have camped near us tonight. They appeared to be gratified to see us actually on the way to their country. Mr. Spalding, Dr. Whitman and Mr. Gray are to have a talk with the chiefs tonight.

JULY 6—We arrived at the rendezvous this evening. Were met by a large party of Nez Percés, men, women, and children. The women not satisfied short of saluting Mrs. Whitman and myself with a kiss. All appear happy to see us. If permitted to reach their country and locate among them, may our labors be blessed to their temporal and spiritual good.

JULY 18—We have commenced our journey for Fort Walla Walla in company with Mr. McLeoud. The Nez Percés seem sadly disappointed because we do not accompany them. All appear very anxious that they may be taught about God; and be instructed in the habits of civilized life. One chief has concluded to go with us, not withstanding it will deprive him of the privilege of securing a supply of meat for the winter.[4]

While the Whitmans are rightly regarded as the leaders of this group of missionaries, the Spaldings are more important in Nez Percé history. Henry Harmon Spalding was born near Wheeler, Pennsylvania, in 1803. His unmarried mother was unable to support her child, who was cared for by neighbors until, at seventeen, he left after a violent quarrel. This early period of neglect and the stigma of his birth explain to a large extent some of the peculiarities in Spalding's temperament and had a direct bearing on his quarrels with his fellow workers in later years. After Spalding had joined the church at the age of twenty-two, he worked his way through Franklin Academy at Prattsburg, New York; Western Reserve College at Hudson, Ohio; and Lane Theological Seminary at Cincinnati, Ohio, graduating from the last in 1835. During this time, he supported himself by teaching three terms of school and by working in the college shops at printing and woodworking. After his marriage to Eliza Hart in 1833, she assisted by keeping boarders. In 1835, Spalding applied for a position as teacher to the Choctaws and this was refused. He then asked the American Board of Missions for an appointment to any Indian tribe. The board assigned him to the Osages, his work to commence the next spring. He spent the winter studying medicine in preparation for work on the frontier. On his way west in the spring, he was overtaken by Marcus Whitman, who had permission from the board to take Spalding to Oregon if he was willing to go. At this time, Spalding is described as a medium-sized, sturdy man with sharp features, dark, bushy hair, large brown eyes, and a hot temper. He was kind and obliging, a true though not very humble Christian. His ex-

4 McBeth, *Nez Percés Since Lewis and Clark*, 38–39.

ploits at Lapwai mark him as a man of considerable strength, endurance, and courage.

Eliza Hart Spalding was born at Kensington, Connecticut, in 1807 and moved with her family to Oneida County, New York, in 1820. She met Henry Spalding through the offices of a mutual friend, who felt that she was just the wife for a young minister. In some of the letters sent to the mission board recommending the Spaldings, special emphasis was placed on Mrs. Spalding's exceptional qualifications as a missionary's wife.[5] William H. Gray described her thus:

"She was above the medium height, slender in form, with coarse features, dark brown hair, blue eyes, rather dark complexion, coarse voice, of a serious turn of mind and quick in understanding language. In fact she was remarkable in acquiring the Nez Percé language so as to understand and converse with the natives quite easily by the time they reached their station at Lapwai. She could paint indifferently in water colors, and had been taught while young, all the useful branches of domestic life; could spin, weave and sew, etc.; could prepare an excellent meal at short notice; was generally sociable, but not forward in conversation with or in attentions to gentlemen. . . . With the native women Mrs. Spalding appeared easy and cheerful and had their unbounded confidence and respect. She was remarkable for her firmness and decision of character in whatever she and her husband undertook. She never appeared alarmed or excited at any difficulty, dispute, or alarms common to the Indian life around her."[6]

An extract from one of her letters home two years after reaching Lapwai gives further insight into her character: "Little Eliza [her first child] is a great favorite with the natives, both old and young, and they are so determined to take her into their arms, that they sometimes almost rend

[5] Based on Drury, *Spalding*, 165-350.
[6] William H. Gray, *History of Oregon*, 110-11.

her from mine, and frequently when I am about my work, take her from the cradle and not unfrequently I have the mortification to pick a flea or a louse from her clothes, but these are little things and I will say no more about them at present."[7]

Marcus Whitman was a country doctor from upstate New York who had wanted to study for the ministry instead of medicine. With him was his wife, Narcissa Prentice Whitman, a pale blond woman, very attractive, and a former friend of Henry Spalding, who had once proposed to her. She liked to talk to men. At the rendezvous in 1836, while Mrs. Spalding was making friends with the Nez Percé women, Narcissa Whitman held court for the mountain men. Many of them later testified that her presence in their midst that summer had a lasting beneficial effect on their lives.[8]

The fifth member of the party was "Oregon's historian," William H. Gray, who had left school because of poor scholarship and had failed later at an attempt to study medicine. He had served an apprenticeship as a cabinetmaker. He went west largely for adventure and was responsible for much of the discord that arose in the mission later. While the missionary helpers who later followed this advance party are important in Northwest history, they have no part in this study of the Nez Percés.

[7] Drury, *Spalding,* 180.
[8] *Ibid.,* 180.

8: The Little Log Schoolhouse

FORT HALL marked the parting of the ways for the missionaries and the main body of Nez Percés, although several of the tribe went as far as Walla Walla with the newcomers, following the old Indian route that later became the Oregon Trail. The rest of the tribe returned to the Clearwater by way of the upper Salmon and the old Nez Percé Trail. After a pleasant visit with Pambrun at Fort Walla Walla, the whites proceeded down the Columbia to Fort Vancouver and the famed hospitality of Dr. John McLoughlin, the "ruler of the Northwest," who gave them a great deal of assistance in establishing their missions. With supplies from the company's posts, Whitman commenced building on the bottom lands of the Walla Walla River about twenty-five miles above the fort. Here he had an ample supply of farming land and water for irrigation and was near the timber of the Blue Mountains. He hoped to collect the Cayuse and Walla Walla tribes around his mission, establishing them as farmers and stock raisers with permanent dwellings.

The Spaldings were to settle among the Nez Percés if a suitable location could be found. They wanted a large tract of good land to take care of the expected converts, who should be numerous in a tribe of 3,000 or 4,000. In the crisp October weather, Spalding and Whitman, with Nez Percé guides, rode over the country searching for the best location. The dry, barren hills, covered with short, scorched range grass, looked very dismal to men raised in the rolling farm lands and wooded hills of the New York lake region, dampening their spirits until the Indians became alarmed. The Nez Percés explained that the land was much better in some of the creek bottoms nearer the mountains. Finally, in the little valley of Lapwai, a sheltered expanse of rich bottom land was found, surrounded on all sides by bleak, forbidding hills. The nearest timber was miles away, up Lapwai Creek. One hundred and twenty miles of rough trail separated the spot from the Whitman mission, where the nearest white people lived, but here the Spaldings decided to begin their work.

As soon as Spalding returned to Lapwai with his building supplies, hundreds of willing helpers gathered to assist him in constructing a house. Logs were cut along the Clearwater and floated down to the mouth of Lapwai Creek, being carried the last two miles up the creek to the building site by gangs of toiling men. Soon Spalding had a combined dwelling and school, eighteen by forty feet, with a mud-daubed fireplace at each end and a partition in the middle. During the winter, until the house was ready, the Spaldings lived in a tipi pitched nearby. While Spalding and his crew of volunteer helpers were busy on the house, Mrs. Spalding began to instruct a large group of eager students in reading and writing.

Several favorable circumstances offered encouragement to her in this herculean task. Many of the tribe were extremely anxious to learn both reading and writing because of the added power it would give their "medicine," and they were willing to work at tasks fit only for women in order to gain their desires. Moreover, Spalding, by the force of his example, made work more respectable in their eyes. As a group, they were clean, moral, industrious, and intelligent, rating above the average Indian in all these respects.

Even with such advantages, there were several formidable difficulties. The Nez Percés had no alphabet, no written language, no system of spelling for their words. While their language was very pleasing and expressive, it was quite different in structure and grammar from English. Some English sounds were entirely lacking in their speech and, conversely, some of their sounds were very difficult to express by the English alphabet. Before she could even begin the most elementary instruction in reading or writing, Mrs. Spalding had to learn a good deal of the Shahaptian language and devise an alphabet that would express all the necessary sounds. Then she would translate short English sentences into Shahaptian, hand print some copies of this lesson for her classes, and she was ready to begin the formal teaching. Imagine a woman with a multitude of household duties, living in a tipi with none of her accustomed conveniences, producing by hand sufficient lessons for a school of two hundred students. Fortunately, the Indians learned printing readily and proved to be very skillful in copying the material furnished them. Each one would then carry his prized copy home each evening and turn his lodge into a schoolroom where he instructed members of his family. With such intense interest and application, there is little wonder that hundreds of the tribe learned to read and write a little in their native tongue and that a few learned some English. Many a modern teacher would be willing to sacrifice some of the present-day aids to teaching if he could have a group of students with the same desire for learning.

In the spring of 1839, with the importation of a small printing press, a gift from the Hawaiian missions, the work of instruction became easier. In all, a dozen books were printed in the Shahaptian language on this little press before it was moved down the river to the settlements. In this way, several books of the Bible were made available for the Indians, who were interested only in religious subjects in their reading.

Another difficulty confronting the teachers was the securing of sufficient food. Not only did the Spaldings have to feed themselves, but they had to plan a food supply for the hundreds of students and their families if the school were to continue. By this time, the Indians had become seminomadic, roaming from fishing camp to camas grounds to buffalo hunting and back in pursuit of their living. If they settled near the mission, they would be cut off from much of their usual food supply. If they did not settle, they could not learn from their new teachers.

Spalding believed the answer to the food problem was the introduction of cultivated crops and the raising of cattle, sheep, and hogs, but he was handicapped in his plans by a lack of tools, seeds, and breeding stock. For a few years, all the cultivated land was wrested from the wild grass by hoes in the hands of the Indians, a most tedious task. While the braves in jest accused Spalding of turning them into women, they worked long hours in their small gardens. In the spring of 1840, there were 150 hoes in constant use from morning until night in the little garden patches along Lapwai Creek, one of the implements commanding the same price as a horse because of the great demand for them.

Potatoes, other vegetables, and a little grain were the first crops. A water-powered grist mill produced a rough meal, very coarse but nutritious and quite palatable, from the grain. Soon the mission was producing practically all the food needed for the Spaldings and their helpers, and many of the Indians raised substantial crops. The cattle, sheep, pigs, and chickens multiplied rapidly once the initial stock had been secured.

Even after he had interested many of the Indians in farming, Spalding had difficulty in keeping his students in the school for any length of time at a stretch. They all liked to roam the country throughout the summer and fall, hunting, visiting, and gathering camas. Now at one swoop, Spalding proposed taking away all their traveling, all their amusements, all their intertribal prestige, and in return offered to aid them in settling down as stodgy farmers. When they had asked for the white man's religion and his arts, it was not with the idea of giving up all their former ways, but to secure "medicine" strong enough to allow them to retain their old culture in the face of white invasion. The vaguely understood spiritual values of the new religion seemed rather small in comparison with the many sacrifices required of them by the missionary.

Spalding's training in medicine, brief as it had been, was of great aid to him in securing a hearing for his teachings. Through many years of experience, the mission board and its field workers had learned that the best immediate benefit they could bestow on uncivilized peoples of all lands was the care of their sick, and it proved true again in the Nez Percé country. Spalding was kept quite busy administering his simple remedies, but in the end his very success in this line raised up enemies to him and his work. He wrote to one of his eastern friends:

"I am no physician but have more or less sickness to look after sometimes eight or ten cases on my hands at once, usually bowel complaints caused by eating bad food or too much of it, or in other words, gluttony, requiring as I suppose cathartics. These I issue at order five or six before I am dressed in the morning, not often finding time to go near the patients, especially if they are any distance off; besides by my ignorance I can do as well by ear as by eye.

"In the winter, however, there are many cases of lung complaint occasioned by bare feet in the wet snow, which often terminates in consumption and death after a lapse of a few years. Blood letting is a favorite remedy among them, and I

85

often go by the lot, opening five or six at a time and go about more pressing business, leaving them to stop the blood when they please. If they cannot get me to open their veins for them, they do it themselves with an arrow, digging away until they find blood from veins or artery which they usually dig for, occasioning swelled arms, legs, and sometimes, I believe death."[1]

Spalding's medical innovations became the fad of the day, much to the detriment of the local medicine men. Even such patients as did come to them had to be taken at reduced rates or they might go on to the mission for treatment. With both his prestige and his income at stake, it is no wonder that the deposed medicine man resorted to intrigue to regain his former position.

Effective instruments ready to their hands were young men who liked to talk big and kick over the traces occasionally, like young men the world over. In addition, the new teachings seemed to be aimed directly at them. They were forbidden to go on the warpath or to the buffalo grounds. The missionaries objected to their ceremonial dances, their gaudily decorated war horses, and their gambling games. Spalding even went so far as to break up some of the gambling by hurling the cards into the fire, and more than once he whipped someone for breaking his puritanical edicts.

By some miracle, Spalding was not killed by any of the men he whipped, degrading as such punishment was in their eyes. They contented themselves for a time by tearing down his fences, using the rails for their fires, riding through his crops, threatening him with bodily harm, and annoying Mrs. Spalding at her school.

It is not clear why Spalding could whip some of the Indians for their offenses, but could not protect himself and Mrs. Spalding from such annoyances. It is quite evident that he

[1] Drury, *Spalding*, 173.

expected the tribe to discipline such cases through gratitude for the work he was doing. He could not understand why the chiefs and leading men were so little interested in protecting the crops raised primarily for their own benefit.

Had Spalding considered the Nez Percés primarily as human beings, he need not have been at all surprised, even though he might well have been disappointed. He had come bearing gifts of food, clothing, and tools, distributing them indiscriminately, contrary to tribal custom, and without securing any adequate return for them. Although the Indians did not know it, and Spalding would never admit it, he expected very definite repayment for his goods and his labors in the form of protection, support, and the acceptance of his doctrine. When these were not forthcoming, he felt defrauded, especially when he found that his prestige had been hurt rather than helped by his generosity, the Indians considering him an easy mark.

On the whole, the picture of the work at the Spalding mission those first few years was one of peace and progress, of willing work and great accomplishment. The achievements of the tribe in reading, writing, agriculture, household arts, and animal husbandry were considered remarkable by all observers. The saw mill, grist mill, blacksmith shop, and various other buildings, the fenced fields under cultivation, and the herds of stock gave the small settlement an air of prosperity and permanence. While many of the tribe were opposed to working in the fields, a majority were either in active support of the new plan or were indifferent onlookers. The most discordant notes of the period were sounded by the missionaries quarreling among themselves. The friction increased rapidly with the arrival of additional workers from the East and had a decidedly detrimental effect on the efficiency of all concerned. The quarrels themselves do not concern us here since the Indians took no part in them. It is only necessary to note that they arose from a clash of personalities, and that they contributed to the ultimate failure of the missions. The unfriendly Indian faction was quick to point out how much the practice of the whites differed from their teachings.

Because of a lack of funds, the mission board found it necessary to curtail their program quite markedly, dismissing Spalding along with several of their other workers in various parts of the world. He was probably chosen of the group in the Northwest because of the letters of criticism sent to the board by the people with whom he had quarreled. The dismissal order was dated February 25, 1842, but before it could reach Spalding some change in the financial outlook led the board to reverse their action on April 28.

Whitman was rather alarmed by these developments and was afraid that there would be more trouble in the future unless the mission board received a clear picture of the work being done by Spalding. He decided to go east that fall to explain matters, to secure additional support for the work, and to have his and Spalding's appointments made permanent. His trip later became the basis of the widespread "Whitman saved Oregon" legend. While the trip was successful in clearing up many of the troubles, the home board censured Whitman for leeaving his post on such an errand. It was during Whitman's absence that Dr. Elijah White introduced his well-known code of laws to aid in keeping peace among the Indians at the missions.

9: Troublesome White Men

SOME of the missionaries' troubles of this period had their roots in the commercial rivalries of the fur trade. Since 1810, the British and Americans, through various organizations, strove to monopolize the rich trade of the Columbia Basin. In their efforts against each other, each side lowered white prestige in the eyes of the Indians, who soon saw that the whites were subject to the same frailties as the red men and were unworthy of the high position in which they had been placed at first. It was but a short step from opposing one set of traders at the instigation of the other to opposing both sets for the benefit of the Indian.

When Benjamin Louis Eulalie de Bonneville and Nathaniel J. Wyeth invaded the Snake Valley in the early thirties in search of fur, the Hudson's Bay Company immediately took steps to drive out the Americans. They established a post at Fort Boise, where the Boise River empties into the Snake, and began to offer better prices for fur. The Americans were handicapped in the price war because their overland transportation from St. Louis was more expensive than the ocean and river transportation of their rivals, and they were small traders operating on shoestring capital while the opposition was a wealthy, well-intrenched organization. The competition soon forced

Wyeth to sell his post, Fort Hall, to the British firm in 1835. The struggle had a logical but unforeseen effect on the Nez Percés. Previously, they had done most of their trading at Fort Walla Walla and Spokane House because those two posts were so convenient and purchased so many horses. Only a minor portion of the trade went to the Americans on the upper Missouri, the Green River rendezvous, and at Fort Hall, but they traded enough in the Snake Valley to learn of the better prices offered there. Later, when they were offered the old prices at Fort Walla Walla, they began to argue with Pambrun, demanding that he pay the same prices that were paid at Fort Boise. When he refused, the Indians became very angry. Finally, they seized him and subjected him to rather rough handling, jumping on his chest, threatening his life, and discussing the advisability of burning the place. In order to save his life and, what was probably more important in his own opinion, to save the company property, Pambrun finally agreed to raise the prices paid for furs and horses. Having succeeded against an agent of the powerful Hudson's Bay Company, the Indians were encouraged to resist the whites in many ways. Spalding mentioned that the group of Nez Percés causing him trouble was led by a man who had helped abuse Pambrun.

While mountain men frequently married Nez Percé women, they usually stayed in the buffalo country or moved west of the Cascades. The first of these to settle on tribal lands came in 1840, with the passing of the rendezvous and the profitable fur trapping. Such men were usually Americans, unfriendly to the Hudson's Bay Company as a result of years of competition, and they opposed the missionaries for their arbitrary and puritanical rules. Such a mountain man was William Craig, the first white man not connected with the mission to take up farming in the Columbia Basin.

William Craig was born in Virginia about 1800. When

he was seventeen he killed a neighbor with a hoe after the latter picked a quarrel with him. He fled to the West, where he had little to say about his early life, possibly fearing arrest for his action. He was reported as a trapper as early as 1829, and from then on his name is frequently connected with those of Kit Carson, Joe Meek, and Jim Bridger. In 1833, he joined the party sent to California by Captain Bonneville under the command of Joe Walker. Craig was the man who tricked Walker into diving headfirst into the Humbolt River where a few inches of turbid water covered a soft mudbank. By the time Walker had scrambled out and had dug the mud from his eyes and nose, he went for his rifle, but the joker managed to keep out of gunshot until the danger was over.

William Craig was well educated for his time. His letters and reports are well composed and well written. He served with some distinction under Governor Isaac Stevens during the Indian troubles of 1855–56 and was Indian agent at Lapwai for many years. He was the first postmaster at Walla Walla, serving only a short period before he returned to his farm, where he ran a hotel and stage station until his death in 1869. He was generally respected by his associates, with the exception of Henry Spalding.

In 1838, at the Wyoming rendezvous, Craig married Isabel, daughter of Chief James of Lapwai. Two years later, in the summer of 1840, he helped Robert Newell and Joe Meek take two wagons from Fort Hall to Walla Walla for Marcus Whitman. Soon after that, he and his wife appeared at her father's village on Lapwai Creek, where Craig began farming a tract of bottom land near the Spalding mission. When Spalding objected, saying that he needed all that land for the mission farm, Craig moved farther up the creek. In 1846, he secured a government deed to his farm, the first deeded land in Idaho.

Chief James and Henry Spalding did not get along too

well. Spalding had taken over the local medicine practice, depriving James of revenue. Spalding told the Indians that James and the other medicine men got their power from the devil and all their patients were in danger of eternal damnation. He also refused to pay James any rent for the land used by the mission. James claimed that Samuel Parker had promised that the mission would pay a yearly rent, and Parker's interpreter supported this claim.[1] It may be that some of Parker's flowery references to spiritual benefits were misinterpreted or misunderstood. Whatever the true explanation, the trouble remained, and when Spalding refused to pay, James considered himself the injured party. Perhaps this hope of payment accounts for some of the eagerness shown by the Nez Percés in welcoming the missionaries.

James had an additional grievance. As chief at Lapwai, he did not approve of the influx of Indians from other villages. The old tribal custom had explicitly reserved a village site for members of the local band. Now there were Indians from many bands living on what he regarded as land belonging to his band and village, but they would not acknowledge him as chief, nor would they obey any of his orders.

Joseph and Timothy, the first two converts, probably irked James most. They ranked highest of all the tribe in the eyes of the Spaldings and had personal prestige in their own right, each being a village chief. Joseph was one of the important fighting men of the tribe, too, sometimes leading a war party of several hundred men. Their continued presence at Lapwai considerably reduced the influence of the local chief, who did not understand how he could regain his prestige until he had shown that he had power over the Spaldings. It is apparent then that Craig did not cause the trouble at the mission. He merely entered the discussion after it had been going on for some time.

[1] Miles Cannon, *Waiilatpu, Its Rise and Fall, 1836–1847*, 38.

Troublesome White Men

Two extracts from Spalding's writings describe how bad the situation had become. On February 2, 1841, he wrote in his diary:

"From what the Indians say, he [Craig] came telling the Indians he would set things right and giving them to understand that I must be sent away and he take the place, mills, property. My heart sickened at the discovery of such a dark plot against the temporal and spiritual good of these benighted ones."[2] In a letter he wrote: "I have had a gun cocked and presented at my head for fifteen or twenty minutes while four of the principal men stood and looked on with as much indifference as if a dog were to be shot down and when the proper moment arrived I arose and walked off, the muzzle of the gun brushing my cheek. At one time probably five hundred people were collected threatening to go to my home tie and whip my wife and for no other reason than because she had sent to the chief of the place requesting him to send away two of his men who had just presented themselves before the school naked and painted with the most horrible figures and continued their indecent gestures until Mrs. S was obliged to leave the house."[3]

In his attempts to protect himself and his wife, Spalding was handicapped by his Christian doctrine of nonresistance to personal attack, although he would sometimes use violence, such as whippings, to punish infractions of his moral code. He was able to carry out such sentences when he had the backing of public opinion, but here he often allowed his anger to bias his judgment. Once he gave an Indian woman seventy lashes for leaving her husband, a white man who was the mission blacksmith at the time. Because he had beat her, some of the Indians thought the husband deserved the whipping more than the wife, but Spalding made no effort to punish him.

[2] Drury, *Spalding*, 262.
[3] *Ibid.*, 294.

Spalding had one unusual punishment to be used against a large group in exceptional cases. He would refuse to hold church services until his wishes had been granted. However one might doubt the efficacy of such an action, more than once it brought a group to repentance and extracted from them a promise to reform very quickly. It was a punishment that had to be used sparingly to remain effective and was of no value against the antimission crowd. It should be kept in mind also that the people punished by Spalding usually had done nothing against their own social standards, which may account in part for his ineffectiveness in many cases.

Because of the loose social organization of the tribe, the chiefs and influential men interested in the church work could not protect the Spaldings from the rough element. While the chief of each village possessed a little authority over his own followers, this came mostly from his own personality. In his own village, with the backing of public opinion, he could keep the young men under control most of the time. Away from the village his authority ceased.

Since the young men causing the trouble at the mission were from several villages, they were subject to no common authority. Even if the chief of each were present, their combined authority would not have been great enough to punish such actions. The jurisdiction, such as it was, rested with the local chief, James, who was unfriendly or indifferent. Even had he chosen to act, there was little he could have done, for the youths had violated no code, and there was no one to judge them. The problem was new and serious.

10: The Law Comes to Lapwai

DR. Elijah White, a missionary in the Willamette Valley, was appointed Indian subagent for Oregon by the United States government in 1842, even before the boundary question with Great Britain had been settled. To him Spalding turned for help, asking that he come to Lapwai to make some arrangements with the Indians that would take care of the changed conditions under which the tribe was then living. There had to be some sort of tribal government adopted if the mission work was to continue, and since Spalding lacked both the influence and the authority to accomplish what he saw was necessary, he wisely called in the direct representative of the federal government, which the Indians still respected.

Dr. White, with a few attendants, reached Lapwai in December, 1842. He was greatly impressed with the results of Spalding's work, particularly with the amount and quality of farming done by the Indians. The accomplishments were all the more impressive to him because he was familiar with the poorer results gained in the Willamette Valley by more mission workers at a greater cost.

In his investigations of the conditions reported by Spalding, Dr. White decided that a code of laws and some sort of

95

central government were needed. He decided that there should be a head chief with a good deal of power, assisted by twelve subchiefs, in addition to the village chiefs under the old plan. Each subchief should be in charge of a district and should have five men as a sort of police force. The head chief and subchiefs should confer on the more important matters and should aid each other in their duties.

To indicate the standard of conduct expected, White proposed a code of ten laws for the consideration of the tribal council, probably choosing the number ten in order to associate the new laws with the Ten Commandments in the minds of the Indians and thus give them greater weight.

Unused to democratic practices, the Indians had some difficulty in selecting their new chief and subchiefs, but the matter was finally arranged. Ellis, an influential young man who had been educated in the Red River Settlement, was chosen chief. The ten proposed laws were carefully discussed and finally adopted with very little change. The Indians added a law of their own devising, concerning the keeping of dogs, and they asked that the penalties be made quite severe. This is the code as it was adopted:

1. Whoever wilfully takes life shall be hung.
2. Whoever burns a dwelling house shall be hung.
3. Whoever burns an outbuilding shall be imprisoned six months, receive 50 lashes, and pay all damages.
4. Whoever carelessly burns a house or any property shall pay damages.
5. If anyone enter a dwelling, without permission of the occupant, the chiefs shall punish him as they think proper.
6. If anyone steal, he shall pay back two fold, and if it be the value of a beaver skin or less, he shall receive 25 lashes and if the value is over a beaver skin he shall pay back two fold and receive 50 lashes.

7. If anyone take a horse, and ride it without permission, or take any article and use it without liberty, he shall pay for the use of it, and receive from 20 to 50 lashes as the chief shall direct.

8. If anyone enter a field and injure the crops, or throw down the fence, so that cattle and horses shall go in and do damage, he shall pay all the damages and receive 25 lashes for every offence.

9. Those only may keep dogs who travel or live among the game. If a dog kill a lamb, calf, or any domestic animal, the owner shall pay the damages and kill the dog. [This is the law proposed by the Indians.]

10. If an Indian raise a gun or other weapon against a white man, it shall be reported to the chiefs and they shall punish him. If a white person do the same to an Indian, it shall be reported to Dr. White and he shall redress it.

11. If an Indian break these laws, he shall be punished by his chief. If a white man break them, he shall be reported to the agent and be punished at his instance.[1]

Under this simple code of laws, with chiefs able to enforce them, the tribe rapidly developed more orderly traits and a sense of group responsibility. During the next year, the mission work went on more smoothly and probably reached its highest point of development. The return of Dr. Whitman from the East the following summer and the great harmony within the ranks of the missionaries also contributed to the progress of the missions.

[1] A. J. Allen, *Ten Years in Oregon: Travels of Dr. E. White and Lady West of the Rocky Mountains*, 182–91.

11: The Waiilatpu Massacre

AFTER Joe Meek and Robert Newell showed that the Blue Mountains could be crossed with wagons, the tide of immigration to Oregon swelled rapidly, one of the early trains being that which Dr. Whitman accompanied on his return trip in 1843. The new settlers reached Fort Boise with their provisions and teams exhausted by the trip across the desert of southern Idaho, with the worst part of the trail still to be traveled. To supply their great demand for fresh horses and food, the Cayuses and Nez Percés assembled in small bands along the trail with horses, meat, salmon, and camas. They usually asked for clothes, tools, or cattle in exchange.[1] One woman traded a worn camp apron for two large salmon, and a man was offered a fine riding horse for two print dresses.[2] Sometimes the Indians would take the exhausted horses of the settlers in trade for fresh ones, with some other goods as "boot." Thus, few of the newcomers reached Oregon without one or two Indian horses.

Most of the settlers made no distinction between the Cayuses and the Nez Percés, many of them not even knowing there were two tribes represented, so they thought all the

[1] Origen Thomson, *Across the Plains in 1852*, 87.
[2] Simeon Ide, *A Biographical Sketch of the Life of William B. Ide*, 33.

horses came from the Cayuse tribe. In this way, horses in the Willamette Valley came to be divided into two classes. Those brought from the East were called American horses, while those acquired from the Indians were known as Cayuse Indian horses, which later shortened to Cayuse horses. This term gradually spread throughout the West and came to mean any western horse, although it is sometimes restricted to saddle horses. Since the Nez Percés were less active in this trading of horses than were the Cayuses, their stock was less well known to those passing through.

After the wagon trains reached the west slopes of the Blue Mountains, the Indians brought them vegetables and grain from their small fields. The Whitman mission, an important station along the trail, had excellent opportunities to sell its produce, the demand for breadstuffs in particular exceeding the supply. The crude mills at Lapwai and Waiilatpu both ground a coarse whole-wheat flour much in demand, and the flour was packed across from Lapwai on horses.[3]

The Nez Percés soon became envious of the trade's flowing to the Cayuses because of their location along the trail, and they considered ways of diverting the tide of travel, with its accompanying profits, to their own country. They wanted the trains to turn aside from the Oregon Trail at Weiser, Idaho, and follow the old war trail up the Weiser River to the head of the Little Salmon and on down to the Clearwater instead of crossing the Snake River for the steep climb up the Blue Mountains. They claimed this would be much easier, but no one seemed willing to break the trail.

A story from Joel Palmer's *Journal of Travels over the Rocky Mountains, 1845–1846* indicates how highly the immigrant trade was regarded by the Nez Percés. Several of the chiefs at Lapwai decided they would prevent Spalding from running the flour mill because of an argument they had with

[3] S. A. Clarke, *Pioneer Days of Oregon History*, II, 497.

him. They thought this would prove embarassing, for they knew he had a rush order for flour to be delivered at Waiilatpu to a party of men who were returning to the States that spring. When Spalding found that he could not grind the flour, instead of giving in to the chiefs, he sent a letter to Whitman explaining the situation and asking that he tell the travelers how it happened that thc flour could not be delivered as promised.

The chiefs suspected that the letter concerned their quarrel, so they intercepted and read it just as Spalding had expected. When they found that their actions would cut off some trade and might also give them a bad reputation with future travelers, they withdrew all objections and the flour was delivered on time.[4]

By this time, the trade of the tribe with the immigrants had reached such a size that its cessation would have been a real blow. While their demand for trade goods had been increasing steadily, the market for horses at the Hudson's Bay Company posts had declined a great deal. Unless they could sell to the immigrants, they would have to do without many of the things they needed.

The Cayuse tribe soon found that the increase in travel brought troubles as well as trade. The large parties of travelers swept the country clear of game, fished out the streams, and left a wide swath of littered campsites through the beautiful Grande Ronde, the favorite summer camping grounds of the tribe. The herds of cattle and horses ruined the pasture that had supplied food for the range horses and numerous herds of deer for which the region had been famous.

Coupled with these annoyances wcre more aggravating incidents. The immigrants, mostly from the Middle West, had been raised on Indian horror stories about what had hap-

[4] Joel Palmer, *Journal of Travels over the Rocky Mountains, 1845–1846,* 238–39.

pened when dad or grandad were little boys, when the savage tribes north of the Ohio had ravaged the borders with fire, rapine, and slaughter for two generations. The last great border conflict in the Middle West had ended less than thirty-five years before, and its details were still fresh in the minds of the people. Whites raised in that section of the country were firmly convinced that all Indians were inherently cruel, thieving, and treacherous. Such contacts as they had made with the scum of the Plains Indians on the westward trip too often confirmed their beliefs. This state of mind found them ready and anxious to retaliate for any wrong, real or fancied, suffered at the hands of the red men, and they did not seem to care so much if they caught the guilty individual as long as they punished one of his detested race. In this they were one step beyond the Indian, who at least confined his vengeance to the clan or tribe of the guilty man. The whites also held to the doctrine that the only good Indian was a dead one, and they had the reforming temperament. It can be seen that they were totally unprepared to appreciate the good qualities of the Cayuses and the Nez Percés.

In the rough terrain of the Blue Mountains, horses and cattle often strayed from the camp herd and were lost in the ravines and wooded draws. Such losses were often blamed on the Indians, and quite rightly, for the Shoshoni delighted to steal stock in Cayuse territory, where the latter would get the blame. In some cases, the thieves were renegade Cayuses or irresponsible young men out for devilment. However, many of the losses were directly due to carelessness on the part of the herder, who escaped blame by accusing the Indians. No matter how the loss occurred, the immigrant, under the pressure of necessity, was apt to make the shortage good from the first herd of range horses he found, not bothered in the least that they belonged to innocent people.

When one of the whites did find an Indian herd, it was

not very difficult to convince himself that his lost stock was very much more valuable than the animals he found running wild on the range, and consequently he felt justified in taking several to make up for the one or two he had lost. This trait of overvaluing lost possessions is proverbial in all communities. One railroad official in Iowa summed up his observations in the matter by saying that nothing so improved the scrub livestock of the Middle West as crossing it with a railroad train. Crossing southern Idaho with stock seemed to have much the same effect.

The immigrants may have believed that their raids on the "wild" horses would pass unnoticed, not knowing that the Indian system of branding and ear marking accurately determined the ownership of their stock, and that stolen animals were easily spotted. The Indians could not recover their stock short of open fighting, something they were loath to do. The various arguments arising from such incidents and from the depredations of the Shoshoni gave the Cayuses an undeserved reputation as troublemakers.

Smallpox, measles, and scarlet fever were quite common in the various wagon trains and were spread to the Indians when they came to trade with the whites. The Indian's lack of acquired immunity, his mode of life, his disregard of the elementary rules of camp sanitation, and his methods of treating disease all helped raise the mortality rate much above that of the whites. In the three diseases mentioned, the vapor-bath treatment was particularly deadly. For a person with a burning fever to steam himself and then plunge into a cold mountain stream was only slightly slower than, but practically as deadly as, a strong dose of poison. Measles often wiped out entire families and destroyed three out of every four persons in a village.

Under ordinary summer conditions, the Indians could avoid the ill effects of unsanitary camps by moving frequently, but when illness struck, they often were forced to camp in one place for weeks. The resulting filth caused typhoid and dysentery that were fatal to the weakened survivors of the epidemic. Many of the northwestern tribes were further weakened by widespread venereal diseases, usually introduced by the whites, but the Cayuses and the Nez Percés were saved from these inflictions by the higher standard of morals among their women. It is too bad that they could not have had some sort of protection against the contagious diseases also.

On the whole, the Nez Percés suffered less from the various causes discussed above than did the Cayuses. They were too far from the trail to catch diseases so readily. Both their pasture lands and their horse herds were safe; their game was undisturbed. During the years of 1844 and 1845, their mission had reached its period of greatest development, with the tribe rapidly learning the ways of the whites, but from then on until the mission was abandoned in 1847 there was a steady deterioration.

This decline may have resulted largely from the ill health of Mrs. Spalding and her forced withdrawal from most of the work. Ever since her first appearance at the rendezvous, the Indian women and many of the men had considered her their especial friend. She had always been kind, sympathetic, and understanding, learning their language almost from the first meeting. She was always calm and patient, working long hours for them in the school, the sewing and household arts classes, and the religious activities. While her husband was a very conscientious man, his effectiveness with the Indians was reduced considerably by his impatience and short temper. Time and again Mrs. Spalding had to act as peacemaker when some violent outburst on his part had aroused the tribesmen. Although neither she nor Spalding mentioned the matter in their accounts, it is evident from various reports that she was more responsible for the success of the mission. Spalding's illness caused little anxiety among the Nez Percés, but when Mrs. Spalding was not expected to live, one of the men, probably the beloved Timothy, expressed his willingness to die in her stead if such a sacrifice would spare her to teach his people.[5] Although other influences were at work undermining the mission during this period, it is significant that interest in the school fell off markedly when Mrs. Spalding had to give up teaching and Spalding took over the work.

In considering William Craig's activities during this period and his possible influence against the Spaldings, it is well to keep in mind that practically all the information on this affair comes either directly or indirectly from Spalding and is obviously biased. The two men disagreed on the right method of handling Indians. Spalding looked on himself as the lawgiver, judge, and ruler of the tribe, an opinion not shared by Craig and many of the Indians. When Spalding criticized Craig as an ungodly man and a bad influence on the Nez Percés, he meant that Craig opposed some of his arbitrary methods.

There is no evidence that Craig ever gave the Nez Percés bad advice, considering the matter from the standpoint of the Indians. Spalding wrote that Craig told the Indians that civilized people paid for land and water privileges and that Spalding was treating them like slaves. Here, again, is the matter of land rent for the missions. Neither Spalding nor Whitman understood the Indian point of view, believing that their mission work should be considered more than enough payment for their farms, but they were wrong in blaming Craig for raising the question. The indications are that the Indians had discussed this topic for some time before Craig's arrival and had merely asked him what the custom was among whites in similar cases.

[5] Drury, *Spalding*, 299.
[6] *Ibid.*, 324.

Spalding also accused Craig of trying to file a claim on the mission property, but he never offered any evidence to support the charge. He did record in Craig's favor that the latter was a good workman and a good neighbor.[6] Other white men considered Craig an honest and responsible man, leaving stock in his care for months at a time while they were away.

A much different type of mountain man was Tom Hill, who had also settled among the Nez Percés. While Craig was a white man with an appreciation of the advantages of white culture, Hill was an Indian with a heritage of bitterness against the Americans. His people were a part of the great Delaware tribe which had been driven steadily westward from their original home on the banks of the Delaware by the encroaching settlers until some of them sought refuge across the Mississippi in Spanish territory, settling near Cape Girardeau with the consent of the governor about 1794. Here they built a prosperous farming settlement, only to have their lands taken by force for American farmers after Louisiana was bought by the United States, while they were driven to the open country in Kansas.

Another portion of the tribe settled with the Wyandots (Hurons) near Sandusky, but their reservation was whittled down by successive treaties until the remnants of the people were moved to Kansas. These events were filled with tragedy and terror for the Indians, as atrocity followed atrocity, and the peaceful Christian members of the tribe were treated more harshly than their wild relatives.

Two Delawares with some white blood, Isaac and John Hill, are mentioned in the treaties with the Sandusky band, and one of them very likely was the father of Tom, who had been under mission influence for a time, probably attending school for a while with William Walker, the interpreter, whose father was in charge of the Sandusky mission during that period. When the Delawares moved to Kansas, young

Tom Hill became a hunter for the mountain men and was soon serving under Kit Carson. In the spring of 1834, he was one of the three Delaware hunters with Kit Carson, Joe Meek, and two other white men who fought off a large band of Comanches in the country between the Cimarron and Arkansas rivers, a fight embellished and recorded by Joe Meek in later years. In 1837, Hill was with Kit Carson on the Yellowstone. When Manhead, leader of the Indian hunters, was killed in a fight with the Blackfeet, Carson appointed Hill to take his place.

Two years later, when Kit Carson disbanded his hunters and trappers, Tom Hill joined a band of Nez Percés in the buffalo country of Montana. He had known these people for some years, since Nez Percé bands often joined forces with the mountain men. Hill married a Nez Percé girl from Kooskia and soon rose to a position of power, being credited with a following of 8 or 9 chiefs and 1,000 Indians, which included almost all of the Nez Percés in the Montana country at that time.

Spalding made no effort to meet Tom Hill or to understand his great popularity. He merely registered complaints against Hill in the reports and letters he sent east. Marcus Whitman followed a different course. He invited Hill to the Waiilatpu mission and treated him well. These two men liked each other as persons even though they disagreed on each other's teachings.

In the summer of 1846, Hill went to California with a band of Wallawallas. There he served with distinction under John C. Frémont in the Bear Flag Revolt. After two years in California, he went back to the Delaware reservation in Kansas and accepted land in recognition of his army service, for he served in California as an enlisted man, not as an Indian scout. He evidently died in Kansas about 1860, as his estate was probated in the fall of that year.

The Waiilatpu Massacre

Tom Hill is an important figure in Nez Percé history because of his violent opposition to white farmers and missionaries. He believed that these people should be driven out of the Indian country or killed off. The rest of his teachings, as recorded by Spalding, Whitman, and Craig, favored keeping the old Indian religion and customs. For this he was called an atheist and a debased infidel by the missionaries, who were too angry with him to be accurate in their epithets.[7]

It is evident, then, that the increased immigration, the rapid growth of Tom Hill's influence, and the poor health of Mrs. Spalding coincided with the decline of the mission, and while each, in some measure, contributed to the decline, it is difficult to assign them any relative rank. It is clearly shown that Hill's prestige grew more rapidly as his predictions concerning the whites came true. How much Mrs. Spalding, unhampered by illness, could have neutralized his teachings is problematical.

The sad state of mission affairs is shown by the decline of interest in the school. Spalding grew discouraged over the prospect. He wrote: "The large and interesting school at this place which once numbered 234 has entirely ceased. No one attends this winter, and there is not the least prospect that there ever will be another school here. The last two winters I took charge of the school myself. But more assembled to disturb, break windows, steal, create every possible confusion than assembled to receive instruction."[8] The Indians broke all the windows in the school and the meeting house, tore shingles off the roof, and used Spalding's fences for firewood to light their gambling games.

During the troubles, Craig proved helpful and sympathetic. He helped repair the mill so grain could be ground

[7] Francis Haines, "Tom Hill, Delaware Scout," *California Historical Society Quarterly*, Vol. XXV, No. 2 (June, 1946), 139–47.

[8] Drury, *Spalding*, 326.

after the Indians had damaged both mill and race considerably, and he took the mission stock to his place so they would not injure the poorly fenced crops of the Indians, receiving $100 for the season's work.[9] This can hardly be considered an excessive charge, for the stock were much safer under Craig's care, and they had much better pasture than was available at Lapwai.

While the depredations and diseases of the immigrants were working such havoc among the Cayuses, Tom Hill was on hand to point out the cause of their troubles and to urge the immediate killing of the whites as the only remedy. To add to the tense situation, Yellow Serpent, or Peu Peu Mox Mox, war chief of the Wallawallas, had a son murdered at Sutter's Fort in the Sacramento Valley, where he had gone to trade for some cattle. When the tribe demanded the punishment of the murderer under the code set up by Dr. White and found that the United States government had no authority over a man on Mexican soil, they proposed raising a war party of 2,000 braves, the pick of the warriors of the entire Columbia Basin, which would sweep northern California with torch and gun. Dr. White, by some fast talking, managed to prevent the raid, but his failure to fulfill the promises given at this time further angered the Indians.[10]

About 200 warriors did go to California in the summer of 1846, where the rumor of their coming created a great scare among the settlers, who thought they were coming for revenge. Instead, the party was quite peaceable and enlisted under Frémont for a time during the Bear Flag Revolt of 1846. About 30 of them died of measles on the trip through the mountains, to the great grief of their families.[11]

[9] *Ibid.,* 326.
[10] Allen, *Ten Years in Oregon,* 243–50.
[11] Paul Kane, *Wanderings of an Artist among the Indian Tribes of North America,* 282–83.

At this stage, Nature took a hand in the game. The winter of 1846–47 was the most severe known in the Northwest since the coming of the whites. Deep snows and weeks of subzero temperatures killed the prized cattle herds, the range horses, and most of the game. The Indians, shivering in their inadequate tipis, lacked food supplies for such a season and died from the cold and hunger. The weakened survivors found no game in their spring hunting. The salmon run was late and the fishing poor because of the excessive spring floods. When the immigrant trains appeared that summer, the poor physical condition of the undernourished survivors made them more susceptible to disease. That year the effects of the measles were more severe, the disease reaching epidemic proportions among the Cayuses, with many of the convalescents dying of the accompanying dysentery.

After the Nez Percés deserted his school and his church, Spalding turned more and more to trading. There is some indication that he opened a small trading post at the mission, and he sometimes stationed himself along the Oregon Trail with various articles to sell to the travelers.[12] By such activities, he lost much of the respect of the small group of loyal church members, who quite properly objected to their minister's acting in such a manner.

To cap it all, there arrived at Waiilatpu that summer a half-blood Maine Indian of low character, Joe Lewis. The wagon train refused him permission to travel any farther and turned him adrift at the mission. Dr. Whitman vainly tried to get Lewis to do some work, finally outfitting him so he could proceed with another westward-bound party. In a few days Lewis was back, continually stirring up trouble. Because Cayuse Indians under the doctor's care died of measles, while most of the whites recovered, Lewis persuaded the tribe that Whitman was poisoning the sick so he might take their lands.

12 J. Ross Browne, *Report*, 35 Cong., 1 sess., *Sen. Exec. Doc. 40*, 64.

On Monday, November 29, 1847, these various causes combined to produce the widely advertised Whitman massacre. Dr. Whitman, his wife, and twelve white men then at the mission were killed by the very Cayuse Indians who owed the Whitmans so much for their years of work in the tribe. Several of the men escaped, some of them wounded. Forty-six women and children were later ransomed from their captors by Peter Skene Ogden, chief factor of the Hudson's Bay Company, whose prompt use of the company's prestige and resources prevented a greater tragedy. Three girls, ill at the time, died from shock and exposure. Three others, taken by various Indians as wives, were given up on demand to Ogden. Most of the atrocity stories connected with the event are either exaggerations or later inventions. No one was tortured. The captives suffered much more from their imaginations than from actual abuse. Compared to massacres of the Middle West or the Great Plains, it was a very tame affair.

Indian Mission church, 1891.

MATTHEWNIM TAAISKT.

WANAHNA I.

TIMASH hiwash Jesus Christpkinih wiautsath kuph. Davidnim miahs awaka Jesus Christ, Abrahamnim miahs awaka David.

2 Abrahamnim miahs autsama Isaac; Isaacnim miahs autsama Jacob; Jacobnim mamaias autsama Judas wak askama;

3 Judasnim autsama mamaias Phares wah Zara, Tharmapkinih; Pharesnim miahs autsama Esrom; Esromnim miahs autsama Aram;

4 Aramnim miahs autsama Aminadab; Aminadabnim miahs autsama Naason; Naasonm miahs autsama Salmon;

5 Salmonm miahs autsama Booz Rachabkinih; Booznim miahs autsama Obed Ruthpkinih; Obednim miahs autsama Jesse;

6 Jessenim miahs autsama David, Miohat; Davidnim Miohatom miahs autsama Solomon, ka yoh awaka iwapna Urianm, kunimpkinih;

7 Solomon miahs autsama Roboam; Roboamnim miahs autsama Abia; Abianm miahs autsama Asa;

8 Asanm miahs autsama Josaphat; Josaphatom miahs autsama Joram; Joramnim miahs autsama Ozias;

9 Oziasnim miahs autsama Joatham; Joa-

The first page of the Gospel of St. Matthew, printed in Shahaption. From the 1871 edition of the New Testament, it was printed from the same type and press used at Lapwai in 1840 by Henry Spalding.

12 : Interlude

SPALDING narrowly missed death at Waiilatpu also. He had been there visiting his oldest child, Eliza, who was attending the school for white children conducted by the Whitmans that fall, but he had gone on down to Umatilla, returning on Wednesday after the massacre. The murderers were waiting on his return to add him to the list of victims. He was saved by a timely warning from Father Brouillet, one of the Jesuit missionaries, and managed to escape his pursuers in the fog and early dusk of the winter evening. Traveling only at night, without food or fire, he approached Lapwai, anxious concerning the fate of his wife and three children there. The second morning he lost his horses. His ill fitting shoes, from some missionary barrel, gave out, and his blankets, soggy from the driving storm, were too heavy to carry. Suffering from cut, bleeding feet and a badly wrenched knee, he finally reached the hills above Lapwai after five days and nights of hardship to find a band of Nez Percés pillaging his home, with no sign of his family.

One of the wounded men from Waiilatpu had reached Lapwai on Saturday, December 4, reporting that Spalding had perished with the Whitmans. Mrs. Spalding immediately took charge of securing the safety of herself and the children by attempting to rally the local chiefs to her support. She decided it would be better to tell them at once of the trouble, and at the same time she sent a messenger to warn Craig. The faithful Timothy went to Waiilatpu to rescue Eliza.

William Craig came down to the mission at once. He and Mrs. Spalding decided that it would be best to assemble all the whites, including three workmen at the mission, in Craig's substantial house, where it would be easier to defend themselves against attack, but Mrs. Spalding refused to move on Sunday, even in the face of danger. Her prompt action in confiding in the chiefs and her bravery in this matter strengthened her influence with the Indians at Lapwai.

Early Monday morning, Mrs. Spalding packed her children and some of her things in the wagon for the trip to Craig's, with Craig and a band of his Indian friends as an escort. Just as they were ready to start, a band of Nez Percé trouble makers rode up, headed by an Indian who had been at Waiilatpu as an onlooker. He suggested that they kill all the mission people except Craig, but James and his followers formed a guard around the wagon and conveyed the party safely to Craig's home.

James had little difficulty in protecting the mission workers, but he could not prevent some looting of the house and farm. As soon as he came back from his escort duty, he was able to calm the looters and thus save the permanent structures. Spalding had no way of knowing that his family was safe as he looked on the pillaging from the hill that afternoon, but one of his Indian friends told him that night as Spalding rested in his lodge, exhausted from his ordeal. Tuesday he arrived at Craig's, his immediate danger over, but he never fully recovered from the effect of those dreadful days.[1]

With the mission in the possession of the Indians, Spalding had no goods with which to pay for a messenger to Fort

[1] Drury, *Spalding*, 333–50.

Walla Walla. He persuaded James to do various errands, promising to pay him as soon as the necessary goods could be obtained from the Hudson's Bay Company. James received his payment at the same time the Cayuses received the ransom payments for their captives. This has caused some confusion among the writers on the subject who assume that the Spaldings were ransomed from the Nez Percés. Spalding, in one of his letters, specified that he needed various articles to pay friendly Indians for their services.[2] The Spaldings came to Fort Nez Percé, not as captives, but with a guard of honor. Many of the tribe sorrowed over their departure and hoped that the mission would be reopened soon, but more than twenty years were to elapse before Spalding resumed his church work at Lapwai.

James took over all the mission property, as was his right under the ancient tribal custom.[3] He divided the stored grain and possibly the cattle with some of the other chiefs. With his increased prestige, he was able to send the Indians at the mission back to their own villages. Among these were Timothy and Joseph.

James had shown his jealousy of the two for many years. As the first two converts, they had ranked high in church circles, and Joseph easily outranked James in the tribal council because of his ability as a war leader. He also had served as one of the twelve subchiefs under Dr. White's plan. Timothy was as important in the church as Joseph, although he was much less important in the tribe. Now, with the mission power broken, the two bowed to the old Nez Percé custom, Timothy returning to his village at Red Wolf crossing, while Joseph settled again in the Wallowa.

The enmity between James and Joseph had an important

---

[2] William Isaac Marshall, *The Acquisition of Oregon and the Long Suppressed Evidence about Marcus Whitman*, II, 220.

[3] Drury, *Spalding*, 343, n. 1.

bearing on later tribal affairs, but their roles have been confused by some careless writers, who assumed that James belonged to the mission group because he protected Mrs. Spalding and the mission property, while Joseph has been accused of helping to loot the mission. Yet James was an important leader of the antimission party and Joseph remained a practicing Christian and a friend of the whites for some fifteen years after he was supposed to have reverted to heathenism.

The mistake grew out of the confused accounts of Henry Spalding. In his first account of the looting, he said he recognized Joseph's brother-in-law as one of the crowd.[4] Years later he changed this to a statement that Joseph himself led the band. In evaluating the confused, garbled, and highly colored statements of Spalding in later years, it is well to keep in mind that the terrible hardships connected with the massacre left his mind somewhat impaired.

Other testimony places Joseph more than 100 miles from Lapwai at the time. Yet had he been present he could not have stopped the looting unless he had a powerful force of fighting men ready to act. With Mrs. Spalding and her children safe at Craig's, it is doubtful that he would have considered the mission property worth a tribal feud.

Although some regular soldiers and several companies of volunteers campaigned against the Cayuses in revenge for the Whitman deaths, the Nez Percés were not bothered. To be sure, some of the volunteers were in favor of attacking the Nez Percé villages when they found that the Cayuses had escaped into the mountains, but the conduct of the Nez Percés prevented any such action. As soon as Colonel Cornelius Gilliam arrived with his troops at Waiilatpu, he was met by William Craig, acting as envoy for the tribe. Craig secured permission for a council to which more than 250 warriors came, led by Joseph, who advanced to the council grounds

[4] *Ibid.*, 343, n. 1.

under an American flag, carrying a New Testament in his hand as a token of his innocence.[5]

General Joel Palmer, Indian agent for Oregon at the time, was quite pleased with this turn of affairs. He granted peace to the tribe and sent them home to their spring planting. He also promised that no white men would be permitted within the Nez Percé borders without the consent of the tribe and appointed William Craig as Indian agent at Lapwai with powers of a magistrate. This was in March, 1848.[6]

Two months later, the Nez Percés were back at Waiilatpu in another council with a new request. Ellis, the head chief appointed by Dr. White in 1842, had antagonized many of the tribe with his pride and arrogance. When they objected to his conduct, he went to the buffalo country, where he stayed until he and sixty of his band died of disease. Now the tribe asked that General Palmer appoint a new head chief.

The whites were more interested in having a head chief they could manage than they were in choosing a good leader. They chose Richard, one of the boys who had gone east with Whitman in 1835. He was a good man but not much of a leader, and soon resigned in favor of Lawyer. In direct opposition to Nez Percé custom, the whites appointed a peaceable man of mediocre ability as war chief. This man, Meaway, made no attempt to act as war chief, leaving all such activities to Lawyer, Joseph, or the great Looking Glass, all of whom had won their rank in many battles.

For the next few years, the Nez Percés are seldom mentioned in the records, indicating a period of peace and progress. Craig remained at Lapwai, a prosperous farmer. Many of the Nez Percés raised grain and vegetables each year. Red Wolf, at the mouth of Alpowa Creek, had a thrifty orchard. When Anson Dart, of the Indian service, held a routine coun-

---

[5] Mrs. Frances Fuller Victor, *Early Indian Wars of Oregon*, 184.
[6] 32 Cong., 1 sess., *House Exec. Doc.* 2, Pt. 1, 450.

cil at Lapwai in 1851, he commented on the fine behavior and unusual progress of the tribe.[7]

About this time, a proposal was made to move all of the Indians living west of the Cascades onto the spare lands in the Columbia Basin in order to make room for more white settlers. Both the Nez Percés and the Cayuses protested vigorously, fearing the spread of venereal infection so common in the Coast tribes.[8]

In 1853, the Indian commissioner proposed using Nez Percés as guards for the Oregon Trail so they could protect the wagon trains in the hazardous stretch from Fort Hall to Burnt River. This scheme to use the ancient enmity between the Nez Percés and the Shoshoni to aid the whites fell through. The next important event concerning the Nez Percés came in 1855.

[7] Palmer to Manypenny, 33 Cong., 1 sess., *House Exec. Doc. 1*, Pt. 1, 450.
[8] Thompson to Palmer, 33 Cong., 1 sess., *House Exec. Doc. 1*, Pt. 1, 488.

13: The Great Council on the Walla Walla

THE importance of the year 1855 in the history of the Nez Percés arises chiefly from the actions of a very able man who was burdened with a great deal of work. In 1853, Isaac Stevens was appointed governor of the newly created Washington Territory and Indian agent for the Northwest. Jefferson Davis, then secretary of war, was interested in building a transcontinental railroad. As Stevens was proceeding west to take up his other duties, Davis gave him the task of surveying a possible route near the northern border. Stevens planned to become acquainted with the various Indians along the route, holding preliminary councils with them from time to time in preparation for his later plans.

The newly appointed governor believed that the best approach to the Indian problem was to get the various tribes to quit fighting one another. Then they could settle down, enjoy some prosperity, and be much less of a bother to the government. Peace in the Northwest would also be of advantage to the traders, road builders, and settlers.[1] In carrying out his ideas, Stevens held various councils, the first of importance to the Nez Percés being the great council held in the valley of the Walla Walla River a few miles above the old Waiilatpu

[1] Hazard Stevens, *Life of Isaac Ingalls Stevens*, II, 54.

mission ruins. The following account of the council is quoted directly from the diary kept by Lieutenant Lawrence Kip, a young army officer with the escorting troops.[2] A few comments are added for clarity.

WEDNESDAY, MAY 23, 1855. At two P.M. we arrived at the ground selected for the Council, having made the march [from The Dalles] in six days. It was in one of the most beautiful spots of the Walla Walla Valley, well wooded and with plenty of water. Ten miles distant is seen the range of the Blue Mountains, forming the southeast boundary of the great plains along the Columbia, whose waters it divides from those of Lewis River. It stretches away along the horizon until it is lost in the dim distance, where the chain unites with the Snake River Mountains.

Here we found General Palmer, the Indian Agent, and Governor Stevens, with their party, who had already pitched their tents. With the latter we dined. As was proper for the highest dignitary on the ground, he had a dining room separate from his tent. An arbor had been erected near it, in which was placed a table, hastily constructed from split pine logs, smoothed off, but not very smooth. Our own preparations were made for a more permanent encampment than we have as yet had: a tent was procured for Lieutenant Gracie and myself, while the men erected for themselves huts of boughs, spreading over them pack covers.

THURSDAY, MAY 24—This has been an exceedingly interesting day, as about twenty-five hundred of the Nez Percé tribe have arrived. It was our first specimen of this Prairie chivalry, and it certainly realized all our conceptions of these wild warriors of the plains. Their coming was announced about ten o'clock, and going out on the plain to where a flag staff had been erected, we saw them approaching on horse-

---

[2] Lawrence Kip, *The Indian Council in the Valley of the Walla Walla, 1855,* 10–24.

back in one long line. They were almost entirely naked, gaudily painted and decorated with their wild trappings. Their plumes fluttered above them, while below, skins and trinkets and all kinds of fantastic embellishments flaunted in the sunshine. Trained from early childhood almost to live upon horseback, they sat upon their fine animals as if they were centaurs. Their horses, too, were arrayed in the most glaring finery. They were painted with such colors as formed the greatest contrast; the white being smeared with crimson in fantastic figures, and the dark colored streaked with white clay. Beads and fringes of gaudy colors were hanging from the bridles, while the plumes of eagle feathers interwoven with the mane and tail, fluttered as the breeze swept over them, and completed their wild and fantastic appearance.

When about a mile distant they halted, and half a dozen chiefs rode forward and were presented to Governor Stevens and General Palmer in the order of their rank. Then on came the rest of the wild horsemen in single file, clashing their shields, singing and beating their drums as they marched past us. Then they formed a circle and dashed around us, while our little group stood there, the centre of their wild evolutions. They would gallop up as if about to make a charge, then wheel round and round, sounding their loud whoops until they had apparently worked themselves up into an intense excitement. Then some score or two dismounted, and forming a ring, danced for about twenty minutes, while those surrounding them beat time on their drums.

After these performances, more than twenty of the chiefs went over to the tent of Governor Stevens, where they sat for sometime, smoking the "pipe of peace," in token of good fellowship, and then returned to their camping ground.

The Nez Percé, or Pierced Nose Indians, received this name from the early traders and trappers, but they call themselves by the name of Chipunnish. While they are the most friendly to the whites of any tribe in this region, they are at the same time one of the most numerous and powerful, roaming over the whole Rocky Mountains, along the streams to the West, and across the almost limitless plains to the East, until they reach the hunting grounds of the tribes of the Missouri. They hunt the elk, the white [grizzly] bear, the mountain sheep and the buffalo, while they trap the beaver to sell the skins to the whites. They are celebrated for their droves of horses, which, after being branded, are turned loose to roam the fertile plains till needed by their owners: when this is the case, it requires but a few days to break them sufficiently to answer the purpose of their bold riders.

About seventy women were seen among the warriors, for their presence is necessary when the tribe is to be encamped for any length of time. They perform all the menial offices, arranging the lodge, cooking and bringing wood, for it would be a disgrace to their lords to be seen engaged in these things. It would procure for them the title of "squaws." Everything but the perils of war and the chase are beneath their attention. When at home and not occupied in preparing their arms, or in feats of horsemanship, they are gambling, lounging in groups on the mounds of the prairie or listening to some story teller who recounts the exploits of the old warriors of the tribe.

The Walla Wallas, another of the principal tribes, is much reduced in numbers and importance since the pioneer trappers first came among them. . . .

In the afternoon I visited the lodge of an old chief of the Nez Percés, named Lawyer. He showed us a wound in his side from which he was yet suffering, although several years had elapsed since it was received. It had been inflicted in a fight with their old hereditary enemies, the Blackfeet Indians. . . . He showed us also, some locks of their hair which he wore about him,—not as love tokens, or presented willingly by their former owners, but rather the reverse; as I presume they are the remains of scalps he had taken.

The Great Council on the Walla Walla

Today Governor Stevens and Mr. Doty, one of his party, dined with us. It was the first dinner party we had given in the wilderness. Yet think not, O ye who dine your friends at Delmonico's, that our entertainment was at all like yours. In the centre of our tent, a buffalo robe was laid on the ground (the luxury of a table being confined to the Governor) on which were placed the tin plates which were our only dishes, for china is not adapted to mule traveling on the plains. About this we reclined rather in the Oriental style. At one end of the table (I mean the buffalo skin), was a beef steak from one of the cattle daily killed at the camp, and at the other end a portion of the same unfortunate animal's liver. One side dish was a plate of potatoes—the other, a plate of bread of leaden heaviness. The second course was—coffee, likewise served in tin cups. Yet we gathered around this feast with appetites which could not be found among the strollers in Broadway, and which it required no French sauces to provoke.

FRIDAY, MAY 25—We woke this morning to hear rain pattering about us, and to be thankful that we were encamped, and not obliged to resume our march. At noon it cleared up, when we procured our horses and rode over to the Indian camp to pay another visit to our friend Lawyer. We found the old chief surrounded by his family and reading a portion of the New Testament, while a German soldier of Governor Stevens' party, was engaged in taking his portrait in crayon. He afterward presented me with a copy, which I keep as a memento of these pleasant days in the wilderness. In the evening he came to our tent to return our visit and we feasted him to the best of our ability, not omitting the indispensable pipe, and he seemed exceedingly gratified with his entertainment.

SATURDAY, MAY 26— . . . Towards evening the Cayuse tribe arrived, numbering about three hundred. They came in whooping and singing in the Indian fashion, and after riding around the camp of the Nez Percés two or three times, they retired to form their own at some little distance. In the evening I again visited Lawyer and also a number of his tribe. Some of them we found singing sacred music to prepare for tomorrow, which is Sunday.

SUNDAY, MAY 27—After riding over to Governor Stevens' to lunch, we went to the Nez Percé camp where we found they were holding services in one of the largest lodges: two of the chiefs were officiating, one of them delivering an address (taking the Ten Commandments for his text) and at the end of each sentence the other chief would repeat it in a louder tone of voice. This is their invariable custom with all their speeches. Every thing was conducted with the greatest propriety, and the singing, in which they all joined, had an exceedingly musical effect. There is an odd mixture of this world and the next in some of the Nez Percés—an equal love for fighting and devotion—the wildest Indian traits with a strictness in some religious rites which might shame those "who profess and call themselves Christians." They have prayers in their lodges every morning and evening—service several times on Sunday—and nothing will induce them on that day to engage in any trading.

At an early day the Roman Catholic Missionaries went among them, and as the tribe seemed blessed with a more tractable disposition than most of their brethren, the laborers of the Fathers appear to have met with considerable success. A kind of Christianity was introduced among them, strangely altered, indeed, in many respects, to make it harmonize with Indian thoughts and actions, yet still retaining many of the great truths of the faith. It exerted, too, a very perceptible influence over their system of morality. The Methodists, I believe, have more recently added their teaching; so that if the theological creed of the Nez Percés was now investigated, it would probably be an odd system which would startle an ordinary D.D.

After service we rode through the Cayuse camp, but saw

no evidence of Sunday there. The young warriors were lounging about their lodges, preparing their arms or taking care of their horses, to be ready for their evening races. The Christianity among these Indians, we suspect, is confined to the Nez Percés.

MONDAY, MAY 28—We spent the afternoon at the Nez Percé camp where a band of some thirty warriors were engaged in dancing and singing. Their musical instruments are few in number and of the rudest kind. The singing is very harsh and to us, who listened to it only as a collection of sounds, seemed utterly discordant. The songs are almost entirely extemporaneous, like the Improvititore recitations of the Italians, a narrative of some past events or perhaps suggested by the sight of persons present, or by trifling circumstances known to the audience. We never saw the women dancing and believe they rarely do, and never with the men.

During the dancing we had a little interlude in the shape of a speech. A young chief delivered it, and at the end of each sentence it was repeated in a louder voice by one of the old men. . . .

Today, leading chiefs belonging to some of the most distant tribes, attended by their followers, have been coming in to the camp, and most of those for which the Commissioners have been waiting are now represented. . . .

TUESDAY, MAY 29—Today the Council was to have met at twelve, but it was two o'clock before it came together. About eight tribes were represented. Nothing, however, was done but to organize the Council and swear in the interpreters. Governor Stevens made them a short address. All this occupied about two hours, when it began to rain and the Council adjourned to meet again at ten o'clock tomorrow morning if the weather should be pleasant; otherwise, on the first pleasant day. A fine prospect for the extension of our stay in the valley! There are about five thousand Indians, including squaws and children, on the ground.

The Nez Percés

WEDNESDAY, MAY 30—At one o'clock this afternoon the Council met and business seems to be really commencing. It was a very striking scene. Directly in front of Governor Stevens' tent a small arbor had been erected, in which, at a table, sat several of his party taking notes of everything said. In front of the arbor on a bench sat Governor Stevens and General Palmer, and before them in the open air, in concentric circles, were ranged the Indians, the chiefs in the front ranks, in the order of their dignity, while the far background was filled with women and children. The Indians sat on the ground, (in their own words) "reposing on the bosom of their Great Mother." There were probably a thousand present at the time.

After smoking for half an hour, (a ceremony which with them precedes all business) the Council was opened by a short address from General Palmer. Governor Stevens then rose and made a long speech setting forth the object of the Council and what was desired of them. As he finished each sentence, the interpreter repeated it to two of the Indians who announced it in a loud voice to the rest—one in Nez Percé and the other in the Walla Walla language. This process necessarily causes the business to move slowly.

THURSDAY, MAY 31—On arriving at Governor Stevens' tent I found that the Council had already met. After the usual preamble of smoking, Governor Stevens and General Palmer, in succession, made long speeches to them, explaining the benefits they would receive from signing this treaty, and the advantages which would result to them from their removal to the new lands offered in exchange for their present hunting grounds. The Council lasted till three o'clock.

This evening we went, as usual, to the Nez Percé camp. There was a foot-race but the great events of the evening were the horse-races. Each of the tribes now here possesses a large number of horses, so that wherever they are, the prairies about them are covered with these animals roaming at large until wanted by their masters. Part of these are derived from the wild horses of the prairies, while some, from the marks with which they are branded, show that they have been stolen from the Spaniards in Upper Mexico. To capture horses is esteemed next in honor to laurels gained in actual war, and they will follow the party of a hostile tribe for weeks, watching for an opportunity to "run off" their horses. It is for this, too, that they are hovering around the emigrants on the plains, who sometimes by a stampede or a single bold dash, lose in a night all their animals and are left helpless on the plains, as a ship at sea without sails.

Living as they do on horseback, racing forms one of their greatest amusements. They will ride for miles, often having heavy bets depending on the result. On this occasion we saw nearly thirty Indians start at once and dash over the plain like the winds, sweeping round in a circle of several miles.

Friday, June 1—The Council did not meet this morning, as the Indians wished time to consider the proposals made them during the last few days. We learned that two or three of the half-civilized Nez Percés, who could write, were keeping a minute account of all that transpired at these meetings.

At the races this evening a serious accident took place, and which had nearly proved fatal. The Indians, as usual, were dashing about on horseback, some going up and others down, when two of them came in collision, knocking down both horses and leaving the riders senseless. No bones happened to be broken; the "medicine men" took charge of them and it is supposed they will recover.

Saturday, June 2—The Council was already assembled, having met at twelve o'clock. The Indian Chiefs had at length begun to reply so another step has been gained. After Governor Stevens' opening speech, several of them followed in short addresses. I arrived just in time to hear the last one, made by one of the Cayuse Chiefs. He did not commit himself as to what they would do, but the whole tenor of his address was unfavorable to the reception of the treaty.

At the Indian camp tonight there was a great foot-race between about a dozen competitors, who ran over two miles. It was a good test of the long-winded endurance of the young warriors.

MONDAY, JUNE 4—The diplomatists met today at half-past one o'clock. After Governor Stevens' address, the old Chief, Lawyer, spoke, which was the first time any thing had been heard from the Nez Percés. Several of the other Chiefs followed, and the Council finally adjourned at five o'clock, without having yet made sensible progress.

Until a late hour we heard from the Indian camps the sound of their singing and the beating of their drums, and could see the figures flit before the fires as the dancing went on.

TUESDAY, JUNE 5— . . . Governor Stevens at the opening gave them the most elaborate address he has yet made, explaining to the Chiefs most definitely, what lands he wishes them to give up, and what their "Great Father" (the President) would give them in return, together with the benefits they would derive from the exchange. General Palmer afterwards made a speech an hour long in which he endeavored to illustrate to his audience the many advantages resulting from their being brought into contact with civilization.

There is evidently a more hostile feeling towards the whites getting up among some of the tribes, of which we had tonight a very unmistakable proof. The Cayuses, we have known, have never been friendly but heretofor they have disguised their feelings. Tonight as Lieutenant Gracie and I attempted as usual to enter their camp, they showed a decided opposition. We were motioned back, and the young warriors threw themselves in the way to obstruct our advance.

WEDNESDAY, JUNE 6—Today the Indians again determined not to meet in Council, as they wished to consult among themselves; so there is another day lost.

The races tonight were the most exciting we have seen, as the Indians had bet some sixteen or eighteen blankets on the result and all the passions of their savage natures were called into play. There was visible none of the Mohawk stoicism of manner which Fennimore Cooper describes.

THURSDAY, JUNE 7—The Council met today at twelve, when I went into the arbor, and taking my seat at the reporters' table, wrote some of the speeches delivered. There is, of course, in those of the Indians, too much repetition to give them fully but a few extracts may show the manner in which these wearisome debates were conducted day after day.

Governor Stevens—My brothers. We expect to have your hearts today. Let us have your hearts straight out.

Lawyer responded with a long speech, ending by approving of the treaty.

Governor Stevens—We now have the hearts of the Nez Percés through their chief. Their hearts and our hearts are one. We want the hearts of the other tribes through their chiefs.

Young Chief, of the Cayuses—I wonder if the ground has anything to say? I wonder if the ground is listening to what is said? ... The ground says, It is the Great Spirit that placed me here. The Great Spirit tells me to take care of the Indians, to feed them aright. The Great Spirit appointed the roots to feed the Indians on. The water says the same thing. The Great Spirit directs me, Feed the Indians well. The grass says the same thing, Feed the horses and cattle. The ground, water and grass say, The Great Spirit has given us our names. We have these names and hold these names. Neither the Indians nor the Whites have a right to change these names. The ground says, The Great Spirit has placed me here to produce all that grows on me, trees and fruit. The same way the ground says, It was from me man was made. The Great Spirit in placing men on earth, desired them to take good care of the ground and to do each other no harm. The Great Spirit said, You Indians who take care of certain portions of the country should not trade it off except you get a fair price.

He could not understand just what payments they were to receive. "When I come to understand your proposition, I will take hold. I do not know when. This is all I have to say."

Five Crows—(A Chief of the Cayuse tribe and half-brother to Joseph) I will speak a few words. My heart is just the same as the Young Chief's.

Peepe-Mox-Mox—(also called Yellow Serpent, of the Walla Wallas) The whites may travel in all directions through our country, we will have nothing to say to them, provided they do not build houses on our land. . . .

Owhi—(of the Umitillas) I am afraid of the Great Spirit. . . . Shall I give the land which is part of my body and leave myself poor and destitute? Shall I say, I will give you my land? I cannot say so. I am afraid of the Great Spirit. . . .

The Council did not adjourn till six o'clock. In the evening I rode over as usual to the Nez Percé camp and found many of them playing cards in their lodges. They are most inveterate gamblers, and a warrior will sometimes stake on successive games, his arms, and horses, and even his wives, so that in a single night he is reduced to a state of primitive poverty and obliged to trust to charity to be remounted for the hunt.

In the other camps, everything seemed to be in violent commotion. The Cayuses and other tribes are very much incensed against the Nez Percés for agreeing to the terms of the treaty, but fortunately for them, and probably for us also, the Nez Percés are as numerous as the others united.

FRIDAY, JUNE 8— . . . Just before the Council adjourned, an Indian runner arrived with the news, that Looking Glass, the war chief of the Nez Percés, was coming. Half an hour afterwards, he, with another chief and about twenty warriors came in. They had just returned from an incursion into the Blackfoot country, where there had been some fighting and they had brought back with them, as a trophy, one scalp which was dangling from a pole. . . . Looking Glass, then without dismounting from his horse, made a short and very violent speech, (The speech: "My people, what have you done? While I was gone you have sold my country. I have come home, and there is not left me a place on which to pitch my lodge. Go home to your lodges. I will talk to you."), which I afterward learned was, as I suspected, an expression of his indignation at their selling the country. The Council then adjourned.

At the races this evening in the Nez Percé camp, we found ten of the young braves who came in that afternoon, basking in the enjoyment of their laurels. . . .

SATURDAY, JUNE 9— . . . Looking Glass then arose and made a strong speech against the treaty, which had such an effect, that not only the Nez Percés but all the other tribes refused to sign it. Looking Glass, although nominally only the second chief, has more influence than Lawyer and is in reality *the* chief of the different Nez Percé tribes. . . .

Near the race grounds this evening we found the women collected in circles on the ground, gambling with the most intense earnestness. Like the men they will spend hours around the lodge fires, staking everything they have on the changes and chances of the game. Near them stood, as on the last evening, the returned warriors, exhibiting their fantastic bravery, and apparently thus challenging the applause of the softer sex.

SUNDAY, JUNE 10—The Nez Percés have been all day holding a council among themselves, and it is represented, the proposition has been made to appoint Looking Glass head Chief over Lawyer. Yesterday, while Looking Glass was speaking, Lawyer left the Council without saying anything; which many of them were disposed to regard as the surrender of his place. Should this proposition be carried into effect, it would give a quietus to the treaty.

MONDAY, JUNE 11—Before breakfast we had a visit from Lawyer with some other Indians. At ten o'clock the Council met. Governor Stevens opened it with a short speech, at the close of which he asked the Chiefs to come forward and sign the papers. This they all did without the least opposition. What he has been doing with Looking Glass since last Saturday, we cannot imagine, but we suppose savage nature in the wilderness is the same as civilized nature was in England in Walpole's day, and "every man has his price." After this was over, the presents which General Palmer had brought with him were distributed, and the Council, like other Legislative bodies, adjourned *sine die*.

As soon as this business was finished, we at once struck our tents and began our march toward the Umatilla. . . .

And so Kip passes from the scene after having recorded a vivid picture of an important Indian council.

There is reason to suppose that the opportune arrival of Looking Glass was prearranged between himself and Lawyer. The plan appears to have been for Lawyer to get the most favorable terms that he could, and when the negotiations were about over, Looking Glass would come in and oppose everything. Then he would have to be bought off by some additional concession, and the tribe would be assured of the best possible bargain. These Indians proved themselves rather clever diplomats on many occasions, and such a scheme was often used when bargaining with outsiders.

*Nez Percé Indians preparing the records of the Walla Walla Council,
1855.*

Sohon

May 1855

Arrival of the Nez Percés at the treaty ground, Walla Walla Valley,
1855.

Chief Looking Glass, Yellowstone River, 1871. (From a photograph
by William Henry Jackson, courtesy Smithsonian Institution)

14: Wars and Rumors of Wars

GOVERNOR STEVENS, in his capacity as superintendent of Indian affairs in the Northwest, strove to secure
a permanent settlement of the Indian problem through his
policy of intertribal peace and definite reservation boundaries.
He saw that the influx of white settlers would continue and
that land disputes would soon arise. Unless the Indians were
segregated, Stevens feared that white encroachment would
inevitably lead to bloody fighting. Symptoms of such a conflict were already noticeable in the Coast area, where the tribes
were more docile. Much less provocation than the Coast tribes
had endured would arouse the mounted Indians of the interior
to war. In order, then, to provide more land for the new settlers, protect the Indians, and lessen the danger of conflict,
Stevens proposed that all the tribes be placed on permanent
reservations.

Up to this time, few settlers had been attracted by the
land east of the Cascades, preferring the moister climate and
the timbered country to the west. With the western valleys
rapidly filling, it was evident that soon there would be a rush
to the fertile river bottoms in the Columbia Basin. The recent
discovery of gold at Colville, Washington, and other places
would aid in turning attention in that direction. By his treaties

made at the Walla Walla council, Stevens hoped to get the reservation lines well established before the trouble could start. To open as much of the basin as possible for white settlement and to remove the Indians to the more remote areas, Stevens first proposed that all the tribes be placed on one big reservation in the Nez Percé country. He expected the large numbers of friendly Nez Percés would dominate the discordant factions of the various other tribes and would gradually absorb them, for the Nez Percés were increasing in numbers while most of the other tribes were wasting away. At that time, the Nez Percés lived farthest from probable white settlement, so their land could best be spared for an Indian reservation. Such a solution would be particularly advantageous to the whites in the case of the Cayuse, Wallawalla, and Umatilla tribes, who had all been unfriendly since the Whitman massacre and who controlled a long section of the Oregon Trail.

Stevens was unprepared for the storm of protest raised by his proposal. Each tribe insisted on keeping some of its ancient tribal lands as a reservation and did not want to submerge itself in the Nez Percé tribe. The latter, in turn, did not care to crowd their country with outsiders, even though they were friends and neighbors. In the face of the united opposition, Stevens was forced to modify his plan. He finally negotiated three treaties instead of one, dealing with the Cayuses, Wallawallas, and Umatillas in one group, the Yakimas, Palouses, and twelve small adjacent tribes in a second group, and leaving the Nez Percés by themselves. In this way, he felt assured of Nez Percé consent to his plans and hoped that their agreement would influence the other tribes.

The Nez Percé Reservation, as defined in the proposed treaty, included most of the land claimed by the tribe, the principal tract surrendered to the government being the grazing land on both sides of the Snake River from the mouth of Alpowa Creek westward. Because of the opposition of Joseph, none of the lower Grande Ronde Valley was given up, the dividing line running along the crest of the Blue Mountains for some distance. In this way, all of the lower Grande Ronde and the entire Wallowa and Imnaha valleys were kept by the Nez Percés.

The Indians did not give up their right to hunt and fish on the lands they surrendered. They specifically reserved the right to use the fishing stations along the Snake River outside the reservation and the right to pasture their horses and cattle on any public lands near the reservation boundaries.

In compensation for the relinquished land, the tribe was promised a total of $200,000 in payments extending over a period of twenty years, the money to be spent on various improvements on the reservation or used to purchase merchandise for distribution to the tribe. In addition, the government agreed to build, furnish, and operate two schools, two blacksmith shops, two mills, one tin shop, one gunsmith shop, one carpenter shop, one wagon and plow shop, and one hospital. No whites, except the necessary employees of the Indian Bureau, were allowed on the reservation without permission of the tribe.

William Craig, at the special request of the Nez Percés, was protected in his holdings near Lapwai by a special clause in the treaty. His ability to retain the confidence of the tribe and of the various government officials would indicate that he was a more honest man than Spalding had believed. He was a useful man too, acting as interpreter and letter writer for the Indians on many occasions.

Lawyer's active support of the treaty has been variously interpreted. Some credit him with great foresight and say his actions were for the best interests of his people since he could see that their only hope in competition with the whites was a rapid adoption of civilization and settled abodes. This may be true, but he might have been interested more in the increased wealth and influence that would accrue to him personally. He was to have a house built and furnished by the government and a yearly salary of $500.[1]

After the Nez Percés signed their treaty, the other tribes followed their example, but rather unwillingly. They had a great deal of dislike and distrust for the whites, acquired over a period of fifty years of association. They knew that the Nez Percés had received a much better bargain. Many of them were plotting open warfare even at the council grounds. Some of them were hostile to Lawyer for his outspoken support of the whites. Lawyer told Stevens that the hostile chiefs were plotting to kill all the commissioners and their escort, and had invited the Nez Percés to join them, but he refused and moved his tipi into the camp of the whites in order to put them under his protection. Some people have suggested that Lawyer might have been more concerned with his own safety than that of Stevens, while others say he exaggerated the affair to gain increased concessions from the commissioners. It was at this time that Kip reported noticing the Cayuse camp's increased hostility toward the soldiers.

Stevens left the Walla Walla Valley as soon as he had concluded the treaties, hoping that the resentments of the various tribes would die down if they were left alone. He next devoted his energies to organizing a council at Fort Benton on the Missouri, where he hoped to get some agreement between the Plains tribes, headed by the Blackfeet, and the western tribes, led by the Nez Percés. Instead of taking a military escort for protection on his journey across the mountains, Stevens relied on the Nez Percé warriors for his guard of honor. Among the famous fighting men who went with him were Looking Glass, Spotted Eagle, Three Feathers, Eagle from the Light, Lone Bird, White Bird, and Plenty Bears.[2]

[1] Charles J. Kappler (ed.), *Indian Affairs, Laws and Treaties*, II, 702, 706.
[2] *Ibid.*, II, 739.

Wars and Rumors of Wars

After several thousand Indians had assembled near Fort Benton, it was discovered that the presents promised for the council had not been shipped from St. Louis on time. The Indians scattered over the country hunting buffalo while scouts went down the Missouri in search of the boats bringing the presents. Soon after, Stevens decided to hold the meeting farther down the Missouri, at the mouth of the Judith River, because he feared that the snows would block the mountain passes and thus prevent his return to the Columbia. Here he negotiated a treaty which was signed on October 17, 1855, after a discussion much like that recorded by Kip at the Walla Walla council.[3]

Since this treaty dealt primarily with the Blackfeet, only the terms that concern the Nez Percés will be mentioned here. The tribes agreed to divide the Montana buffalo country, the tribes from west of the mountains hunting south of the Missouri and going to their hunting grounds by a southern trail past Three Forks and across Bozeman Pass to the Yellowstone. The Blackfeet were to stay north of the Missouri and were to remain at peace with the western tribes as long as the latter did not trespass on their hunting grounds.[4]

This treaty established friendly relations between the Nez Percés and the Blackfeet after a century of conflict. From then on it was not uncommon for the Blackfeet to invite their former enemies to spend a season visiting them for the summer hunt. The southward movement of the Nez Percés brought them into closer relations with the Crows and gave them the westward-moving Sioux as enemies in place of the Blackfeet.

Scarcely had the treaty been signed when the first October snows fell in the mountains, warning Stevens that he must hurry if he wished to avoid difficulty in the passes. By this time, the western country was ablaze with revolts headed by

[3] Stevens, *Life of Isaac Ingals Stevens*, II, 110–19.
[4] Kappler (ed.), *Indian Affairs, Laws and Treaties*, II, 738–39.

141

the Rogue River and Yakima tribes, giving Stevens 100 miles of hostile country to cross with no protection but the Nez Percé forces. Timorous souls from Seattle advised Stevens that he should return by way of St. Louis, New Orleans, Panama, and the West Coast to prevent his being captured, but he counted on baffling his enemies by the speed of his movements. He crossed rapidly to the country of the Coeur d'Alênes and the Spokans, who were wavering in their allegiance to the whites but had not yet taken to the warpath. Stevens' sudden daring appearance among them convinced them that they should renew their peace pledges, and Stevens moved on to Lapwai where he could obtain an escort of several hundred warriors willing to fight to open a path for him to The Dalles.

At Lapwai, news of the victory of the Oregon volunteers under Colonel James K. Kelly showed that a large force was unnecessary, so Stevens took only 100 picked men, who served as his bodyguard when he rode gaily into the camp of the troops on the Walla Walla River, December 20, 1855.[5]

During the following two summers of conflict, the Nez Percés occupied the uncomfortable position of opposing their neighbors and former allies in order to keep the treaty they signed in 1855. All the neighboring tribes sought their support and threatened them if they did not join the revolt. At times, about two-thirds of the tribe favored doing so, but the most important chiefs held firmly to their treaty obligations. In the actual fighting, Nez Percés served on both sides. When William Craig joined the Washington volunteers as a lieutenant colonel, one troop of cavalry under Stevens was composed entirely of Nez Percé volunteers, among whom was Joseph, and seventy more served as scouts. These men supplied their own horses and equipment and served well for several months.[6] Because their customary trade sources for

[5] Stevens to Manypenny, 34 Cong., 2 sess., *House Exec. Doc. 93*, 137–40.
[6] Stevens, *Life of Isaac Ingalls Stevens*, II, 169.

such supplies had been closed by the war, the friendly portion of the tribe were supplied through Craig's influence with arms and ammunition to enable them to defend themselves against possible attack. They also maintained a band of tribal police to watch the trails and crossings on their reservation, thus hindering the movement of hostile bands across the country.[7]

The greatest heights of Nez Percé disaffection were reached the summer of 1856. When Stevens called a council at the Walla Walla grounds that August in an effort to end the fighting, he found even the friendly chiefs were beginning to grumble. Eagle from the Light explained that they objected to the hanging of one of Red Wolf's band by the volunteers the previous winter. When Stevens proved that the man had been acting as a spy for the Yakimas and his hanging was allowed under the rules of war, they admitted the justice of the sentence and brought out their real grievance. The hanging incident had been used merely to put Stevens on the defensive and to make him more ready to grant concessions. When the Nez Percés saw that their ruse had failed, Joseph and Red Wolf explained that they thought the treaty unfair to them because they had surrendered all the land taken from the tribe by the government, but Lawyer, who had not lost any land, was getting all the benefits. All the buildings and improvements promised under the treaty were being put at Lapwai, where Joseph and Red Wolf could not use them. Supporting them in this protest against Lawyer were Eagle from the Light and Speaking Owl, who represented Looking Glass.[8] It was obvious that Looking Glass had planned the whole matter in order to secure Lawyer's position as head chief, but another great warrior, Spotted Eagle, joined the Lawyer faction, keeping him in power. This incident indicates that the friction between Joseph and the Lapwai band was still great,

[7] Victor, *Early Indian Wars of Oregon*, 477–78.
[8] Stevens, *Life of Isaac Ingalls Stevens*, II, 217.

and it offers a clue to the sharp division of the tribe over the treaty signed in 1863.

While Stevens conducted the council with his customary tact and friendliness, he was greatly handicapped because the treaties of the previous summer had not been ratified by Congress. The Indians had expected the promised payments to begin at once, and the hostiles had been making a good deal of fun of the Nez Percés for selling their land and not getting anything for it. As the discussion became more and more heated, it appeared that the governor was losing all the Nez Percé support until Spotted Eagle made an impassioned speech that induced the chiefs to vote to uphold the treaty. He stressed the necessity of keeping their pledged word and of acting like honorable men and promised his protection to all the whites.[9]

In all other respects, the council was a failure. The other tribes refused to attend the meetings and massed to attack the governor's party as it left for The Dalles. Because of the loyalty of Spotted Eagle, Nez Percé participation in the attack was rather weak, and the fight ended with the Indians' retreating, few casualties being suffered on either side. It is interesting to note that, contrary to popular tradition, at this time 120 of the Nez Percés who had attended the council were in the attacking party under their regular chiefs.[10]

The struggle with the hostile Indians dragged on because of a lack of agreement between the two men in charge. Governor Stevens believed that he, as governor of all the territory and Indian superintendent as well, should have command of all the troops in the Northwest during the fighting. General John E. Wool, commander of the Department of the Pacific, maintained that he should determine how the soldiers should be used and that he took orders only from the War Department. While General Wool was technically in the right, he

9 *Ibid.*, II, 219.
10 *Ibid.*, II, 221–22.

allowed his personal animosity toward Stevens to bias him on Indian matters which were outside his jurisdiction, so the futile struggle between these two prolonged the war.

Governor Stevens wanted to pen the Indians on their reservations as determined by treaties not yet ratified and so not in force. Wool, looking at the situation from a strictly military point of view, wanted to use the natural barrier of the Cascades as the dividing line between whites and Indians, with the passes guarded by his soldiers. However, such a solution did not provide for the development of the Columbia Basin with its recently discovered gold mines and its potentially rich farming areas.

When Stevens found that he could not command the federal troops, he raised several companies of volunteers, among them the Nez Percés mentioned above. The volunteers were effective Indian fighters, but they did not discriminate between friendly and hostile bands, holding to the theory that any Indian was greatly improved by being thoroughly shot. When the news of their irregularities reached General Wool, he sent troops into the Walla Walla country to protect the peaceful Indians from the volunteers.

Reports from both the regular troops and the volunteers show that the Indians needed such protection. The volunteers were out to subdue the tribes and to live off the country. Having suffered at various times from Indian depredations, they refused to believe that the Indians could be justified in any way. It was easy for them to believe that all food caches, cattle, and horses belonged to hostile Indians and were fair spoils of war. Their raids on the stock of the neutral and friendly Indians finally became so bad that General Wool ordered them to leave the country, threatening them with arrest if they refused,[11] but they managed to take away a large herd of stock

[11] *Topographical Memoir, Department of the Pacific*, 35 Cong., 2 sess., *House Exec. Doc. 114*, 114.

which was sold at The Dalles to help pay the expenses of the expedition. The friendly portions of the Cayuse and Walla-walla tribes were left destitute, and all the Indians received a lesson of what they might expect from white troops who passed through their country.

Because of the personal animosity between Stevens and Wool, stemming from an incident at a banquet in San Francisco, they insisted on taking opposite sides on almost every question. When Stevens sent messages to Congress urging that the treaties be ratified, Wool sent reports against ratification. The Senate, unable to choose between the conflicting statements, ended by doing nothing. Finally, the situation was clarified by the transfer of General Wool and the replacement of Stevens as Indian agent by Edward R. Geary, who was to be in charge of the Indian affairs of the entire Northwest.

As soon as the treaties were removed from the factional struggle, it was evident that a majority of the people involved favored ratification. The Senate finally voted approval in 1859, and the first appropriations were made available in 1860.

Geary decided that the Indians needed a more positive program than just being confined to reservations. If they quit their roving habits, their hunting would be seriously reduced. Then they would need a new source of food and permanent homes. Geary outlined a policy for his own guidance, the principal features of which were:

1. Land should be assigned to the individuals, so that each Indian could have a permanent, fixed home and an individual right to a portion of the soil.
2. Indians should be compelled to do regular labor for their own support, instead of being furnished rations by the government.
3. The agent should be permitted to find homes in suitable white families for neglected Indian orphans.

4. Industrial schools should be established "where habits of cleanliness, punctuality, and order should be carefully cultivated."
5. Only men "of pure morals and correct deportment" should be employed on the reservations.[12]

[12] *Report of the Commissioner of Indian Affairs, 1859, 191–92.*

15: The Treaty at Last

ONE constant factor in the history of the Nez Percés from the founding of the Spalding mission in 1836 until the final breakup of the tribe was its division into two rather antagonistic groups, at various times called the prowhite and antiwhite, the Christians and the heathens, or the treaty and antitreaty. From 1855 on, the latter designation was the more accurate. As conditions on the reservation changed, many Indians changed from one group to the other, but the wild young men were always in the antitreaty party, while the leading chiefs were usually in the treaty party, especially those getting government favors. Usually, the conservatives, the sedentary people, were treaty, while the adventurous buffalo hunters were antitreaty.

At the council in 1855, the opposition group was small and disorganized, probably the weakest it ever became. Most of the group opposing Spalding had been won over by the closing of the mission and by the influence of William Craig. From this low point to the height of the antitreaty movement was a period of just a year. In 1856 Craig estimated that two-thirds of the Nez Percés favored joining the hostile tribes.[1]

After the council with Stevens in the summer of 1856, the

[1] *Report of the Commissioner of Indian Affairs, 1859,* 191–92.

The Treaty at Last

Nez Percé chiefs regained their confidence in him, carrying with them a majority of the tribe, a development that had an important bearing on the campaign of 1858. The Nez Percé aid to Colonel E. J. Steptoe in his disastrous campaign can best be shown by extracts from Steptoe's reports and from the letters of Lieutenant John Mullan. The latter had excellent opportunities to observe the Nez Percés while he was in command of the group of scouts which served under Colonel George Wright the same summer and who were equipped with uniforms by order of the colonel so they could be distinguished readily from the hostiles.[2] After Mullan had been in command of his scouts for more than three weeks, he wrote:

"And thirty bold warriors, marshalling themselves under brave war chiefs were placed at his [Wright's] disposal to assist him in finding and fighting the enemy. This is the same people who, meeting the flying columns of Colonel Steptoe in hot night retreat, having abandoned animals, provisions, and guns, behind them, received him with open arms, succored his wounded men, and crossed in safety the whole command over the difficult and dangerous south fork of the Columbia [the Snake River] at a time when no other means whatever, to out reach a foe, who already triumphant with success had determined his complete destruction."[3]

While Mullan's construction is a bit involved at times, it is clear that he thought well of his Nez Percés. Colonel Steptoe also gave them much credit for their help to him. His official report reads in part: "Without the assistance of Timothy's Nez Percés it would have been utterly impossible for us to cross [the Snake River] either going or returning."[4]

[2] Lawrence Kip, *Army Life on the Pacific, a Journal of the Expedition Against the Northern Indians, the Tribes of the Coeur d' Alênes, Spokanes, and Pelouzes, in the Summer of 1858,* 46.

[3] *Report of the Commissioner of Indian Affairs, 1858,* 277.

[4] Benjamin Franklin Manring, *The Conquest of the Coeur d'Alênes, Spokanes and Palouses,* 133–34.

The Nez Percés

When the Nez Percés could have insured the destruction of Steptoe's entire command merely by withholding assistance, they braved the certain disapproval of their neighbors by furnishing aid to the soldiers. Lawyer even offered to gather his band and go at once with Colonel Steptoe to wipe out the hostile force, but the colonel realized that punishment would have to wait until the soldiers could be reorganized and re-equipped.

Later that summer, when Colonel Wright won notable success in the same region, the uniformed Nez Percé scouts under Lieutenant Mullan distinguished themselves in two battles. After the battle of Four Lakes, they received mention in the dispatches for their bravery and ability. In the next engagement, they again rendered good service, acting as spies, guides, and guards for the pack train and the spare horses. Wright wrote: "As usual they behaved well."[5] Later, when he asked Lawyer what the chiefs desired for their people, Lawyer replied, "Peace, plows, and schools."[6] That fall, the Indian expressed much the same sentiment in a letter to Governor Stevens:

"At this place about three years since we had our talk, and since that time I have been waiting to hear from our big father. We are very poor. It is other peoples' badness. It is not our fault and I would like to hear what he has to say. If he thinks our agreement good, I will be thankful.

"Colonel Wright has been over after the bad people and has killed some of the bad people and hung sixteen, and now I am in hopes we will have peace."[7]

When the next spring brought word that the treaty had been ratified, and the payments still did not come, the renegades and the antitreaty crowd again became active, pointing

[5] *Ibid.*, 122.
[6] *Ibid.*, 206.
[7] *Report of the Commissioner of Indian Affairs, 1858,* 277.

out that the tribe had been tricked by the government. To counteract this argument and to explain the cause of the delay in payments, A. J. Cain, now agent at Lapwai, met with the Nez Percés during the great summer encampment at the Weippe camas grounds.

"I found there had been great dissatisfaction—not in regard to the treaty—but from the circulation of false rumors amongst them by renegades from the other tribes, to the effect they were being deluded with the idea that their 'treaty' was any good, and would be carried out until the whites and soldiers were strong enough to take their lands by force. . . . I had but little trouble in refuting these rumors with all but one chief [Eagle from the Light] who claimed to the last they had not been treated properly by the whites. He said my talk was good, but he did not know whether I was telling the truth, or was afraid and wanted to scare them. He has always been opposed to the treaty, but has few followers, and no influence with the tribe, with whom he lives but seldom, spending most of his time in the buffalo country with the Blackfeet.

"Some few of the reckless young men, actuated by a filibustering feeling have engaged in hostilities against the whites for which the tribe should not be held responsible."[8]

Although Agent Cain had little difficulty in refuting the "rumors," subsequent events showed that the renegades had been very accurate in their prophecies, for the land was taken by force in less than four years.

The account of this council shows clearly that Joseph considered himself to be one of the friendly treaty Indians opposed to the agitators and that the whites shared his opinion. Cain reported the chief's speech to the council:

"I want to tell you my heart. I am a red man. I have my own opinion about this country. We should make up our minds before we talk. When we made the treaty with Governor

[8] *Report of the Commissioner of Indian Affairs, 1859, 415.*

Stevens the line was drawn. I know where it is. You told us right yesterday. It is as you said. When Governor Stevens made the line, he wanted a certain chain of mountains. I said no, I wanted it to hunt in, not for myself, but for my children: but my word was doubted.

"The line was made as I wanted it; not for me but my children that will follow me. There is where I live and there is where I want to leave my body. The land on the other side is what we gave to the Great Father.

"You told us yesterday if there was anything we do not understand, you will explain. I will tell you one thing. I have a great many bad young men. I don't want them all to live together in one place; it will not do. We have too many horses and cattle to feed on one piece of land; and I am afraid that my young men and young men of other parties will not get along together. I don't only talk so today, but I will tell you the same some other time. We will talk this matter over some other time.

"My young men get drunk, quarrel and fight, and I don't know how to stop it. A great many of my men have been killed by it; and I am afraid of liquor.

"I think we cannot all live in one place. It is better for each tribe to live in their own country. We will talk this matter over some other time.

"This summer some of my children were mixed up with other tribes and some of them done wrong; and if the buildings you spoke of, and are mentioned in the treaty, were divided, it would be better for us all. I have told you my mind as it is. I wish you could arrange it so we could live in our own country. I know my young men are wild, and it is better to keep them separated. It is better for all to live as we are. That is all I have to say."[9]

Joseph had a good understanding of the difficulties in-

[9] *Ibid.*, 420-21.

volved in concentrating too many of the tribe at Lapwai. Always it had been the young men who stirred up the trouble, and grouping all of them from the various bands would make the problem worse. On the other hand, Lawyer was in favor of building up Lapwai, the center of his power, and Kamiah, his home village. In this he agreed with the agents, who felt it would be easier to manage affairs for their charges if they kept them near at hand. For some reason, they did not seem to encourage stock raising by the Indians as a means of making a living.

The long-awaited first payment due under the treaty arrived in the spring of 1860, greatly strengthening the treaty party. Now the chiefs could point to visible evidence of treaty benefits. That summer, too, brought the first test of the treaty restrictions on the whites. Many prospectors were anxious to explore the mountains in the reservation in search of precious metals. The Indians knew this and policed the main trails, turning back all such parties before they reached the reservation. To be ordered out of any place by Indians proved quite galling to the prospectors, and for a time they contemplated armed invasion, hoping that the troops would support them as soon as the fighting started. Agent Cain convinced them that he would call out the troops to act on the side of the Indians in such an emergency, since the prospectors would be violating the laws of the United States.

Cain's opposition to the miners gave the Indians a great deal of satisfaction, convincing them that they were safe under the protection of the treaty.[10] But soon the confidence of the tribe in the good intentions of the government was rudely shattered, and their whole scheme of living was changed by the discovery of gold on their lands, a discovery made possible through the aid of a traitor in their own ranks.

[10] *Report of the Commissioner of Indian Affairs, 1860, 178 79, 210*

16: Gold Is a Curse

UNTIL the first prospecting parties had been turned back by the Nez Percé guards, the reservation had no more appeal to the adventurous than any other unexplored area, but now, because it was forbidden ground, in their excited imaginations it became the most desirable area in the entire Northwest, and they devised many schemes for reaching its forbidden creeks. The vigilance of the guards frustrated all such attempts until the hidden trails of the reservation were disclosed by a traitor in the tribe and the white men were led by devious paths to their goal. To Jane, the eighteen-year-old daughter of Chief Timothy, was given the distinction of betraying her people merely to gain the temporary friendship of a band of strangers of another race.

One party of prospectors, more persistent than the rest, had been turned back on every known trail before they could even cross the Snake River, until they finally camped near Timothy's village, ready to give it up as a bad job. Here something happened to make them try once more, and when they finally left the village one night in a last effort, they were accompanied by Jane, who defied the conventions of both her own people and the whites by strolling off across the hills for a lengthy trip with a group of men. Under most circumstances, such conduct might bring a maiden censure and reproof, and for the betrayal of her tribe she might even be called a traitor. But Jane was far above all such criticism. For her exploit, she is ranked, by some of the whites, with Charbonneau's wife, Sacagawea.[1]

However unconventional her conduct might have been, Jane proved a most efficient guide and soon led her party to the banks of a creek not far from the western end of the Lolo Trail. Here, the first evening, gold was discovered in paying quantities, but it was very fine and hard to collect. Since most of the party had come from the California fields, they named the creek Oro Fino. When news of their strike reached Walla Walla late that fall, 1860, it caused little excitement. Richer diggings than that would be necessary to start a stampede across 150 miles of snow-swept plateau with winter at hand and the dreaded Nez Percé gauntlet to be run.

Quite surprisingly, the Indians who had guarded the trails so carefully against white invasion took no action against the small party of successful miners when they were finally discovered. They were allowed to leave the country peaceably by the main trail down the Clearwater and to return later by the same route with their winter supplies. The Indian agent inspected their camp, complimented them on their good behavior, and advised the Indians to accept the situation. This the Nez Percés seemed quite willing to do when they found that the miners were interested only in the back country, caring nothing for farming and furnishing a profitable cash market for beef and horses. The great fear of the tribe was that a swarm of white farmers would seize their good farm lands, leaving them practically destitute. Seemingly, miners were different, and less to be feared.

Springtime brought many changes. One of the miners went

[1] Robert G. Bailey, *River of No Return*, 102–109; Byron Defenbach, *Red Heroines of the Northwest*, 227–90.

to Walla Walla with $800 in dust for supplies and told how friendly the Indians had acted. At once the rush was on, hundreds flocking to the new diggings. Agent Cain had foreseen such a stampede, with its many complications, and had attempted to prevent some of its worst effects. At a tribal council, he convinced the Nez Percés of the desirability of making concessions to the miners. The tribe willingly agreed to allow prospecting and mining on all their land north of the Clearwater River if the miners would promise to disturb none of the farm land or camas fields. They also insisted that no farmers be allowed anywhere on the reservation, even near the mines.[2]

By this time, the rush to the gold fields was in full swing. The prospectors made no effort to stay inside the generous boundaries granted them. Their spread to the south was hastened by the discovery of richer diggings on the South Fork of the Clearwater and on the lower Salmon. When the winter snows blocked the mountain trails that year, hundreds of miners were snowbound with insufficient supplies. Only the prompt aid of various Indians saved many of them from starvation.

Up to this time, the head of navigation and the depot for supplies had been at Wallula, but the increased demands for goods along the Snake River soon induced the steamboats to ascend as far as the mouth of the Clearwater. Here a new difficulty arose, for the ground to the north of the Clearwater was unsuitable for a boat landing and a warehouse. In view of this, the Nez Percés granted special permission that the landing and warehouse might be built on the tongue of land between the two rivers, provided no other buildings were

[2] H. Clay Wood, *The Treaty Status of Young Joseph and His Band of Nez Percé Indians under the Treaties between the United States and the Nez Percé Tribe of Indians, and the Indian Title to the Land*, 25–26.

placed there.[3] In return, the tribe asked nothing except that the government supply a force of regulars sufficient to enforce the terms of the new agreements and of the treaty of 1855. It is evident that the Indians had no intention of violating any of the terms, or they would not have wanted the soldiers at hand.

It will surprise no student of Indian history to learn that the agreement so freely given and so scrupulously kept by the Nez Percés was ruthlessly violated by the whites as soon as they felt confidence in their numbers:

"No sooner had these privileges been granted than the landing and warehouse became a town, now known as Lewiston; their reservation was overrun; the enclosed lands taken from them; stock turned into their grain fields and gardens; their fences taken and used by persons to enclose lands to which they laid claim, or torn down, burned, or otherwise destroyed. . . . I have thus given a plain statement of facts. Would they were otherwise, as they are only calculated to make us blush with shame. . . . Along the roads on the reservation to all the mines, at the crossing of every stream or fresh-water spring, and near the principal Indian villages, an inn or 'Shebang' is established, ostensibly for the entertainment of travelers, but almost universally used as a den for supplying liquor to the Indians. The class of men that pursue this infamous traffic are, as might be expected, the most abandoned wretches of society."[4]

"Horses or mules, only strayed from lack of herding, were supposed to have been stolen by the Indians; and the reckless owner would often indulge in rash measures for their recovery.

"Broken miners, who were leaving the mines disgusted, would sometimes appropriate an Indian pony on which to

[3] *Ibid.*, 26.
[4] *Ibid.*, 27.

leave the country respectably. 'Road Agents' would often steal horses from whites and Indians alike and the Indians generally got the credit, or discredit, for the theft."[5]

When the angry Nez Percés demanded that the treaty terms be enforced to prevent such actions, the whites were indignant. The Lewiston paper, *The Golden Age*, advised the whites to settle, occupy, plow up, and cultivate the lands on the reservation without regard to the Indian title and in contempt of all treaty terms.[6] Even this is mild compared to the writings of a Boise editor who asked for a shipment of blankets infected with smallpox. He guaranteed that such blankets would be distributed to the Indians in his neighborhood where they would be the most effective.[7] These two editors reflect the sentiment of their readers concerning the proper treatment of Indians in the Northwest and show how high they held Indian rights.

Some of the more farsighted men preferred a peaceful settlement of the difficulty, particularly since the United States was in the midst of the Civil War and no government troops could be spared from the major conflict to fight Indians in a remote corner of the country. These men arranged for another treaty council to be held at Lapwai in the spring of 1863, where the Nez Percés could be induced to "adjust the boundaries of the reservation." In a pleasant meadow between the agency and the fort, they laid out a camp for the expected guests, with the tents in neat rows.

The commissioner expected some trouble with the Indians when he asked them to surrender most of their tribal lands for the benefit of the whites who had been causing so much trouble. They might even ask how they could hope for any more

---

[5] W. V. Rinehart, "Oregon Cavalry" (MS in the Bancroft Library, the University of California).

[6] Wood, *Status of Young Joseph*, 27.

[7] Chester Anders Fee, *Chief Joseph: The Biography of a Great Indian*, 64.

protection under the new treaty than under the old one. To impress the Nez Percés and to keep them under control, six companies of volunteers were stationed at the fort for the duration of the council. They were drilled and paraded during the council meetings in the open space between the fort and the Indian camp.

Since the Nez Percés were coming to the council in an attempt to solve their problems without fighting, such a show of force was rather futile. The Indian leaders were as outspoken in debate and as firm in their opinions as before. Many of them could see no advantage in making a new treaty with a government that made little effort to enforce the old one. What reason was there to believe that the new treaty would prove any more binding on the whites? As the discussion progressed, it was apparent that the tribe was divided into three groups, each representing a different point of view. One group, headed by Chief Lawyer, favored the new treaty with its promise of cash payments, schools, shops, fences, plowed lands, and the like. These payments and improvements were to go largely to Lawyer's village. In addition, the treaty provided for a salary for the head chief and his two assistant chiefs. Lawyer needed the support of the government officials if he was to remain head chief. Such considerations might have influenced his attitude.

While the second group showed no animosity toward the whites, they refused to give up any more land. They asked the government to enforce the treaty of 1855 by removing all the whites who were trespassing on the reservation. When the officials indicated that the government was in no position to take such action, the Nez Percés maintained that there was no assurance it could enforce a new treaty, and what good would it do the Indians to sign a new treaty that could not be enforced? Big Thunder, now chief at Lapwai, was the leader of this group. He hoped in time to become head chief if he could just get Lawyer sent back to his home at Kamiah. Joseph joined with Big Thunder because he also opposed both Lawyer and the new treaty. The rest of this second party was made up of bands of Indians living along the Salmon and Snake rivers who would lose their lands under the proposed treaty.

The third group was much smaller than either of the first two and was composed chiefly of men who still followed the teachings of Tom Hill, the Delaware. They objected to any agreement, even the favorable treaty of 1855. Their leader was Eagle from the Light, who favored driving out or killing off all the whites in the entire Northwest and giving the country back to the Indians. Most of his following consisted of restless young men from the various bands. This small group furnished the only real threat to the safety of the commissioners during the council.

Day after day, the council dragged on, with Lawyer and Big Thunder each struggling for his program, while Eagle from the Light stayed hostile to all proposals. Day after day, the breach widened between the rival chiefs. The tense situation and the open opposition of Eagle from the Light and his followers led the commissioners to fear some plot against themselves, or even a general uprising. One evening they were alarmed to learn that fifty-three important men of the Nez Percé tribe were holding a meeting in one of the tents. Captain George Curry, of the Oregon volunteers, was detailed with his company to investigate.

Captain Curry had no difficulty in locating the meeting and in learning that no plotting was being done. He was invited into the tent with a brother officer, and the two were given places at the council fire, where they listened to the discussion for several hours. The chiefs were debating the terms of the proposed treaty in an effort to reach some compromise, but neither group would yield, so they decided to disband the tribe and go back to the old way, before 1842, when each chief was the independent leader of his own village, owing no allegiance to the head chief. They thought that each chief would be free then to negotiate a separate treaty with the commissioners in respect to the village holdings and his action would bind only his own village.

Once this momentous decision had been reached, the chiefs staged a dramatic farewell scene, emotionally shaking hands all around as they pledged eternal friendship between the various bands. Captain Curry finished his account of the meeting: "I withdrew my detachment, having accomplished nothing but that of witnessing the extinguishment of the last council fires of the most powerful Indian nation on the sunset side of the Rocky Mountains."[8]

After this meeting, the council progressed more smoothly. All the antitreaty group withdrew or remained silent while the Lawyer group concluded the negotiations with the commissioners, signing an agreement reducing the size of the reservation by three-fourths in return for some cash payments and various new buildings. Curry had this to say of the treaty:

"Although the treaty goes out to the world as the concurrent agreement of the tribe, it is in reality nothing more than the agreement of Lawyer and his band, numbering in the aggregate not a third part of the Nez Percés tribe."[9]

A map showing both the old and new reservation boundaries is helpful in understanding the situation. Except for Big Thunder, every nontreaty chief held lands outside the new boundaries, while every chief who signed, except Timothy, lived within the new boundaries. However, there is nothing in this to indicate that Lawyer and his followers deliberately sold out the rest of the tribe. Being shrewd traders, they got what they could for themselves, sincerely believing that chiefs who did not sign would not be bound. Under the

[8] *Oregon Adjutant-General's Report, 1866,* 18.
[9] *Ibid.,* 18.

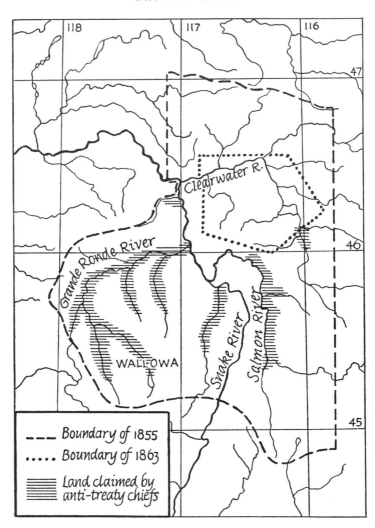

118	117	116

47

Clearwater R.

46

Grande Ronde River

WALLOWA

Snake River

Salmon River

45

- - - Boundary of 1855
..... Boundary of 1863
≡ Land claimed by anti-treaty chiefs

Nez Percé Reservation Boundaries

treaty of 1855, the entire reservation had been held jointly by the whole tribe, but by disbanding the tribe, the individual chiefs gave up all claims to any lands outside the holdings of his village. In 1863, each chief who signed believed that he was signing only for his own village lands and that his action would not affect the lands of the other chiefs.

Some trickery on the part of the commissioners was necessary even after Lawyer and his men agreed to sign. In 1855, fifty-eight chiefs had been important enough to sign the treaty for Governor Stevens, and fifty-three rated seats at the council attended by Captain Curry. Now, after more than half of these fifty-three had withdrawn from the council, the commissioners managed to secure fifty-one names.[10] This would indicate that the commissioners induced twenty-five or more unqualified Indians to sign in place of the dissenting chiefs in order to show the necessary number of signatures and then announced that the entire tribe had accepted the treaty terms, a bit of sharp practice often used in negotiating Indian treaties.

No further effort was made to conciliate the antitreaty chiefs. The officials claimed that the treaty bound the entire tribe, since head chief Lawyer had signed for all the Nez Percés. Then it was that Joseph, convinced that his people could expect no justice from the whites, tore up a copy of the treaty and destroyed his long-treasured New Testament, declaring he would have nothing more to do with the white man and his ways.[11] This marks his first break, in any form, with the whites. For nearly thirty years, he had been a staunch friend to them. He had welcomed Parker and Spalding, aided in the mission work, accepted the new religion, and adopted many of the ways of the white men. He had served as a volunteer in the white man's army against other Indians, furnished his own horse and equipment, yet after a lapse of seven

[10] Kappler (ed.), *Indian Affairs, Laws and Treaties*, II, 847-48.
[11] Monteith to Walker, August 27, 1872, Lapwai Agency files.

163

years he had not been paid. Now, as a reward for his loyalty and service, he was defrauded of his lands and his home.

His New Testament, received from the Spaldings years before when he and Timothy had been the first two converts baptized at Lapwai, had always been to him a symbol of his faith. This book he carried in his hand as a token of his innocence when, in 1848, he went forth to face the angry white troops bent on avenging the Whitmans. In thus destroying the cherished book, he emphasized the finality of his decision. From that time until the day of his death, he never wavered. He had once put his faith in the white man and the Christian religion and they had failed him.

LAWYER and his party, after working so hard for the new treaty, found themselves in a rather awkward situation. Four long years the treaty lay in Washington before the Senate finally ratified it in 1867. Meanwhile, payments due under the first treaty were not made and no improvements were begun at Lapwai or Kamiah. Congress had appropriated only a part of the necessary funds, but the money it did appropriate usually ended up in the pockets of the agents and their friends. Each new agent reported, with a great wealth of detail, how his predecessor had wasted the funds and had accomplished nothing, while he in turn was busy lining his pockets with Indian money, setting an example which was followed in both respects by his successor. This sort of thing was common throughout the Indian service at the time, finally leading to a congressional investigation, the findings of which were published in 1867. A few extracts indicate the situation at Lapwai:

"For the last three or four years the reservation has been overrun with white people, not only those in search of gold, but by others who have made locations there for agricultural purposes, and who have erected buildings, enclosed lands, and exercised all the rights of ownership over it. . . .

"Under the leadership of Big Thunder, a principal chief,

a party is forming which is hostile to the government, and if something is not speedily done to remove the causes of complaint, there is great danger to be apprehended of their resorting to open hostility. . . .

"The credit of the Indian Department is utterly destroyed, and the tribe greatly disaffected toward the government, and I think it safe to assert that there is no portion of the United States in which Indian affairs are in so chaotic and disorganized a state as in Idaho Territory. Mr. O'Neill, who is the only Indian agent within the territory, is utterly powerless to remedy the evils. The regulations of the department require him to conduct his correspondence through the Superintendent of Indian Affairs for his district. 'Caleb Lyon, of Lyondale,' who is governor and ex-officio superintendent of Indian affairs, has not been heard of in Idaho since early last spring.

"His absence from his post, however, seems to entail no embarrassment upon the management of Indian affairs. When present, he conducted them with an ignorance unparalleled, and a disregard of the rights and wants of the Indians, and of the laws regulating intercourse with them, deserving the severest rebuke. . . .

"I was unable to find any records in Idaho connected with or pertaining to the office of Superintendent of Indian Affairs. . . .

"I have examined invoices and purchases made by the department or its agents in eastern cities, where the prices charged were from fifty to one hundred percent above the market value of good articles. Upon examination of the goods I have found them, as a general thing, worthless and deficient in quantity. 'Steel spades,' made of sheet iron; 'chopping axes' which were purely cast iron; 'best brogans' with paper soles; 'blankets' made of shoddy and glue, which came to shreds the first time they were wet. . . . Many articles are purchased which would be utterly useless to the Indian . . . in one case forty dozen pairs of elastic garters were sent to a tribe in which there was not a single pair of stockings."[1]

Such a state of affairs did not arise from mere ignorance on the part of the employees of the department. Not only had the treaties stated definitely the kind of goods to be supplied, but the men in the field had sent in detailed requisitions, yet both the treaties and the requisitions were disregarded. The Indians, particularly the Nez Percés, wanted good tools, farm implements, household goods, and hunting equipment. They had been accustomed to buy for themselves from the Hudson's Bay Company and later from the American stores and trading posts and they knew the difference between good and poor quality. They also knew exactly what things had been specified in the treaty. Such barefaced fraud both angered and disgusted them, but their pride kept the treaty crowd from complaining much, for the nontreaty Indians were only too anxious to point out that the government was not to be trusted and should not have been given a second chance to cheat the tribe. The Indians took their troubles to the agent.

"They do not grumble so much on account of their absolute want of goods . . . but it is with the desire of doing away with the reports that are being circulated by the Big Thunder or non-treaty side. . . . One great cause of the disagreement and split among this people is the non-payment of their annuities. The non-treaty side throw it up to the other side now that they have sold their country and have got nothing but promises. . . .

"Many say they had rather be with the non-treaty side and not expect anything than to remain with the Lawyer side and have, every few days, these promises repeated to them."[2]

One item that was particularly resented by treaty and nontreaty Indians alike was the government's failure to pay for

---

[1] *Special Report* (of the Commissioner of Indian Affairs, 1867), 10–12.
[2] *Report of the Commissioner of Indian Affairs, 1865*, 237–38.

horses purchased from the Nez Percés during the war with the Yakimas. Joseph and the other volunteers had furnished their own horses and had also sold many horses for the use of the whites. Although the purchases had been duly certified and acknowledged as a just debt, a total of more than $4,600 was still due the Indians. The treaty commissioners, at the council in 1863, had promised faithfully that the debt would be paid and even included a clause in the treaty to that effect, but the Indians were still waiting for their money.[3]

In 1868, the government officials wanted to change the treaty again to give some of the reservation lands to the military forces. This time no council was held, but four Nez Percés were taken to Washington, D. C., by Agent Robert Newell. They were Lawyer, Jason, Timothy, and Utsinmalihkin. From the West Coast, they went by steamer to Panama, crossed the isthmus, and took another steamer to New York City. Utsinmalihkin became ill in New York and died the day after the group reached Washington. The other three signed a supplementary treaty in August which gave the army its military reservations and contained a promise that Congress would restore the squandered school funds.[4]

The inefficiency, disorder, and corruption of the Idaho Indian agencies should not be considered unusual for the period. Agent O'Neill had been rated by the investigators as one of the best servants in the Indian service, so a person hesitates to say what the worst might have been. During this period following the Civil War, the entire government was honeycombed with graft, especially the Indian Bureau, but this explains rather than excuses such a condition. To the Indians who had given up their lands on the solemn promise of the government that they would be paid a set price, the turmoil

[3] *Report of the Commissioner of Indian Affairs, 1866,* 194.
[4] Robert Newell Diary, 1868.

Right: *Timothy, photographed in Washington, D.C., 1868.* (Courtesy Smithsonian Institution)

of Reconstruction appeared an inadequate explanation for dishonest agents or breaches of faith.

Following the disclosures of the investigating committee, a sincere effort at reform was attempted in the Indian Bureau, spurred on by public pressure. One of the interested groups was the Society of Friends, who argued that if the red men were treated fairly and if honest, efficient agents were appointed, savings could be made in both the Indian Bureau and the War Department. The old policy of attempting to civilize the Indians by using soldiers against them had resulted in costly failure. Peaceful means could do no worse, and might easily do better. President Grant was interested in their plan and offered to let them try it at one agency. Men who wanted to keep the old plan saw to it that the Quakers were given the Kiowas, the most troublesome of all the tribes in the West, hoping thus to insure failure.

Instead, within a year, the Kiowas were one of the least troublesome of the tribes, and President Grant was greatly impressed. Meanwhile, he tried to improve several of the other agencies by appointing some of his surplus army officers as agents.

At Lapwai, two army officers, Lieutenant J. W. Wham and Captain D. M. Sells, his successor, were accused of large-scale frauds, but they had some definite improvements on the reservation to show for the money spent. They repaired agency buildings, fenced many fields, and had them plowed for the Indians to use. The fencing and plowing were poorly done at a high cost, indicating possible collusion between the officers and the contractors. However, the chiefs were better satisfied under the new management than under the old, for they had more to show for their funds and they were more willing to take direction from army officers than from civilians.

Congress made no objection to placing the Society of Friends in charge of the Indians, but they feared that Grant

Left: *Jason, in Washington, D.C., in 1868.* (Courtesy Smithsonian Institution)

was trying to pave the way for a military dictatorship by using army officers for civilian jobs. To eliminate such a possibility, a bill was passed in 1870 prohibiting an army officer from holding any civilian position under the government. As a result, many new agents had to be found quickly for the posts thus made vacant.

Grant hoped that the best answer to the Indian problem was to place all the agencies in the care of the various religious groups which had missions. Under Grant's plan, the Nez Percés were first assigned to the Catholics because that faith had the only active mission on the reservation. The Presbyterians immediately protested, claiming prior right because of the mission established by Spalding from 1836 to 1847. They finally won, and the Catholics were given the Umatilla reservation instead.

The first agent at Lapwai under the new arrangement was appointed jointly by the Presbyterian Church and the Indian Bureau and was under the supervision of both. This man, John Monteith, was a conscientious and careful worker who accomplished a great deal during his term of service. From his official correspondence during the years from 1871 to 1876, many details of the agency work have been taken. These records also contain many items bearing on the causes of the Nez Percé War.

Nez Percés painting a robe. Note shells for mixing and holding paint.

Upper right: *Nez Percé men threshing wheat with horses.*

Lower right: *Nez Percé woman winnowing wheat.*

Kentuck, a Nez Percé man.

176

18: Compulsory Civilization

FOR half a century, the Nez Percés had sought teachers and schools that they might learn to read and write. One of the impelling forces of the famous delegation to St. Louis in 1831 was the desire for knowledge. In 1836, they had warmly welcomed the Spaldings, flocking to the little log schoolhouse to receive instruction. In 1858, Lawyer had defined the tribal needs as peace, plows, and schools. With a tribe so consistently in favor of education, one might suppose that the new agent would need only to provide buildings and teachers to insure a successful school program, but actually there were many difficulties to be overcome.

An important factor interfering with a program of formal instruction was the Indian way of living. The treaty Indians, for the most part, had settled on small patches of farm land along the creek and river bottoms, about twenty acres of land being allotted to each family. Most of them lived in tipis, raising small quantities of garden truck, potatoes, and grain. Their horses and cattle grazed unattended on the neighboring hills and the plateau. The small crops were supplemented by supplies of fish, game, and camas roots. Spending money and goods were secured by selling horses to the people in Lewiston or in the mining camps. When there was little to do at home, the men often worked at odd jobs for the whites, cutting timber, herding stock, driving pack trains, and the like.

Grain proved the ideal crop from the Indian point of view. The most laborious part of the work could be done with teams. After a brief interval of intensive labor in the planting season, no further attention was required until harvest time, except for a little irrigation during the periods of drought. Thus, with twenty or thirty days of concentrated effort, in two widely separated periods, the grain farmer had a staple crop that could be sold for cash at any time or easily stored for his own use. The agency mill would convert it into flour at small cost if he wanted to eat it. In most cases, the Indian showed little interest in the eastern type of farm, with its milk cows, pigs, and chickens, requiring an endless round of tedious chores every day in the year. Crops requiring constant attention throughout a long growing season also had little appeal for him.

The concentrated seasonal work in planting and harvesting grain left the Nez Percé families with a great deal of leisure time for the normal pursuits of Indian life. After the spring work was done, they were free to visit friends or to move to one of the fishing stations on the lower river for the early salmon run or even to travel as far as the camas grounds in the Yakima Valley. Then about the first of July, when the summer heat had evaporated the excess moisture from their own camas meadows, the entire tribe would assemble at Weippe to harvest the crop. Two or three days' labor would supply enough bulbs for the season, but the camp lasted for many days while the men indulged in horse racing, gambling, drinking, and trading and the chiefs debated plans for the coming year. Here, too, were recruited the bands which planned to make the long trek to the Montana buffalo grounds that fall, usually starting in August or early September for a stay of one or two years.[1] Meanwhile, the women, in their periods of leisure, had their own gambling games, dances, and social groups. The young people quite naturally turned to love-making, while the children ran wild in their own games.

Another popular summer excursion was to the great meadows near the head of the Little Salmon River. Large numbers of salmon reached this point during late July and early August and were easy to catch in the small streams. Convenient timber supplied the necessary fuel for the smoking process and for camp use. The ridges and berry patches had fruit and game of various kinds. Here the high altitude provided pleasant weather quite different from the sweltering heat of the sheltered river bottoms near the agency.

The ripened grain was usually harvested during August, leaving the farmer free until the following spring. During the fine fall weather, he rode with his friends on hunting or trading trips or worked a little for additional winter supplies. Then when the northern wind swirled snows across the open plateaus, it was much simpler to move the family tipi to the woods than to haul fuel so many miles to the tipi. The de luxe winter resort of the tribe was located in the sheltered valley of the Salmon River from the mouth of the Little Salmon to White Bird Canyon.[2] Here the camps were well protected from the winds, firewood was plentiful, fish and game were close at hand. The winter passed pleasantly with a little hunting, a little fishing, and a great deal of visiting from lodge to lodge until the warm March sun sent the families back to Kamiah and Lapwai in time for spring plowing and planting.

When a Nez Percé family left the agency on a pleasure trip, all the children went along. They worried not at all over a few days of school missed. In their school, there was no systematic promotion, no division into grades, no necessity for a child to make a certain amount of progress each year, and it

---

[1] Monteith to Walker, December 22, 1871, Lapwai Agency files.
[2] Monteith to Walker, February 14, 1873, Lapwai Agency files.

is doubtful that such a system would have caused the parents any additional worry in any case. From the point of view of the teachers, the recurring absences were exasperating. After they had worked for weeks trying to adjust a child to the school, he would leave on a trip that might last three or four months, and by the time he returned he had forgotten all that the school had taught him.

Even the children who were regular in attendance did not progress as rapidly as the teachers wished. They might prepare the classroom lessons well, but they insisted on talking their own language on the playground and at home. As the children crossed the threshold to freedom, the slight veneer of white ways so painstakingly imposed at school vanished almost without a trace, as though it was blown away by the first breath of fresh air.

The teachers finally decided that boarding schools offered the best solution to the problem, since they could then dominate the child twenty-four hours a day and thus insure compliance with their arbitrary standards of conduct through a system of penalties and punishments. The added cost of such a program was ignored. The sufferings of lonely little prisoners from homesickness and rigid supervision were considered beneficial to the improvement of their souls. Illness arising from the radical change of diet or the abrupt shift from free outdoor life to close confinement was disregarded. One matron even expected the children's health to improve rapidly because she fed them so well.[3]

After the boarding schools had been established according to the plans, the problem was only partially solved. Occasionally, a boy or girl was permitted to visit his family for an afternoon or for overnight. The teachers asked that all such visits be forbidden, insisting that those few hours at home could, and usually did, undo all the results of many

[3] *Report of the Commissioner of Indian Affairs, 1870,* 187.

days of school. They proposed that the children be taken from the parents for a period of several years, during which time there would be no visiting and no holidays.[4] One might suspect that the teachers considered the children to be government property rather than people.

Although both the treaty of 1855 and of 1863 provided for the establishment of schools, and funds were allocated for that purpose, the investigators in 1867 found no schools in operation. When the delegation of chiefs went to Washington in 1868 to write a supplementary treaty, they asked about this, with the result that a clause concerning the restoring of these funds was incorporated in the new treaty, which was ratified by the Senate in February, 1869. The regular funds were available before then, however, and the first school was opened in the fall of 1868.

No great rush of students resulted. Fifteen came the first day, with a few more drifting in from time to time, until a smallpox scare in Lewiston, fifteen miles away, caused the parents to withdraw their children in January, 1869.[5] School was reopened in April with some success.

The first boarding school was opened in the fall of 1869, and school attendance grew, but the students made much slower progress in their studies than had been made at Mrs. Spalding's school some thirty years earlier, chiefly because of the short period of service for each teacher. At Lapwai, this was more detrimental than in an ordinary village school on account of the language difficulty. The teacher usually arrived from some distant point just in time for the opening of school, poorly trained, unfamiliar with Nez Percé traits and customs, unable to speak or understand a word of their language, and interested in collecting his salary for the least possible work. Since the children had to learn English first,

[4] *Ibid.*, 185–86.
[5] *Report of the Commissioner of Indian Affairs, 1869*, 285.

several months were used in establishing some sort of communication between teacher and students before instruction could be given in the formal subjects. By the time the mutual adjustments had been partially completed, the school year was over. The children returned to their homes and to the use of their native tongue, while the teacher passed out of their lives, to be replaced the following fall by another complete stranger. Such schools did not win tribal confidence.

Lieutenant Wham and Captain Sells had worked to correct these poor conditions and had made some progress by the time the latter was replaced by John Monteith. The new agent was able to make more rapid changes because he had more authority, he was held strictly responsible for the schools by the mission board, and, on account of the religious element involved, he was able to secure a higher type of teacher who had a keener interest in the work and who was assured of a longer tenure. Because the agency was under a church board interested in the moral education of the Indians, a decided effort was made to employ teachers of good moral character who, by their conduct, would serve as examples for their charges. Similar precautions were taken in hiring other agency employees also, for Monteith wanted no repetition of the scandals of the previous decade, when most of the agency workers had mated informally with Nez Percé women during their term of service.

It proved difficult to find many people in the Northwest qualified to supervise the schools who were also acceptable to the mission board and were willing to work in such a remote location at the low salary offered. Finally, Henry Spalding, the founder of the Lapwai mission, was chosen for the work. He was anxious to resume the labors so rudely interrupted by the Whitman massacre some twenty-five years before. His previous work at Lapwai, his knowledge of the Nez Percé language, his education, and his friendship for many of the older Nez Percés were all points in his favor, but his work proved a disappointment. Spalding had never fully recovered from his terrible trip in the fall of 1847, and he had developed some marked peculiarities of temperament as he grew older. Now he had to work without the support of his wife, who had died twenty years before. Although he had been hired as a subordinate of Monteith, with his authority limited to the educational work, he tried to dominate the younger man in everything. He interfered with agency matters and gave much harmful advice to the Indians at various times. His peculiar idea of allowing the primer classes no reading material except the New Testament seriously retarded their schoolwork. Finally he had to be gently removed from the school and placed in charge of the local church, where he could do less harm.[6] Here he labored happily until his death in 1874, baptizing hundreds of converts.

Monteith and his teachers were either ministers or from the immediate families of ministers. Their influence on the religious life of the community was marked and aided in building up a large church membership. In some ways, though, their outlook seems to have been too narrow for the best interests of their charges. Their concept of an educated, Christian Indian was that he should resemble, as far as possible, a pillar of the church in some settled eastern farm community. These roving horsemen of the western plateaus were expected to give up entirely their old ways, their native tongue, all their amusements, and most of their freedom of thought if they hoped to be classed as good church members, the *ne plus ultra* of the new dispensation. Children, to be educated, must be confined for years in boarding schools, must be taught to be subservient to the whites, and must be removed as far as pos-

[6] Monteith to Smith, January 8, 1874, Lapwai Agency files.

sible from their parents. The entire social structure of the tribe must be recast, councils and bands must be eliminated, the mild rule of the chiefs must give way to the benevolent despotism of the agent and the ministers of the church.

Right: *Nez Percé woman making pemmican, Yellowstone River, 1871.* (From a photograph by William Henry Jackson, courtesy Smithsonian Institution)

A fish trap on Lapwai Creek.

Nez Percés roasting salmon.

Nez Percé food cache near Lapwai about 1891.

19: Benevolent Despots

MONTEITH and his little group of earnest reformers felt that their prestige was seriously threatened by the conduct of the nontreaty group, whose comments on their efforts proved most annoying. Serious souls such as these can endure, nay, even welcome martyrdom more calmly than they can suffer their cause to be ridiculed or ignored. Whether the nontreaty bands realized this is open to question, but their course of action proved most effective none the less. They assumed an attitude of superiority to the poor, benighted strangers who called them heathen, and indicated that keen minded, independent chiefs could not be deceived by the strangers' doctrines even though they were accepted by the not-too-bright, docile treaty-signers. They also ridiculed all arguments against horse racing, gambling, buffalo hunting, and other popular pastimes of the tribe. They even argued that if the missionaries really believed that gamblers, thieves, drunkards, and Sabbath-breakers were so in need of religion to save themselves from eternal damnation, why did they not first reform the white men of the mining camps, who were far worse in all these respects than the Nez Percés?

Not only did the Indians disregard suggestions, advice, and teachings, but they even disobeyed direct orders from the agent, knowing themselves to be perfectly safe from reprisal. It was no punishment for them to be excluded from the churches and schools when they objected to both institutions and all their teachings. The usual handy and effective punishment of the Indian agent, the withholding of annuities and treaty payments, would not work here, since the nontreaty group steadily and consistently refused all money, goods, food, and tools offered them in any guise. They owned no land or stock on the reservation and never used the agency mills or shops. Their trading was done at Lewiston or Walla Walla, leaving them independent of the agency store. Their evasion of orders was never serious enough to warrant calling out the troops, and what else could the agent do to harm them?

Such a stand on the part of the dissenting Indians was both logical and farsighted. Any payment made to the tribe or its individual members was in return for the land surrendered by the treaties. Since these Indians had never signed the second treaty, and since no one else had had authority to sign for them, they had never given up title to their lands. If they now accepted any goods, presumably as payments on the first treaty, there was great danger that the government would again resort to trickery, claiming that the goods included payments due under the second treaty and that by accepting them the Indians had tacitly accepted the terms of the second treaty. Available accounts indicate that this analysis of the situation was the work of Joseph. Monteith testified to the fidelity of the nontreaty bands in upholding these principles, saying in one report that they had refused to accept any gift of any sort from the agency, except a little tobacco.[1] Under the old custom observed by both red man and white, acceptance of such a gift entailed no obligation on either side except temporary friendship.

Throughout this period, the tribe was divided quite evenly

[1] *Report of the Commissioner of Indian Affairs, 1872, 271.*

between treaty and nontreaty, with Big Thunder always mentioned as the leader of the latter group. Associated with him
was another chief, Red Heart, who had gained distinction as
a war leader since the death of Looking Glass. His reputation
was earned on the Montana plains, where the Nez Percés,
as allies of the Crows, had lately come into conflict with
the Sioux.

Except that they did less farming, the nontreaty bands
lived in much the same fashion as the treaty Indians. They
hunted, fished, visited the camas grounds in summer and the
sheltered valleys in winter. They formed a large majority of
all parties heading for the buffalo country in Montana, and
they furnished the warriors who fought against the Sioux. For
spending money, they relied on the sale of their surplus stock
from the large herds of horses and cattle which they tended.

For many years, the chief source of argument between the
two factions had been that the treaty group had unfairly sold
the land belonging to all, and for a very inadequate amount
which was not even paid. Now that the treaty payments were
being received regularly and the reservation improvements
were being made under Monteith's supervision, the heathen
crowd switched to a new angle of attack. A part of young men
liked to ride by a farm where the owner was sweating over his
farm work and make choice comments on the obvious lack of
intelligence or sanity in a man who would so waste his time
and the fine weather. Or they might point out to him that
such work was degrading to a Nez Percé warrior, injuring his
health and leaving him an easy prey to disease.[2] At the campgrounds, they painted such glowing pictures of the joys and
excitements of buffalo hunting, the free life of the Plains, and
the thrilling deeds against their enemies that they were the
center of feminine admiration. Many a man, seemingly settled for life on his little agency farm, abandoned his crops,

[2] *Ibid.*, 271.

191

improvements, and prestige with the whites for another year or two of such life, much to the disgust of the agent and his helpers.[3]

In their opposition to all white innovations, the heathen party felt the need of some method of combating the religious teachings of the church, now growing rapidly in members and influence. The primitive beliefs of their ancestors were inadequate and lacked the necessary dynamic appeal. At this juncture, there arose a new cult, based on the old beliefs and headed by an Indian messiah, Smohalla, who first rose to prominence as a medicine man in a little fishing village on the Columbia River near Priest Rapids. His band was an unimportant, poverty-stricken branch of Shahaptian stock usually overlooked by the lordly Nez Percés.[4]

Smohalla himself was a short, thick-set man with a noble head, an alert mind, and an intelligent eye. His contemporaries have mentioned his likeness to Daniel Webster in appearance and in oratorical ability. He enjoyed considerable distinction up and down the river as a medicine man and for his brilliant speeches until, about 1860, he quarreled with Chief Moses from farther up the river. Moses believed that Smohalla possessed the power to send sickness or death to his enemies and sought to forestall such a calamity by killing the medicine man. After quite a fight, he left Smohalla for dead on the riverbank, but the latter revived sufficiently during the night to climb into a canoe which he then cast adrift. His prestige had vanished because of the defeat, and he feared he also might well lose his life if Moses ever heard of his recovery.

This fight and its consequences turned the unimportant village medicine man into a messiah for his race. After he had

---

[3] *Report of the Commissioner of Indian Affairs, 1874,* 285–86.

[4] James Mooney, "The Ghost-dance Religion and the Sioux Outbreak of 1890," Bureau of American Ethnology *Fourteenth Annual Report* (1892–93), Part II, 708.

recovered from his wounds under the care of a kindly white man farther down the Columbia, Smohalla set out on a journey to the far places of the West Coast. He went to Portland, San Francisco, San Diego, then east into Mexico, north through Arizona, Utah, and Nevada before he finally appeared at his home village after an absence of five years. Here he was looked on as a man who had returned from the dead, a belief he was careful to foster. He explained that he had gone to heaven, but the Great Chief Above had selected him to serve as the messenger to the red men of the Northwest. In obedience to divine commands, he had returned to instruct them all in the new religion and to deliver to them messages from the Great Chief.

Possibly the Great Chief Above liked white religions and had guided Smohalla on his travels, for the religion as revealed by him had a ritual with features borrowed from Catholic, Mormon, and military ceremonies on a base of primitive, aboriginal mythology. A part of the basic doctrine came from the teachings of Tom Hill, the Delaware, stressing the necessity of driving out or killing off all the whites as the first step toward a paradise on earth. Smohalla, by a new, spectacular revelation, explained how such a difficult task could be accomplished. Soon, at a time to be revealed by the Great Chief Above, all the Indians who had died would be resurrected and by their great numbers would overwhelm the whites. They would then repossess the land, which would become their hunting grounds for all eternity. To supply the vast quantities of game needed for the hunting, all game animals were to be resurrected also, that they might be killed by the hunters.

The Great Chief Above was bitterly opposed to all white ways, particularly to mining and farming, for these changed the surface of the country and had a degrading effect on the men who practiced them. Smohalla explained it thus:

"My young men shall never work. Men who work can

not dream, and wisdom comes to us in dreams. . . . You ask me to plough the ground. Shall I take a knife and tear my mother's bosom? You ask me to dig for stone. Shall I dig under her skin for her bones? You ask me to cut the grass and make hay and sell it and be rich like white men. But dare I cut off my mother's hair?"[5]

It was in trances, probably epileptic in nature, that Smohalla experienced the dreams to which he referred. Immediately on awakening from one of these, he would give his followers the instructions which he had just received from the Great Chief Above. From these trances of the leader, the followers of the cult came to be called Too-ats or Dreamers.

In their criticism of white ways, the Dreamers focused much of their attack on the agency boarding school. They claimed that the high mortality rate among the students was caused directly by their change from the free, outdoor life of the Indian to the confined existence recommended by the teachers. This point was emphasized by the sudden death of the brightest scholar at Lapwai in the summer of 1872.[6] Although the teachers insisted the death was just a coincidence, many of the parents who were perfectly willing to have their children educated hesitated to send them to the boarding school. Modern medical science has demonstrated that the uneducated Indian was right in his conclusions, even though he gave the wrong reasons for them, and that many of the Indian children died in the boarding schools because of too abrupt a change in their habits.

The heathen, antitreaty Nez Percés joined the new Dreamer cult by the hundreds. The pomp and ceremony, so dear to their barbaric natures, contrasted strongly with the colorless meetings in the agency churches. The Nez Percés had reached the point where a new religion preached by a red man,

[5] *Ibid.*, 708.
[6] *Report of the Commissioner of Indian Affairs, 1872,* 271.

for the red men, and prophesying their ultimate domination of the whites, had fundamental appeal. The conflict between the Dreamers and the Christians rapidly widened the breach between the two factions of the tribe. The Dreamers ridiculed the Christians for being the dupes of the whites, while the latter, encouraged by their teachers, assumed a "holier than thou" attitude. Since the ultimate purpose of the government was to settle the nontreaty element among the treaty Indians on the reservation, any aggravation of the discord between the two groups was bound to make for future trouble. When the nontreaty Dreamers were finally rounded up and herded onto the reservation by the soldiers, did Monteith and his helpers expect all discord to vanish at once, or did they perhaps have plans to force the heathens into a definitely inferior position as punishment for past misdeeds?

From his reports and letters, it is evident that Monteith wanted more power over his charges in order to accomplish his aims more rapidly. He thought the Indians should be forced to work for a living instead of having so much leisure for roaming around the country. Two particular practices that annoyed him were camas gathering and buffalo hunting, partly because they encouraged habits which he disliked, and partly because they took the Indians from their farms for long periods, making it impossible for them to raise chickens, pigs, and milk cows, all of which required frequent attention. The annual assemblage at the Weippe camas meadows also fostered laziness, because the bulbs were too abundant and too easily secured.[7]

Buffalo hunting was much worse in the opinion of the agent. People making the trip to the Plains neglected their farms for an entire year and reverted to their "heathen" ways. Their fights with the Sioux might build up a strong war party under a great leader and produce a bloody border war in Idaho. First, Monteith asked for troops to guard the trails

[7] *Report of the Commissioner of Indian Affairs, 1874,* 285–86.

and turn back all eastward-bound bands. When this was refused, he ruled, on his own authority, that anyone going to Montana would forfeit his plot of ground and all improvements on it.[8] This threat, approved by the treaty chiefs, was quite effective for the more settled farmers, but it meant little to the families living in tipis and subsisting for the most part on game, salmon, and camas, or to the unencumbered young men.

To make his charges more dependent on their crops and more under his power, Monteith wanted to restrict the number of range horses they might raise. A man with plenty of horses had little need of a farm or a job. If he wanted some spending money, he could sell one of his herd in Lewiston for ten or fifteen dollars and buy what he needed.[9] Such easily acquired funds often were spent on whiskey, to the detriment of the man and his friends.

The Dreamers and their teachings greatly hindered the young men of the tribe who might have learned trades. Monteith tried several times to teach blacksmithing to some of the youths living at Lapwai, but with little success.[10] They made excellent progress as long as they could be kept on the job, but some of the wild bunch would tell them how degrading the work was, unworthy of a warrior, or they would coax the apprentice to go on a trip to the fishing grounds or to the camas meadows. Evidently, Monteith felt that he could turn all these people into sedate farmers more quickly if he had more authority to prevent such occurrences.

Even without the added authority, Monteith had accomplished some remarkable results, overcoming many of the difficulties in his way. It is to be regretted that he was not successful in his work with the nontreaty bands.

[8] Monteith to Smith, July 20, 1874, Lapwai Agency files.
[9] Monteith to Smith, September 7, 1874, Lapwai Agency files.
[10] Monteith to Smith, September 7, 1874, Lapwai Agency files.

Smohalla (seated, front right, dressed in light shirt), the prophet of the Columbia River Indians, and his priests inside a lodge. (Courtesy Smithsonian Institution, B.A.E. Collection)

Nez Percé camp on the Yellowstone, 1871. (Photograph by William H. Jackson, courtesy Smithsonian Institution, B.A.E. Collection)

Nez Percé camp photographed on the Yellowstone, 1871. (Photograph by William H. Jackson, courtesy Smithsonian Institution, B.A.E. Collection)

20: A Question of Property Rights

TAKE a vast stretch of open range, well watered and covered with abundant grass. Across this range stretch an imaginary line, the exact location of which is unknown. On one side of the line place a proud, intelligent, independent tribe of Indians, insistent on their rights, dependent on large herds of horses and cattle for the major part of their living. Across the line place a community of aggressive, greedy white settlers, convinced that they are a superior race, entitled to disregard all Indian rights, and also engaged in raising large herds of stock. Explain that the stock of the white settlers must in no case cross the imaginary line, because the grass over there belongs to the Indians, whether they use it or not, but that the Indian herds are free to feed over the entire range with no regard for the line. Make no provision for enforcing the regulations, inflict no penalty for trespassing, provide no police force, no police powers. Can anyone doubt that these circumstances contain all the elements necessary to produce constant friction and probably open conflict?

Such was the situation along the borders of the Nez Percé Reservation during the eighteen seventies. Agent Monteith soon perceived the inherent dangers in the setup and the inevitable encroachment on Indian rights that must follow. He suggested several schemes to improve matters, such as providing a boundary patrol, impounding all stock trespassing on the reservation, fining negligent owners of such stock, and other similar devices,[1] but none of them was adopted by the Indian Bureau. Monteith also attempted to secure the co-operation of the stockmen, urging them to keep their herds farther from the line, to provide for a patrol, and to round up strays, but they refused to be bothered. They were well within their rights in turning their stock loose along the boundary. If the government objected to a few thousand cattle straying across into Indian territory, let it erect a suitable fence or maintain a patrol of its own. No one was required to provide a herder for stock on the open range. Besides, there was more grass on the reservation than the Indian stock used. It was unjust for all that good pasture to go to waste while cattle went hungry, all on account of governmental red tape and the Indian Bureau's attempts to coddle a tribe of lazy savages who should have been shipped off to some remote mountain valley long ago, leaving the good land for farmers who knew how to make the best use of it. Such pampering of the red men was a great hindrance to the proper development of the western country.

Friction between the rival groups of stockmen increased each year. Possibly the worst feature was not the hard feelings thus engendered, but the realization on the part of the Indians that the government, through either fear or negligence, would not enforce any treaty regulations that would injure the white settlers. The Nez Percés did not wish to precipitate a war over such matters, but neither would they submit tamely to such impositions. Finally they took to burning the grass on the hills each summer as soon as it had dried. While this put their own herds on short rations, it proved very effective in getting rid of the stray stock.[2] The whites protested loud and long

[1] Monteith to Walker, August 22, 1872, Lapwai Agency files.

against such a waste, convinced that by rights the grass belonged to them even though it was on Indian land, but they were powerless to stop the Indians, which, of course, made them all the more angry.

Illegal use of the Nez Percé pasture lands was but one of many ways the whites infringed on the reservation. Another was the stealing of timber. There were vast quantities of free timber for all on the public lands of Idaho in those days before the establishment of forest reserves, but most of it was located too far from the settlements or from the rivers, and consequently it was difficult to transport to market. Some of the timber on the reservation was close to both the river and the market, making it very attractive to timber thieves. Year after year, Monteith complained to his superiors of the thefts and asked for an effective police force at the agency to prevent such things, with no results.

Another popular device of the whites was to erect an inn or stage station on reservation land along one of the roads, as the treaty permitted. To feed the horses of the travelers and a milk cow or two, the innkeeper was allowed to put up a little hay. The hay lands thus cropped grew rapidly in area from year to year, for the milk cows were increasing to great herds and customers for hay were easy to find. Here again the agent was helpless.

If the settlers felt justified in stealing from the Indians on the reservation, technically under the protection of the government, imagine their attitude toward the nontreaty bands who were under no protection of any kind and indeed were in disfavor with the agent for their refusal to move to the reservation. Many of the nontreaty Indians held small farms or garden plots along the creek and river bottoms, on land declared open to white settlement. It was provided that the Indians could gain title to their holdings if they would comply

2 Monteith to Smith, November 2, 1874, Lapwai Agency files.

with the homestead law,[3] but few of them could understand the necessity for such formalities regarding land which they had always owned. The government, in the treaties, had promised to pay them for their improvements if they would move to allotments at Lapwai, but the necessary funds never reached the agent so that the Indians could take advantage of the offer.

Two effective methods were used by the whites to induce the Indians to surrender their holdings. The more common was to burn the fences or turn stock in on the crops during the owner's absence. After a period of such persecution, the Indian would usually move away. A more direct method was to "jump" the claim, moving in while the owner was off on a trip, and hold the place by force, shooting any misguided redskin who ventured to "trespass" on the farm. "Jumping" was usually done just after the Indian family had left on a visit or a trip to the camas grounds. When they returned after an absence of several days or weeks, they would find some white man securely in possession with his gun handy.

Monteith mentioned one man who secured a piece of land by paying the Indian occupant a small fraction of the value of his improvements. However, he was not indignant at the low price. He explained that where one man was willing to pay such a small fraction of the value there were twenty who would take everything without making any payment.[4] There is no record of anyone's having offered an Indian a reasonable sum. If such a thing had happened and the neighbors had found out about it, in all probability the man would have been mobbed or forced to submit to an examination to test his sanity.

Even in the most flagrant cases, the Indian could not secure justice from the local courts. The grand jury and trial jury would be composed of men who had secured holdings in

[3] H. C. Wood, *Status of Young Joseph*, 30.
[4] Monteith to Smith, January 22, 1876, Lapwai Agency files.

the same fashion, or they would be friends of such men. Even if the grand jury should indict, the trial jury would not convict. But should an Indian, in revenge for such treatment, venture to burn a fence or drive off some stock, the entire white population would rise in wrath and demand that he be severely punished, while the newspapers would carry wild stories of bloody savages attacking peaceful citizens, and burning editorials would demand instant action by the entire army against the culprits and their friends.

The western habit of embroidering and enlarging stories of any Indian misdeed can well be illustrated by an incident in the summer of 1872. A large camp of Nez Percés had assembled, as was their custom and their treaty right, at one of the camas meadows north of the reservation for their yearly root digging. They found that, since the previous year, settlers had fenced some of the meadows, including one customarily used for horse racing. The Indians raised no protest because they knew the settlers had a right to the land.

When the camas harvest had been gathered and the time for the usual horse racing had come, the Nez Percés prepared to hold their meet on another meadow some distance away. The settlers were interested in watching the races and offered to take down some of their fence around the old race track if the Indians would race there. The offer was accepted and the races passed off smoothly. Before the fence was replaced, some stray stock, probably from the Indian camp, got through the gap and damaged some crops. The settlers sent in a hurried call for the cavalry to drive off these terrible savages who were destroying so much property and might start killing people any minute. Monteith immediately rode over to investigate the trouble and was able to adjust the matter singlehanded. The Nez Percés took their supplies of camas and departed as peaceably as they had come, slightly puzzled at all the commotion, and the settlers subsided, possibly just a little ashamed of themselves.[5] The local press chalked up another Indian outrage against the whites, telegraphing a wild version of the affair to the eastern papers.

A constant source of irritation to the thrifty farmers was the sight of droves of Indian horses pasturing on the public lands. Because the horses were western and different, they were considered to be of little value compared to the slow, clumsy, big-footed, big-boned farm animals from the East. Farmers did not like to have their horses mingled with the range herds. It taught them wild ways and made them too hard to catch. The whites also believed that crossing one of their mares with a range stallion would "taint" the blood of all subsequent colts foaled by that mare.

Fencing pasture land, in those days before barbed wire was common, was tedious and expensive, and if the settler kept his stock in a fenced pasture all the time, he lost the advantage of having free range surrounding his farm. Even if he did keep his horses up, a range stallion sometimes broke through the fences and led the mares away to add to his harem. Often the exasperated farmers retaliated by castrating any stallions they could catch, an action greatly resented by the Nez Percés.[6]

Just as the herds of range horses irritated the farmers, so did the droves of hogs affect the Indians. A few hogs turned in on a camas meadow would fatten well with little care, but they rooted up all the bulbs, destroying the crop for years to come and leaving a barren expanse of unsightly holes. Since the hogs were allowed to roam the country, their depredations were not confined to the privately owned fields.

In 1874, a portion of the Nez Percé tribe assembled at their favorite camas meadow and found it completely ruined by the hogs. The settlers had the same right to pasture their hogs on the open range as the Indians had to pasture their

[5] Monteith to Walker, July 1, 1872, Lapwai Agency files.
[6] Monteith to Walker, April 25, 1872, Lapwai Agency files.

horses, but the latter were so angry that they tore down some fencing in protest.[7] By this unlawful act, they gave the settlers grounds for demanding the protection of the cavalry during the root-digging season the following year.[8]

[7] Monteith to Smith, June 29, 1874, Lapwai Agency files.
[8] Monteith to Smith, June 16, 1875, Lapwai Agency files.

21: Sample Atrocities

W HEN the whites in the Northwest kept agitating for the government to protect them from the savages, Congress asked the Indian Bureau for a list of white men killed in that section. The agency reports from Lapwai listed a total of four white men killed by Indians in the Nez Percé country. All of these killings occurred during the first gold rush, and in only one case did the agent give any details. Sapoon-mas, of Big Thunder's band, confessed to the slaying of a man named Varble. He was tried for the crime at Vancouver, Washington, and was acquitted largely through the efforts of a lawyer from Walla Walla. In another case, a miner had been killed and robbed by an Indian supposed to be the son of Peu Peu Mox Mox, war chief of the Wallawallas who was murdered by the soldiers in 1848. No details were given in the other two cases, indicating that no one knew just how the men had met their death.[1]

Cases of Indians killed by whites were more numerous and detailed. Some writers list as many as thirty-three victims for the period from 1860 to 1877. Sample case: In the fall of 1864, a band under Three Feathers was in southern Montana, heading for the buffalo country, where they expected to join

[1] Monteith to Walker, September 13, 1872, Lapwai Agency files.

Sample Atrocities

Eagle from the Light and his followers. One morning eight white men came to camp and accused the Nez Percés of having stolen their horses. It happened that the Indians had seen the missing animals in the herd of a band of Flatheads they had met a short time before, so they told the whites of this and pointed out the direction taken by the thieves. The whites left, apparently satisfied, but they returned the next morning and shot down a Lapwai Indian, brother of Te-a-po-o-hike. The Nez Percés did not attack the whites in revenge.[2]

In 1873, the report of a special investigating committee mentioned that a white man was then in the Boise penitentiary under a sentence of death for killing a Nez Percé woman. The unusual feature of the case was the severe punishment inflicted on the murderer. In all the other cases listed, there is no record of any punishment and very few instances of the guilty men even standing trial.

Usually there was a camp of nontreaty Nez Percés across the Snake River from Lewiston. Many of the renegades from the Palouse River hide-out visited it at various times. The crowd appeared to have been wilder and more violent than was usual among the Nez Percés. A great deal of gambling and drinking was carried on, the liquor being supplied illegally by a low class of whites from Lewiston. In February of 1874, one of the gamblers killed another in a dispute over a game. When news of the brawl reached Lewiston, a self-appointed posse of roughs, just a mob without a shred of authority even in Lewiston, decided to arrest and possibly to lynch the guilty man. Quite naturally, the men at camp refused to recognize the authority of the whites to make the arrest, and in the resulting argument one of them was shot. From Monteith's reports of the affair,[3] it is not clear whether

[2] O'Neill to Dole, August 3, 1865, *Report of the Commissioner of Indian Affairs, 1865.*

[3] Monteith to Smith, February 14, 1874, Lapwai Agency files.

the man shot was the one involved in the brawl or a by-stander. Perhaps this is the same incident to which the Indians referred when they blamed Spalding's son for accidentally shooting Cass-say-u when he was aiming at a gambler. No action was taken against the gang of roughs.[4]

Later that spring, there was trouble on the lower Salmon. A member of the nontreaty band under White Bird had a small garden spot and camping place along White Bird Creek. This man, Eagle Blanket, returned from a trip in the spring of 1874 to find that his white neighbor, Larry Ott, had extended his fence to include this land. Ott was busy with his spring plowing when Eagle Blanket came to protest against what appeared to him to be an outright theft of his garden spot. Ott claimed that the land was open to settlement as a part of the public domain and that Eagle Blanket had no claim to any land off the reservation. After a bitter argument, Ott resumed his plowing and later claimed that Eagle Blanket then threw rocks at his horses, although it is not claimed that the rocks hit the horses. Ott then drew his revolver and shot the Indian. For this he was later tried but was acquitted on a plea of self-defense.[5] Before he died some hours later, Eagle Blanket asked his son, Wal-lait-its, to promise that he would not try to avenge the death.

Harry Mason whipped two Indians because they did not get off the trail at once when he rode up.[6] Samuel Benedict had a place at the mouth of White Bird Creek where he sold whiskey to the Indians and cheated them out of their change when they bought goods from him. He killed one Indian and wounded two more in disputes with them after they became drunk on his illegal liquor.[7] Although the Nez Percés lodged

[4] McDonald letter in *New Northwest*, October 18, 1878.

[5] Monteith to Smith, April 7, 1874, Lapwai Agency files.

[6] General O. O. Howard, *Nez Percé Joseph: An Account of His Ancestors, His Lands, His Confederates, His Enemies, His Murders, His War, His Pursuit and Capture*, 102.

complaints with their agent in all these cases, they did not succeed in getting any of the white men punished, as the jury failed to convict in the few cases that came to trial. More often the charges were dismissed after a perfunctory investigation.[8]

Even a cursory review of these cases gives a fair indication of how much justice an Indian might expect from the courts of Idaho during this period. Whites guilty of horse and cattle stealing, fence burning, rape, assault, fraud, and various other crimes were in little danger as long as their accusers were Indians. Usually, such cases did not even come to trial, and when they did the defendants easily won their freedom because Indians were not allowed to testify against a white man. To insure his escaping punishment, the white criminal had only to wait until he had no other white man as a witness before going into action.

Many of the local people felt that the whites needed even more advantage over their red brothers, for federal regulations offered a little protection to the government's wards. With the help of the local officials and the state legislature, which often passed acts contrary to Indian Bureau regulations, they strove to nullify any protective measures. Local courts rendered verdicts against the federal government in cases outside their jurisdiction and local law officers tried to enforce such verdicts. At times, it was necessary for the agent to use federal troops for his own personal protection while he was engaged in his official duties on the reservation; troops to protect him, not from Indians or outlaws, but from the leading citizens and businessmen of Lewiston.

Lest anyone feel that the above is an overstatement, let him examine some of the cases such as the trial of John Brady for the murder of Bruno Jim in 1868,[9] or W. G. Langford's

[7] *Ibid.*, 101.
[8] *Ibid.*, 102.
[9] *Report of the Commissioner of Indian Affairs, 1868,* 200–201.

suit for the possession of the Lapwai Agency during Monteith's term of service.

The crimes mentioned indicate the sources of the more important quarrels between the two races: stock, land, women, and liquor, or a combination of these items. Such differences arose more frequently between the whites and the nontreaty bands because they were in more intimate contact and because the whites considered the nontreaty Indians entirely in the wrong when they did not remove to the reservation. Another point to be noticed, in view of later events, is that most of the friction was in the Salmon River country between White Bird Creek and Slate Creek. This was the country claimed by Chief White Bird and by that stubborn foe of the white settlers, Eagle from the Light.

22: Wallowa, Valley of the Winding Water

WEALTHIEST of the Nez Percé bands was that led by Chief Joseph, friend and convert of the Spaldings. He and his people claimed the Wallowa country, a stockman's paradise southwest of Lapwai across the Snake River Canyon. This was a remnant of the old lava plateau, protected on the south and west by the high, rough Wallowa Range which towered some 4,000 feet above the grasslands. Its glacier-carved canyons contained many little mountain lakes and rushing streams which provided ample water for the meadowlands through the long summer months. The streams united to form the Wallowa River, chief tributary of the Grande Ronde. Trout and salmon in the pools, deer and elk in the hills, berries on the mountain slopes, and camas in the meadows made this a desirable habitation for man. To the north lay the deep, tortuous canyon of the Grande Ronde River; to the east, the famous Hell's Canyon of the Snake. The rivers were barriers for the stock, while their deep, sheltered nooks were snow-free and grass-covered during most winters.

Joseph was an intelligent and resourceful leader in peace-time, inducing his followers to trade with the wagon trains on the Oregon Trail for cattle to pasture on the Wallowa ranges. With a substantial herd of cattle and their thousands of horses, the Wallowa band could trade surplus stock for all the goods they needed from the white men.

Guarded on all sides by mountains and canyons and miles from the main travel routes, the Wallowa country was safe from white encroachment for many years. Even the gold rush passed it by. But Old Chief Joseph saw trouble brewing for his people. The trickery of the commissioners in the treaty council at Lapwai in 1863 and the hostility of the white settlers at Lewiston convinced him that white men would be invading the Wallowa soon, looking for farms.

In his village, Joseph had three children, now adults, all of them born after he joined the mission. The oldest son, Heinmot Tooyalakekt (Hinmaton-yalatkit), is known to history as Chief Joseph or Young Joseph, a name given to him by the white men and not used by the Nez Percés. He was born about 1840 and spent several years of his life at the Spalding mission until his father returned to the Wallowa in 1847. As his father grew more feeble with age, Young Joseph, at thirty-one, was accepted as the peacetime chief and village leader. He was a sturdy, well-proportioned man, six feet in height, strong and active. He had been to the buffalo country at least once with his father, in 1868, but he had no reputation as a warrior or buffalo hunter. His strength of character and pleasant personality brought him the friendship of many important white men.

The second son, Ollikut, was taller than his brother and a remarkable athlete. After his father's death, Ollikut was sometimes called Young Joseph by army men and reporters, thus adding to the confusion of the various accounts of these famous men. Ollikut had a reputation as a hunter and fighter and was the leader of the young men of the band on their forays. The third child, Sarah, married a member of the Asotin band shortly after the 1855 treaty council.

By 1871, Old Joseph had become quite feeble and almost

blind. As his strength failed, he gave instructions to his older son to help him through the stormy period ahead:

"My son, my body is returning to my mother earth, and my spirit is going very soon to see the Great Spirit Chief. When I am gone, think of your country. You are the chief of these people. They look to you to guide them. Always remember that your father never sold his country. You must stop your ears whenever you are asked to sign a treaty selling your home. A few more years and the white men will be all around you. They have their eyes on this land. My son, never forget my dying words. This country holds your father's body. Never sell the bones of your father and mother."[1]

Young Joseph later said: "I buried him in that beautiful valley of the winding waters. I love that land more than all the rest of the world."[2]

Scarcely had the young chief taken up his new duties when the trouble began. State officials of Oregon and newspaper editors throughout the Northwest insisted that the Nez Percés must be moved from the Wallowa country and placed on the Lapwai Reservation, as provided by the treaty of 1863. They claimed that the Indians were hindering the growth of the state by excluding settlers from one of the best potential farming areas. As a result of this pressure, the Wallowa country was thrown open to homesteaders, and the influx of settlers began. They occupied most of the meadowlands and put in a few crops.

The Nez Percés tried to prevent this invasion, but their protests were ignored. They did not want to kill the trespassers, so instead Joseph lodged a protest with the Bureau of Indian Affairs through Agent Monteith. Monteith and T.

---

[1] Chief Joseph, "An Indian's View of Indian Affairs," often known as "Chief Joseph's Own Story," *North American Review*, Vol. CCLXIX (April, 1879), 419.

[2] *Ibid.*, 419.

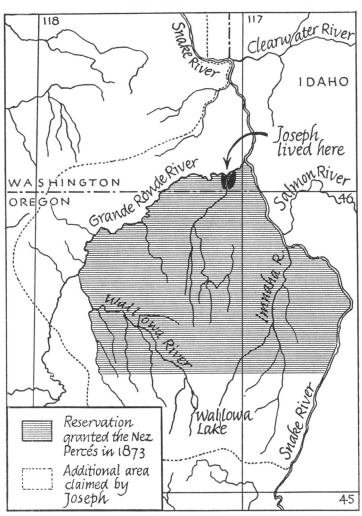

Reservation granted the Nez Percés in 1873

Additional area claimed by Joseph

Joseph's Claim & the Reserve of 1873

B. Odeneal, Indian superintendent of Oregon, were appointed a committee of two to investigate and held a joint meeting with the settlers and Indians in August, 1872. The settlers, accustomed to the mild climate of the Willamette country, had found the Wallowa less of an agricultural paradise than they had been led to expect. An unseasonable early frost had nipped their wheat and gardens. Monteith and Odeneal, who had come to the council planning to move Joseph and his band to the reservation, finally decided that the disputed land was valuable only for stock raising because it was too high and cold for farming. They recommended in their report that the entire area of the upper Wallowa Valley and Wallowa Lake be set aside permanently as a hunting reserve for the whole Nez Percé tribe and be considered a part of the Nez Percé Reservation, open to summer use by any of the tribe. The government should move the new settlers out of the valley, paying them for the improvements they had made on their homesteads.[3] The Indian Bureau approved this report and sent it to President Grant for his consideration.

On June 16, 1873, the President signed an executive order setting aside a part of the Wallowa Valley as a hunting reserve,[4] but the land in this reserve was not the same area recommended by Monteith and Odeneal. Perhaps this error resulted from the lack of accurate maps of the region, but, whatever the reason, the reserve proved unsatisfactory. Joseph was given the northern half of the land he claimed, while the committee had recommended he be given the southern half, which included higher ground, Wallowa Lake, and the headwaters of the Wallowa and Imnaha rivers. The new reserve included the lower Wallowa, the right bank of the lower Grande Ronde, and the plateau between the Grande Ronde and Snake rivers. The net result was to give Joseph and his

---

[3] *Report of the Commissioner of Indian Affairs, 1873*, 18.
[4] H. C. Wood, *Status of Young Joseph*, 31–32.

band a large area covered mostly with pine forests. Very little of this land could be farmed. Almost all the farm land along the Wallowa River was outside the reserve boundaries and still open to white settlement, with the only practical routes to the outside crossing the new reserve.

Since Joseph and his band claimed the entire Wallowa area, the return of half of it did not satisfy them. They continued to ask for the removal of the white settlers and the return of the rest of their land. State officials of Oregon and the area newspapers were dissatisfied too. They claimed that the future of Oregon was imperiled by this new reservation and asked that their state be freed from this obstacle to progress by the removal of the Wallowa Nez Percés to the Lapwai Reservation, as provided in the treaty of 1863.

Meanwhile, Agent Monteith made a strong effort to get Joseph and his people to settle permanently near Wallowa Lake. It is possible, of course, that he did not know that this was outside the reserve, but it is hard to understand why the Indians should not be allowed to choose their own location. Also, Monteith himself had stated that the upper Wallowa Valley was too high and cold for stock in the winter, yet he opposed the use of the lower canyons and valleys on the reserve for winter range.

By this time, some tension had developed between the agent and the chief. Joseph decided that he could get no satisfaction from Monteith in the matter and asked permission to go to Washington to present his case in person to the top officials in the Indian Bureau. Although it was the custom to allow several delegations of Indians from the various tribes to visit the capital each year, Monteith arbitrarily denied Joseph's request.[5]

The settlers in the valley also seemed confused about the boundaries of the new reserve. They did not want the Indians

[5] Monteith to Walker, November 22, 1873, Lapwai Agency files.

to spend the winter in the lower Grande Ronde, which was on the new reserve, but they did not object to the Indians' using the summer pasture. Some of the difficulty seems to stem from the different concepts the red men and white men had of the meaning of home. To most of the white men, home meant a permanent structure, a house, where his family stayed while he was out with his stock or hunting or even working for several months at some distance place. To the Indian, home meant a locality, a familiar round of camping places to be used in turn with the changing seasons. When the Indian went hunting or to the summer pasture, he took his dwelling and his family along. Thus he, with his portable tipi, and the white settler, with his log cabin, each looked down on the other for being different.

Working on the theme of the future development of Oregon, Governor Leonard F. Grover finally convinced the President and his advisors that Joseph's band had forfeited all claim to the Wallowa by their refusal to live in one spot the year around. In June, 1875, two years after it was signed, the original executive order was rescinded, and the Wallowa was again declared open to homesteading. An army officer in the valley at the time said that this was a grievous disappointment to the farmers there, for they, believing that the land would eventually be returned to the Indians, had been holding on in hopes of selling out to the government at a good price.

Meanwhile, friction between the Indians and whites had increased to a dangerous level. In the summer of 1874, the settlers refused to allow the Indians to proceed to the summer pasture with their herds. The Indians declined to start the firing, but neither would they retreat. After a time, the settlers thought it prudent to withdraw, and the danger was over for a while. They demanded and secured two companies of cavalry to protect them the rest of the summer.[6]

---

[6] Monteith to Smith, August 4, 1874, Lapwai Agency files.

Monteith asked for the two companies of cavalry again the next year, more to protect the Indians from the whites during the summer than to protect the whites from the Indians.[7] He continued his efforts to remove Joseph's band to the reservation at Lapwai, even before the Wallowa was reopened to settlement in 1875. The Indians around Lapwai protested bringing the Wallowa band there, stating that the land was fully occupied.[8]

The settlers aided Monteith in his efforts to collect all the nontreaty bands on the reservation by reporting and exaggerating every incident or misdeed until an outsider might have concluded that the entire white population was in danger of being slaughtered. The following incident illustrates this.

In January, 1876, the governor of Oregon received an urgent telegram asking that troops be sent at once to protect the farmers in the Wallowa from Joseph and his warriors, who were reported to be driving off and killing stock and threatening to kill all the settlers. Two companies of cavalry made a forced march in the bitterest winter weather to the scene of the troubles, finding everything quiet. Agent Monteith also arrived, for the Indians were in his charge. The investigation conducted by him and the cavalry officers disclosed an interesting story.

Monteith knew in advance that an error had been made, for Joseph and his band had been under the agent's observation for several weeks. They had arrived at Lapwai before Christmas to visit with friends during the holidays and had not been more than twenty miles from the agency buildings in that time. It would have taken them a week to make the round trip to the Wallowa, and their absence would have been quite noticeable. A search of the country finally unearthed the guilty parties.

[7] Monteith to Smith, July 3, 1875, Lapwai Agency files.
[8] Monteith to Smith, March 11, 1874, Lapwai Agency files.

Wallowa, Valley of the Winding Water

The only Indians in the district were a few old people holed up for the winter in the secluded, sheltered valley of the Imnaha. They had been more interested in staying in their tipis around the fires than in traveling across the snow-covered hills to Lapwai with the rest of the band. But they had encountered one difficulty in their chosen retreat. Stray cattle belonging to the Wallowa settlers insisted on mingling with the Indian horses and eating their food. The cattle could be identified easily by their brands, so they were cut out of the herd and driven toward their own country. In this way, the Indians hoped to be rid of the nuisance and also to avoid any possible charge of cattle stealing.[9] From this slight foundation, the entire Indian scare had been manufactured by the settlers, and two companies of cavalry had gone chasing around the mountains in the dead of winter. Were the brave farmers really so frightened? It would seem that they were only seeking a market for their hay, grain, and food at speculator prices, for they knew that the cavalrymen could not transport sufficient supplies on their mounts for man and beast on a forced march through the snow. This time the farmers were disappointed. The government contractor had anticipated the possibility of a winter march to Wallowa and had taken options on hay and grain the preceding fall.[10] The newspapers which had featured the original scare were not interested in publishing the true account later.

If this winter interlude was mostly comedy, the summer brought grim tragedy. Two white men, looking for their lost horses, came on a hunting camp of several Indians. All but one of the Indians withdrew to avoid any possible trouble. For some reason, an Indian named Wilhautyah remained in the camp. The two white men, McNall and Findley, accused him of stealing some of their horses and McNall grabbed him, but

[9] Monteith to Smith, February 2, 1874, Lapwai Agency files.
[10] Cyrus Townsend Brady, *Northwestern Fights and Fighters*, 91.

soon found himself being worsted in the tussle. He called for Findley to shoot, which he did, killing Wilhautyah at once. Later, the men found their supposedly stolen horses. Although this killing was reported by Agent Monteith, no effort was made by the authorities to punish McNall and Findley.[11]

Everyone realized that such a state of affairs could not continue without leading to serious trouble. Rumors of what the Indians might do spread over a wide area. Nez Percé horse traders carried accounts of their land troubles as far as Fort Peck in northeastern Montana that summer.[12] To appreciate the gravity of the situation, one should keep in mind that this same summer of 1876 witnessed the great Indian uprising east of the Rockies that wiped out the forces under General Custer on the Little Bighorn.

[11] Monteith to Howard, July 3, 1876, Lapwai Agency files.
[12] A. J. Noyes, *In the Land of the Chinook,* 94–95.

23: A Trap Is Set

DEATH finally took Lawyer, head chief of the Nez Percés. He had won fame in fighting the Blackfeet in the buffalo country, and his record as a fighting man added to his prestige as a chief. The whites opposed any of the fighting men as the new chief and used their influence to have Reuben, a rather docile man living near the agency, named as official head chief of the tribe. The Nez Percés never accepted Reuben as their leader, and the real leadership devolved on three of the chiefs of the nontreaty bands. Most important of these was Looking Glass, fighting son of the great war chief of the former generation. The young Looking Glass had enhanced his own record by his conduct in a battle in southern Montana when he helped the Crows defeat the Sioux. His village was on the Middle Fork of the Clearwater above Kooskia.

Another high-ranking chief, and an important medicine man as well, was White Bird, or, more correctly, White Goose. Past seventy, but still erect and alert, he had earned his warrior rank in the buffalo country. His band lived on White Bird Creek below the canyon.

Another of the important chiefs was Toohoolhoolzote, whose band lived in the rough country between the Salmon and the Snake and hunted the rugged Seven Devils country. He was a large, well-built man, supposedly the strongest in the tribe in his younger days. He is said to have carried two large deer to camp at one time, one on each shoulder. He too had fought in the buffalo country.

Four younger nontreaty leaders had not yet earned the right to sit as equals with these chiefs around the council fires. They were Hahtalekin and Hushhushcute of the Palouse band and Joseph and Ollikut of the Wallowa band. The officials and many of the newspapers disregarded this ranking of the chiefs and placed Reuben at the top of the treaty Indians, with Jonah next to him. They rated Joseph, in their reports, letters, and orders, as top man among the nontreaty leaders. This rating was given Joseph more on account of the wealth of his band than for its size, for he had a total of only fifty-five men in his group. Several of these were elderly and had never taken any part in fighting. Yet this band controlled about a million acres of grazing land and timbered mountains, an area nearly twice the size of the entire Lapwai Reservation. Here they grazed thousands of horses and hundreds of cattle, about fifteen head of stock for each man, woman, and child in the band. They were well equipped with arms, ammunition, clothing, and camp goods and had a reserve supply of gold and currency obtained through the sale of stock.

Also impressive to the whites was the dominant personality of Joseph, who was much like his father before him. To the Indians who had known his father, Joseph did not appear so impressive. They considered him more as his father's deputy. To the whites who had not known the older man, Joseph's qualities were quite evident. However, this very strength of character proved to be an important source of trouble for him in his struggle to retain his home. Government officials, impressed against their will, disliked this man who had the knack of putting them in the wrong, of winning his arguments, and

224

A Trap Is Set

who refused to acknowledge white superiority in any fashion. Monteith, General O. O. Howard, and others who met Joseph in council found him too great a man for them to dominate. This aroused in them a feeling of resentment, subconscious for the most part, which flashes forth now and then in their accounts of the meetings, in their estimates of his character, or in their insistence on his complete subjugation.

Joseph's attitude, so exasperating to the whites, was one of quiet strength and dignity. He felt no awe of any man, red or white, and owed none of them allegiance. Hence he could ignore orders from government officials, even from the President, with a clear conscience. To all their arguments, orders, and threats he simply said no, he did not agree; no, he would not obey; no, he was not afraid. Time and again they insisted that he was bound by the treaty of 1863 because it had been signed by the tribal chiefs, but to this he had a very simple and effective reply:

"I believe the old treaty has never been correctly reported. If we ever owned the land we own it still for we never sold it. In the treaty councils the commissioners have claimed that our country has been sold to the government. Suppose a white man should come to me and say, 'Joseph, I like your horses, and I want to buy them.' I say to him, 'No, my horses suit me, I will not sell them.' Then he goes to my neighbor, and says to him, 'Joseph has some good horses. I want to buy them but he refuses to sell.' My neighbor answers, 'Pay me the money, and I will sell you Joseph's horses.' The white man returns to me and says, 'Joseph, I have bought your horses and you must let me have them.' If we sold our lands to the government, this is the way they were bought."[1]

This argument sounds like some of Old Joseph's teachings, for while Young Joseph was like his father in intelligence,

[1] Chief Joseph, "An Indian's View of Indian Affairs," *North American Review*, Vol. CCLXIX (April, 1879), 419.

personality, and dignity, he did not have the older man's reasoning power, just as the latter lacked the spark necessary to make him a great leader of men.

Old Joseph's highly developed sense of responsibility for his country and his people may have been sharpened by his twenty-five years as a Christian and a leader in the Indian church. He passed on to his son this sense of responsibility, a great love of country, and a distrust of the white race. Because of his fine training from his father and his own wisdom and strength, Joseph was soon accepted by his band as leader in fact as well as name, but he never held any tribal office. He was not classed as a fighting man although he had been to the buffalo country at least twice, in 1868 with his father, and again in 1874 at the invitation of the Crows, but there is no record that he fought in the great battle that year against the Sioux.

With the shadow of impending danger constantly hanging over the Wallowa country, it was difficult for Joseph to decide what course of action would bring the most benefit to his people. When his man had been shot in the quarrel with the white hunters, he used the incident as a basis for demanding the entire Wallowa country as an indemnity, as though he were the foreign secretary of some great power dealing with a backward race. General Howard, commander of the Department of the Columbia, did make an effort to bring the murderer to trial, but the local officials, backed by public sentiment, easily checkmated this attempt. Can anyone blame the Indians if they failed to understand why it was so easy to punish a red man for the slightest offense, while white criminals went free?

Agitation over this murder finally attracted the attention of the officials in Washington, impressing them with the necessity of making a permanent settlement of the entire Wallowa question. They finally appointed a committee of five to investigate all phases of the matter and to propose a course of action based on their findings. Two of the five were army men, General Howard and Major H. Clay Wood, a member of his staff, both well acquainted with the problem. The remaining three were civilians, D. H. Jerome of Michigan, A. C. Barstow of Rhode Island, and W. Stickney of Washington.

After a leisurely journey from Chicago to Lapwai by way of San Francisco and Portland, the commission was finally ready for work at the agency on November 6, 1876. They had sent word ahead for the nontreaty chiefs to assemble and await their arrival, but the chiefs had other views of the matter and the appointed day found none of them at hand. Joseph was reported to be on his way, traveling at an unhurried pace, thus asserting his independence and his disregard for official orders. He knew that nothing could be done without him and took advantage of the situation to emphasize the fact that he was coming to the meeting as an equal of the commissioners, and not as a subordinate obeying the call of his superiors.

When he reached the agency after having delayed affairs for nearly a week, he conducted himself in a very courteous manner. He was polite, dignified, agreeable, pleasantly conforming to the best diplomatic standards, willing to exchange endless compliments and light conversation with the officials, but when the question of the Wallowa was broached, he would not budge from his previous position, he would not compromise, he would not submit to white authority. To every proposition, he politely but firmly answered, "No." Imagine the exasperation of the worthy commissioners, resplendent in all their dignity as representatives of the government of the United States of America, defied by an ignorant savage, and in such a way that they could not openly resent it. After Joseph had gone, though, these worthies vented their spleen on him in their final recommendations. How else is it possible to explain the conclusions they reached, the plan of action they proposed?

About six months earlier, Major Wood had written, after a detailed study of the Wallowa: "The non-treaty Nez Percés cannot in law be regarded as bound by the treaty of 1863, and insofar as it attempts to deprive them of the right to occupancy of any land, its provisions are null and void.

"The Nez Percés, undoubtedly, were at liberty to renounce the treaty of 1855, the government having violated the treaty obligations."[2]

General Howard had stated that he thought the Nez Percés had been treated unfairly by the rescinding of the presidential order establishing the Wallowa reserve in 1873. The other three commissioners had not worked on this problem before, so they should have approached it with open minds. But examine the program which they believed to be just and fair to all concerned.

FIRST: That the leaders and teachers of what is known as the Dreamer belief be required to return to the agencies where they belong forthwith, and in case of refusal that they be removed from further contact with the roving Indians by immediate transportation to Indian Territory. [The commissioners were particularly bitter against a Dreamer of Joseph's band.]

SECOND: With this pregnant cause of trouble removed, so long as Joseph and his band remain in the Imnaha Valley and visit the Wallowa for hunting, fishing, and grazing only a short time each year, we recommend a speedy military occupancy of the valley by an adequate force to prevent the recurrence of past difficulties between the whites and the Indians. Meanwhile, the agent of the Nez Percés should continue his efforts to settle these Indians in severalty upon the lands of the reservation which are still vacant.

[2] H. C. Wood, *Status of Young Joseph*, 45.

A Trap Is Set

THIRD: Unless they should conclude to settle quietly as above indicated, within a reasonable time in the judgment of the department, *they should then be placed by force* upon the Nez Percé Reservation. [This meant that in return for their million acres of land the tribe would receive about sixty plots of twenty acres each on the reservation, where all the best land had been allotted or had been seized illegally by the whites.]

FOURTH: If these Indians overrun land belonging to the whites and commit depredations upon their property, disturb the peace by threats or otherwise, or commit any overt act of hostility, we recommend the employment of sufficient force to bring them into subjection and to place them upon the Nez Percé Reservation. [This clause permitted the use of cavalry against Joseph if he again went to the Wallowa, since such an action would surely disturb the peace.]

The Indian agent at Lapwai should be fully instructed to carry into execution these suggestions, relying at all times on the department commander when necessary.[3]

Do not these findings indicate a desire on the part of the commissioners to punish Joseph and his little band? Although two of the commissioners had conceded previously that Joseph had a good claim to part of Wallowa, when they reached their final decision they decided every point against the chief and his people, whose only crime had been that they wanted to keep their homes and had dared say so in council.

Once they had settled the Wallowa question, the commissioners added, seemingly as an afterthought, that the same provisions should apply to all other nontreaty Nez Percés, the Palouse River renegades, the Yakimas, and the Umatillas. It was quite clear, though, that their first thought was of Joseph.

For years, Monteith had insisted that the agent needed more power. Granted this, he could solve all the Nez Percé

[3] *Report of the Commissioner of Indian Affairs, 1877, 212.*

problems. Specifically, he wanted soldiers to prevent any of the tribe from going buffalo hunting or camas gathering. He wanted to take away the Indian herds, particularly the horses, so the Nez Percés would have to hire out at day labor to obtain their spending money. He wanted to take the children from their parents and place them in the agency boarding school under strict discipline in order to "reform" them. And, above all, he wanted to stamp out the Dreamer doctrines so he could increase the membership of the agency church. Here at last was his golden opportunity. Now he had full authority to say what should be done, when it should be done, and he had the United States Army at his call to enforce his decrees. It was a good example of despotism on a small scale, pregnant with possibilities for good or evil.

24: Monteith Gives Orders

"WE do not want schools or schoolhouses on the Wallowa Reservation. . . . They will teach us to have churches. We do not want churches. . . . They will teach us to quarrel about God as the Catholics and Protestants do on the reservation, and at other places. We do not want to learn that. We may quarrel with men sometimes about things on this earth, but we never quarrel about God. We do not want to learn that."[1]

Thus Joseph explained in council his antagonism toward the white man's education and his religion. Old Joseph had been an active Christian for twenty-seven years, from his first contact with the Spaldings until the betrayal of his people at the treaty council in 1863. Much of his bitterness toward the Christians and their teachings in the last years of his life probably came from his great disappointment. The religion which he had hoped would serve as a shield for his people had proved but a screen for the rapacious greed of their enemies. Young Joseph had taken his father's teachings to heart and had tested their truth by many observations. His clear vision could see no benefits for the red men in the interdenominational fights with their petty jealousies and un-Christian conduct. His

[1] *Report of the Commissioner of Indian Affairs, 1873, 159.*

speech came from the depths of his convictions, but Monteith may have taken it as a personal attack on himself.

Monteith's predecessor, Captain Sells, had recommended that all the educational work on the reservation be turned over to the Catholics, who had been conducting active missionary work in the tribe during the years it had been neglected by the Presbyterians. Sentiment alone had given the agency to the latter in 1871. During the first part of Monteith's work as agent, the Catholics had more converts than did the Presbyterians, and the new agent was expected by his church to use his official influence to reverse the situation.

In 1869, the Catholics had established a small mission a few miles above Lapwai on a branch of Lapwai Creek. Here they built a chapel to care for the converts, who were rather slow in joining, but the work went on under the direction of the priests from the Coeur d'Alêne mission. The Catholic Indians asked that their share of the tribal funds for the building of churches and schools be used to develop their mission rather than the Presbyterian mission at Lapwai, but their request was refused.

Finally, in November, 1875, two priests came to the Nez Percé mission. They planned to erect a house for themselves and a school building, greatly alarming Monteith, who as agent forbade them to build anything. After a lengthy wrangle, the Indian commissioner decided that the Catholics were entitled to build a church and a dwelling house for the priests, but no school. Again the struggle went on, for Monteith was convinced that the dwelling was being made larger than was necessary so the extra room could be used for the forbidden school.[2] Most of the Indians were highly amused at this conflict between two groups of whites, and the nontreaty group was quick to point out the weakness of such a religion and such a government. Joseph's remarks concerning religious quarrels

[2] *Ibid.*, 157.

rubbed Monteith the wrong way, for he knew they referred to the above affair.

In addition to opposing Monteith's religious views, Joseph ventured to disagree with him about the proper way for an Indian to make a living. While it is doubtful that Joseph completely accepted the Dreamer doctrines of Smohalla which were against all farming and all white ways, he delighted to use them to annoy the officials, and he was opposed to giving up his herds of stock so he would be forced to earn his living on a twenty-acre patch of crops directly under the agent's eye and the agent's thumb. If stock raising was so good for a white man, why should it not be good for Joseph? Whether or not Joseph knew of Monteith's plans to force the Indians to give up their herds, he could see that if he moved to the reservation the shortage of suitable range would drastically reduce the number of horses and cattle he could raise.

As his burden of responsibility grew, Joseph came to realize that he would have to adopt a new program. No longer could he hope to retain all the country of the winding waters. The rapid influx of white farmers and the increasing use of troops pointed to the necessity for some compromise with the invaders. His new attitude was noticed by Monteith, who possibly thought the change much greater than it really was. He wrote:

"I think from Joseph's actions he will not come on the reserve until compelled to. He has said so much to the Indians who have moved on the reserve, calling them cowards etc. that he would be lowering himself in his own estimation as well as in that of his immediate followers, did he not make some show of resistance. By making such resistance he could say to the other Indians, 'I was overpowered, and did not come of my own choice,' in case he is forced on the reserve."[3]

By such arguments, Monteith justified his request for

[3] *Report of the Secretary of War, 1877,* 115.

troops to bring an end to the matter in the spring of 1877. He was probably justified in his reasoning that far, but his further statement is either inexcusable ignorance or deliberate falsehood: "I have given Joseph until April 1, 1877, to come on the reserve peaceably. *They can come at one time just as well as at another, having nothing to hinder them in moving.*"[4]

When he wrote this, Monteith had been in the country nearly six years. He was familiar with the great floods that roared through the Grand Canyon of the Snake, since renamed Hell's Canyon, from April until July. He also knew that the Indians allowed their stock to scatter to the sheltered valleys and canyons during the winter, where the spring crop of calves and colts were dropped in April and May. Melting snows and spring rains would hinder the stockmen in an early roundup. Much of the range could not be searched adequately until the June sun dried some of the moisture and the heat of the lower canyons drove the stock to the plateau. Mares and colts and cows and calves would need two or three months to gain the strength needed to swim the mountain rivers even in midsummer. All this pointed to mid-July or later as the appropriate time for the Indians to move their herds from the Wallowa to Lapwai, but Monteith brushed away all arguments with the statement, "If he [Joseph] is allowed to have his own way at this time, it will only make him more stubborn in the future." This arbitrary stand of Monteith was an important obstacle to a peaceful solution of the Nez Percé problem.

Joseph was confronted with the difficult task of convincing his people that moving to the reservation was the only solution to their problem. Many of his band were followers of Smohalla and all were opposed to surrendering tamely their homes to the settlers. They counseled further resistance, even open warfare, rather than submission to white dictation. They reminded their leader how he had promised his father he

[4] *Ibid.*, 115.

234

would never sell the land. On this point, Joseph's conscience was clear, since he had no intention of selling any land. He would claim ownership of the Wallowa as long as he lived, but if he should be ejected forcibly, he would be breaking no promise in securing the best possible terms for his people.

While Joseph was discussing matters with his followers and making plans with his younger brother, Monteith was busy with his own scheme. As early as January, 1877, he requested two companies of cavalry to be sent to the Wallowa as soon as the melting snows would permit their movement. He also sent Joseph orders to come to Lapwai.

General Howard believed that Joseph would not submit meekly to such orders. He expected to see the entire band on the warpath and all the discontented Indians in the Northwest rallying to their cause as soon as Monteith began to put on the pressure. In the event of a general uprising, the troops might find themselves the victims of such a combination as had wiped out General Custer the previous summer, leaving the settlers exposed to a long, bloody war. He was certain that any outbreak started by Joseph would center in the Wallowa. Hence he planned to establish a strong post at the confluence of the Wallowa River and the Grande Ronde. Two full companies of cavalry, two of the new Gatling guns, an ample supply of ammunition, and a supply of food sufficient for thirty days were to be placed in a well-built camp designed for several months of occupancy.[5] An additional company of infantry was to be held ready if reinforcements were necessary. Thus Howard would have more than 100 regular troops with the most modern equipment and another 100 armed civilians to withstand a band of Indians mustering about 55 fighting men.

When the news of the proposed troop movement leaked out about March 1, 1877, the newspapers were full of articles on the coming campaign against Joseph. Howard immediately

[5] *Ibid.*, 586–88.

corrected the report, stating definitely that it was merely a precautionary measure and that he did not plan to attack anyone.[6] He feared that the wild stories and wilder rumors, growing from the untimely, but truthful report, might incite the Indians to attack the settlers before the troops could reach their position. The deep snows in the Blue Mountains would delay the construction of the post until at least the middle of April. The delay annoyed Montieth, who appeared anxious to begin cracking the whip over his charges.

On March 12, Howard wrote in reply to Monteith's protest over the delay: "I do not understand how we can take the offensive at all until further instructions from Washington. I am glad indeed you did not fix any time for the ultimatum of Joseph's coming."[7] Yet a month earlier Monteith had fixed April 1 as the date. Why did he conceal this from Howard?

Army officers began to fear that Monteith might precipitate unnecessary trouble. The division commander, General Irwin McDowell, instructed Howard: "As this question of the removal of Joseph's band is a very delicate and important one, the division commander directs it to be done under your personal direction if practicable. . . . It is, therefore, of paramount importance that none of the responsibility of any step which may lead to hostilities shall be initiated by the military authorities."[8]

Evidently, Joseph was keeping in touch with the various developments during this time. He managed to prevent any rash action on the part of the young men that spring, but he was worried about the future. He sent word to General Howard that he desired a personal interview as soon as possible because he feared that the interpreter at Fort Lapwai the previous fall had not done his translating accurately and it was

[6] *Ibid.*, 586.
[7] *Ibid.*, 587.
[8] *Ibid.*, 587.

important that the Indians know exactly what was expected of them that spring. Joseph set the meeting for April 1 at Walla Walla. Howard was busy with other matters at the time and did not reach Walla Walla by that date, but he sent his aide-de-camp, Lieutenant William H. Boyle, to talk to the chief. Joseph evidently knew that Howard had not come, for he sent Ollikut to talk to Lieutenant Boyle. These two agreed that Howard should meet Joseph at Walla Walla on April 19. Again Joseph did not come.[9]

At the second meeting, a group of Nez Percés and Umatillas under the leadership of Ollikut sought a modification of the order for their removal, but General Howard quite properly refused to make any change since he lacked the necessary authority. His duty was to carry out the orders which came to him from Washington through Agent Monteith. The Indians then proposed that the Umatilla Reservation be traded for all of the Wallowa and that the Umatillas be allowed to live there with Joseph's people. Howard thought this a poor plan, but he did not take the proposal seriously because he was sure the Indians had suggested it at the instigation of some whites who had been striving for years to have the Umatillas moved to some other place.[10]

Howard tempered his refusals to make any changes by promising to talk with all the Indians again at Lapwai two weeks later, when the details of the removal would be explained and the various chiefs would choose the lands on which their people would settle. He also explained that the Indians would be given permission to make yearly hunting and fishing trips to the Imnaha country if they would first get passes from the agent, but this privilege was only for those who obeyed orders.[11]

9 *Ibid.*, 590.
10 *Ibid.*, 590.
11 *Ibid.*, 590.

Since the gathering at Lapwai in May was for the purpose of giving orders to the Indians rather than securing concessions from them, the preparations were less elaborate than for a treaty council. A large hospital tent was pitched near the barracks with the sides rolled up and the fly extended, making a cool, airy pavilion that could shelter the assembly from both sunshine and rain.

First to reach the meeting place was Joseph, who lived farthest away. Soon after his arrival, the other chiefs came in one by one, as though they had been waiting to see what Joseph would do before they decided to come. While they waited for the others, the whites made efforts to secure Joseph's assent to the orders. He was promised his choice of all available land, and his right to hunt and fish in the Imnaha was again stressed, but he paid little attention to their persuasions, preferring to wait for the other chiefs.[12]

When the various chiefs had assembled, Monteith addressed the council with obvious satisfaction. His long-awaited hour had come. At last he could give orders to these arrogant nontreaty Indians and know that he had the power to enforce them:

"I sent out Reuben and some others to your camp and invited you to come in. . . . Now you must come in and there is no getting out of it. You and White Bird's Indians can pick up all your horses and cattle and come on the reservation. I have land for all of you. Joseph can pick the place he wants if he will come at once. General Howard will stay until matters are settled."[13]

The chiefs did not want to decide at once and asked for time to talk among themselves. Howard cheerfully assented to this delay. His troops were not yet in position,[14] and he was

12 *Ibid.*, 590.
13 *Ibid.*, 593.
14 *Ibid.*, 593.

not ready to put on the pressure. As long as he could keep the chiefs in council, everyone would be watching events at Lapwai while his troops gained their posts. The late spring had delayed the troops ordered to the Wallowa and they had not been able to start until May 1, just two days before the council opened. Now they were nearing Joseph's country while he, totally unaware of the danger, was striving to delay the date of moving to avoid crossing the Snake River at the height of the spring flood. Howard knew that word of the arrival of his troops in the Wallowa would soon reach the Indians, but then it would be too late. The news would only hasten their compliance with his orders.

As the council progressed, Howard became more stern. The influence of his military rank gave him dominance over the agent, whose authority had been flouted successfully on more than one occasion. The general was a great believer in army discipline and in the Christian religion. Both of his beliefs were rudely challanged by the Dreamers, the most talkative and troublesome being Toohoolhoolzote, who acted as spokesman for the entire nontreaty group. If his fiery speeches could gain any concessions from the whites, the chiefs would back him. If the whites continued firm, the chiefs would take a new line of attack.

Howard feared that he could secure no decision from the council until he had nullified the Dreamer influence. With this in mind, his speech grew severe. "If they continue turbulent and disobedient they will be sent to the Indian country [Oklahoma]. I reiterated the orders to them with as much severity of manner as I could command to give good advice, until I saw they were alarmed for their personal safety."[15]

By "good advice," Howard meant that the Dreamers should cease all opposition to his plans and should support the proposals of the whites. He indicated that he took this stand

[15] *Ibid.*, 594.

because he feared an immediate outbreak of hostilities if the Dreamers continued their speeches. When Toohoolhoolzote still demanded by what right Howard was ordering the Indians around, he was told, "Our old friend does not seem to understand the question is, will the Indians come peaceably on the reservation or do they want me to put them there by force?" but he defiantly asserted that he could not be frightened by threats. Howard then ordered him imprisoned until the council was over.[16]

The wiser chiefs saw that Howard was seeking an excuse to force the issue. They agreed to pick out land for their followers and to discuss the final arrangements. Their compliance was hastened by the report of new troops approaching Lapwai and news that the two companies of cavalry under Captain S. C. Whipple were encamped at the crossing of the Grande Ronde,[17] quite near Joseph's home camp, where he had left the women and children practically undefended. Joseph had much more reason to fear a treacherous attack than did Howard, who constantly played up the dangers he was undergoing at Lapwai and how his bravery protected the white people there.

As the sun broke through the clouds after a warm spring rain, a group of the chiefs left Lapwai with Howard about noon on May 15, 1877, to make their final selections of land. It had been planned to settle Joseph on Lapwai Creek above the agency and to put White Bird on the Clearwater near Kamiah. Howard promised to remove the two white men on Lapwai Creek, whose combined holdings totaled more than 700 acres and to relocate the several Indian families settled in the same area.

Joseph objected to such an arrangement, saying it would be unjust to the settlers, both red and white. He knew that the

[16] *Ibid.,* 593.
[17] *Ibid.,* 594.

Indians near Lapwai and all the whites as far as Lewiston were objecting to his band's being located anywhere near there. Later he said that these considerations led him to request an allotment near Kamiah, where the Indians were more friendly to him.[18]

General Howard and Agent Monteith granted his request at once. They had been wondering how they could dispossess the two white men who had no legal right on the reservation.[19] Also, they thought it would be better for Joseph to be as far as possible from Lewiston, since the people there were openly hostile to even the peaceful reservation Indians.[20]

The people of Lewiston made no attempt to help secure a fair or peaceful solution of the Indian problem. While Monteith was so busy with his problem, some of the Lewiston businessmen and the local press brought charges of graft, theft, mismanagement, and the like against him in an effort to secure his dismissal. Howard was convinced that the furor was caused by speculators who hoped to make a profit from their illegal holdings of Indian land if they could get rid of Monteith.[21] A new agent, arriving during a period of disorder, would of necessity have to rely on the local citizens for information concerning the various claims, and the whites all worked quite well together when it came to defrauding the Indians or the government.

As soon as Joseph had made his choice of land, Howard warned him that he had just thirty days to move all his band and their belongings to their new home. "If you are not here in that time, I shall consider that you want to fight, and will send my soldiers to drive you on."

---

[18] Chief Joseph, "An Indian's View of Indian Affairs," *North American Review*, Vol. CCLXIX (April, 1879), 422.

[19] *Ibid.*, 796.

[20] *Report of the Secretary of War, 1877*, 595-96.

[21] Howard, *Nez Percé Joseph*, 72.

Joseph replied: "War can be avoided and ought to be avoided. I want no war. My people have always been friends of the white men. Why are you in such a hurry? I can not get ready to move in thirty days. Our stock is scattered and the Snake River is very high. Let us wait till fall, then the river will be low. We want time to hunt up our stock and gather supplies for the winter."

General Howard refused. "If you let the time run over one day, the soldiers will be there to drive you on the reservation and cattle outside the reservation at that time will fall into the hands of the white men."[22]

With this ultimatum ringing in his ears, Joseph hastened home to comply as best he could, while Howard, well satisfied with the results he had attained, turned to the other chiefs. To White Bird, who had no Snake River to cross and who lived within a day's travel of the reservation, he likewise allowed thirty days. To Hushhushcute, a constant troublemaker from the Palouse, he granted thirty-five days, with the added privilege of keeping a few men at the village site most of the summer to look after a few scanty crops and the stock. Shortly after this, at another council, he allowed some of the Yakimas until September to comply with his orders. Does not all of this look as though Howard was either trying to force Joseph into some rash act, or that he was striking back at a man who had irritated him, or possibly both? Surely it would have answered the purpose of the government just as well if most of the band, particularly the women, children, and aged, had moved at once, while a small crew of men stayed on through the early summer, rounding up the stray stock and guarding the herds until the low water of late August permitted their safe removal.

[22] Chief Joseph, "An Indian's View of Indian Affairs," *North American Review*, Vol. CCLXIX (April, 1879), 422–23.

25: Murders on the Salmon

FROM the conference tent at Lapwai, Joseph rode across the hills to Lewiston, crossed the Snake there, and followed the rugged trail along the west bank of the Grande Ronde River and two miles up that stream to his camp just below the mouth of Joseph Creek. His decision had removed one problem, but many more still faced him. The soldiers were camped near his people and some of them did not respect Indian property rights or the virtue of their women. Some reckless act by a soldier, a settler, or one of his own young men might easily bring disaster, yet he needed time to gain the consent of his people to the new status.

The time had come to repudiate some of his former teachings and to disregard his father's instructions. His people were to adopt the way of the white man, surrendering forever their beautiful homeland, their parents' graves, the free life, to settle as intruders among neighbors latently hostile. Here they would till scanty patches of soil under white domination, giving up most of their horses and cattle for lack of pasture. When Joseph presented this program in council, he could expect accusations of cowardice, of unfilial behavior, of meek submission to unjust orders, yet he must win them over quickly, for each day lost in debate would increase the difficulty of getting to the reservation within the time allowed.

Some white man might ask: "Why did he not just order them to move? Was he not their chief?" He was the chief, but in all the Nez Percé tribe no chief had ever had the power to say to his people, "Come" or "Go" according to his wish. They were not rulers giving orders, but leaders who must gain consent to their plans by persuasion, by reasonable arguments, by force of personality.

"In their institutions, the autonomy of the individual is so complete that a chief approaches absolutism only in proportion to his strength of character, and the strongest never dreams of such an attempt at power, but acts upon the will of the people expressed in council; and if there be but one man who dissents, his right to depart from the action of the others is unquestioned."[1]

"If in council the tribe or band are pleased with the counsel and advice of their chiefs and head men they follow it. If it does not accord with their feelings, it is disregarded."[2]

It speaks well for Joseph's personality and his ability as a speaker that on this occasion he was able to persuade the entire band to accept his advice after a short discussion. Once the decision was reached, the work of moving got under way. This involved sorting all their belongings into what could be carried along on pack animals and what had to be thrown away. This time, they could not follow their custom of caching surplus articles against the day of their return, for they were not coming back.

Meanwhile, every available rider was busy combing the million acres of ridge and ravine, upland meadow and brushy creek bottom, forest, park, valley, and hill for the thousands

[1] C. E. S. Wood, "Chief Joseph, the Nez Percé," *Century Magazine,* Vol. XXVIII, No. 1 (May, 1884), 135.
[2] Monteith to Walker, August 31, 1872, Lapwai Agency files.

of horses and cattle that had roamed unchecked all winter and spring. In the rush and hurry, hundreds of animals escaped the roundup and were appropriated by the settlers as soon as the Indians had gone.

After two weeks of exhausting work, the little band of exiles gathered their herds on the west bank of the Snake River at the mouth of the Imnaha and faced an angry yellow flood swollen by spring rains and melting snows from a thousand mountain slopes, an icy torrent swirling, boiling, and roaring through the rocky defiles. Across a quarter of a mile of treacherous currents, the Indians had to transport all their families and all their possessions—old people, invalids, cripples, little children, hundreds of packs of goods, hundreds of wobbly colts and calves, thousands of horses and cattle—with two companies of cavalry at their backs to force them along should they hesitate.

Rafts were made of tightly rolled skins lashed together and loaded with the packs. Riders on the best horses, four to a raft, held ropes to tow them across, the men naked and the horses wearing only a thong bridle.[3] Hundreds of yards they would be swept downstream on the swift tide before they could gain footing on the steep bank and drag the goods to safety, with possibly a child or two or an aged Indian clinging to the lashings. Very young children rode strapped to their mothers' backs. Sometimes a canoe could be found for ferrying the sick.

In this sort of work, the sturdy, range-bred horses proved their worth. Only the best were ridden, for human lives depended on their ability. Through the exercise of fine horsemanship, the crossing was completed without loss of life. Meanwhile, the herds of stock were held under a small guard on the nearby slopes. It is said that some of the settlers from Wallowa, taking advantage of the situation, managed to stampede a portion of the herds and escape with several hundred

[3] Howard, *Nez Percé Joseph*, 150.

head while the main body of Nez Percés were engaged in swimming the river.

Finally, the horses were again rounded up and headed for the river, being driven faster and faster until they took the water in one grand rush and were swimming boldly for the opposite shore before they had time to break. After they were well under way, the cattle were handled in similar fashion, the herders following closely in their wake. The stronger and hardier animals soon reached the far shore in safety, but the brood mares, the fresh cows, and the little calves and colts were drowned by hundreds in the wild rapids or were tossed, weak and helpless, against the rocks.

Cold, wet, dispirited, and smarting under heavy losses caused by the greed of the settlers and the impatience of the officials, the Indians drove the remnants of their tired herds up the steep trails to the plateau above, where they might find food and rest. Here the herds were left with a few of the young men as guards while the band went on to the Salmon River Canyon and crossed that flooded torrent. They climbed the slope to the north and finally reached a campsite on the shore of Lake Tolo at the head of Rocky Canyon and a few miles west of Grangeville. Here they were within two miles of the reservation boundary, and they decided to camp until the final day to enjoy their last few hours of freedom before submitting to the arbitrary rule of Monteith.

For ten days, the camp basked in the pleasant June sunshine, scarcely disturbed by the occasional showers. While the elders spent many long hours around the council fires, the rest of the people played games, danced, and staged parades and horse races. It appeared that the whole affair would end peacefully.

Then one afternoon a grand parade was held. Most of the men in camp decked themselves in their best and rode their finest horses in a long procession around the tipis. Near the end of the long line came Wal-lait-its and his cousin, Red Moccasin Tops, both on one horse which pranced and cavorted under the restraining rein. The horse disturbed some cowish roots drying in the sun and brought angry reproof on the young riders. "See what you do. Playing brave you ride over my woman's hardworked food. If you so brave, why you not go kill the white man who killed your father?"[4]

This criticism caused Wal-lait-its to forget his promise to his father and to think only of instant, drastic action. With Red Moccasin Tops and another close friend and relative, Swan Necklace, he rode down to the Salmon River on the afternoon of June 13, 1877.

Larry Ott was not to be found at his ranch nor anywhere along the valley, although they searched carefully for twenty miles upstream. The Nez Percés say that he had disguised himself as a Chinese miner and stayed hidden in a Chinese group until the trouble had passed. The young men did find and kill Richard Divine, a retired English sailor who had a small place some six miles above Slate Creek. He had taken over some Indian land and liked to set his fierce dogs on any Indian passing his place in the narrow canyon. Then they turned back down the river and killed Henry Elfers, who had helped Henry Mason escape punishment for whipping Indians. They also killed Robert Bland and Burn (Harry) Beckroge.

The three then rode back toward camp, meeting Samuel Benedict, the bootlegger, near his home at the mouth of White Bird Creek. They wounded him, but he managed to reach shelter. That night the youths camped on Camas Prairie, away from the main camp, sending Swan Necklace in to tell the people what they had done so that anyone who wanted to stay out of the fighting would have a chance to leave and not

[4] L. V. McWhorter, *Hear Me, My Chiefs! Nez Percé Legend and History*, 190.

become implicated. Several hours later Wal-lait-its and Red Moccasin Tops rode in.[5]

Two Moons, one of the fighting men, then mounted his horse and rode through the camp, calling for volunteers for another foray. A war party was soon recruited, including the original three and about seventeen more, mostly from the Salmon River bands. Later, General Howard and others blamed Chief Joseph for allowing the raids, but both Joseph and Ollikut were away from the camp at the time and did not learn of the events until after the second raid had started.

About a year earlier, one of the Nez Percé stockmen had died. Before his death, he set aside eleven of his cattle to be killed by his brother and ten more men chosen by the brother. Now the time had come to carry out the terms of the bequest, so the brother chose the ten, including Joseph and Ollikut, and the party had crossed the Salmon River to the cattle herd to do the butchering. They returned to camp with the meat just after the second foray had begun. Even had they been in camp, they could have done nothing under Indian custom, for none of the raiders was from the Wallowa band.[6]

On this raid, the young men found supplies of whiskey both at Samuel Benedict's and in a freight train bound for Grangeville. In the resulting drunken frenzy, they committed all the atrocities proved against them during the entire war. Fourteen or fifteen men were killed, women and children were mistreated, houses were plundered. One woman and one boy were among the missing and presumably were killed. Samuel Benedict was routed out of his hiding place and shot. Ad Chapman, on the Indian black list for selling Indian beef to Chinese miners and for "jumping" Indian lands along the Salmon, fled to Lapwai and offered his services to General Howard as a scout.

[5] *Ibid.*, 194.
[6] *Ibid.*, 197.

Murders on the Salmon

The camp at Lake Tolo was shocked at the many killings. Family after family hastily struck their tipis and moved away, anxious to avoid being classed with the guilty. Most of the Wallowa band sought refuge with Chief Looking Glass on the Middle Fork of the Clearwater. White Bird and Toohoolhoolzote, with their bands, moved across the ridge to the south, making camp on White Bird Creek about two miles below the canyon. After some delay, Joseph and Ollikut reluctantly followed them. Although none of his band had gone on the raids, Joseph expected to be blamed for some of the trouble because of his past defiance. His estimate of white reaction proved accurate. The official correspondence of the period indicates clearly that Generals McDowell and Howard and Agent Monteith all expected Joseph to fight, and they seemed sure that if any fighting broke out, Joseph's men would start it. Possibly their belief in the certainty of war caused them to issue their harsh orders that spring so Joseph might be defeated quickly by a superior force and thus serve as an example to the other unruly Indians of the Northwest.

General Howard had expected the outbreak to start in the Wallowa and had arranged his forces accordingly. When Joseph's band left their homeland without resistance, he thought the crisis was over. Howard evidently had overlooked the possibility that some other band might break loose. Hence, the Salmon River killings found the general unprepared, his available forces few. However, he should not be criticized too severely for this. He took a calculated risk, for he might have alarmed and irritated the Indians by assembling his forces when things were going smoothly and peace seemed in sight.

News of the raids reached Lapwai by an Indian messenger, one of the treaty group visiting relatives at the nontreaty camp. He reported to Howard that the raid was one of private revenge and not a declaration of war by the nontreaty bands. Howard believed this until he received a letter from L. P.

Brown, hotelkeeper at Mount Idaho, just east of Grangeville. On the unsupported testimony of this one man that the country was in the midst of an Indian war, General Howard assembled his forces for an attack on the Indian camp.

Nez Percé men photographed on the Yellowstone in 1871. (Photograph by William H. Jackson, courtesy Smithsonian Institution, B.A.E. Collection)

Mounted warriors photographed July 4, 1906, by Major Lee Moor-house. (Courtesy Smithsonian Institution, B.A.E. Collection)

Warrior carrying Nez Percé War Pole.

26: War

ASSURANCES from Mount Idaho that war had begun reached General Howard at Lapwai at 4:30 P.M., June 15, 1877. In three and one-half hours, he had made his plans, outfitted ninety-nine men for the field, and started them up the trail toward the Indian camp, each man carrying his field equipment, forty rounds of ammunition, and cooked rations for three days. Five pack mules followed, loaded with additional food.[1] These forces consisted of companies F. and H, First Cavalry, under the command of Captain David Perry. Many of them were recruits from the large eastern cities, secured the previous winter in a vigorous recruiting campaign that brought in the needed numbers, but many of them of mediocre caliber. As this column moved to the attack, Howard ordered up his reserves. From the post at the mouth of the Wallowa River, Captain Whipple came with two companies of cavalry. Infantry was brought from Walla Walla by steamer, and additional troops and supplies were requested from Fort Vancouver. It is obvious that General Howard expected serious fighting.

From Lapwai to the plateau far above and eastward across rough, broken country, Captain Perry led his men along the

[1] Brady, *Northwestern Fights and Fighters*, 112.

muddy trails through the rain. They paused for breakfast and an hour's rest for the horses at Cottonwood, forty-five miles away, and rode on into Grangeville, another twenty miles, by evening.[2] Here Captain Perry had planned to rest his men for the night, but the local citizens objected. They insisted that he must march at once on the Indian camp so he could mount a surprise attack before the Indians could cross the Salmon River to safety, and they promised a large force of civilian volunteers to help him. Perry finally gave in and set nine o'clock as the starting time.

When Perry was ready to move, he found only eleven civilians instead of the large number promised.[3] He set off with his weary men and reached the ridge high above White Bird Creek a little after midnight. Here they rested and waited for the summer dawn to light their way down the steep, grassy slopes that dropped sharply 3,000 feet to the creek below.

The ridge on which Perry's command rested extended a mile or so to the west of the mountain spur south of Grangeville. Here it became lower and free of timber, curving several miles to the south and ending abruptly at the Salmon River Canyon just below the mouth of White Bird Creek. In the huge bow of the ridge, the grassy slopes dropped steeply for the first mile, then more gently for two miles to the bottom land along White Bird Creek. The course of the creek followed the same curve, breaking from a deep, narrow canyon in the mountain spur to sweep from west to south. Below the canyon mouth, it flowed through a valley whose grassy slopes were broken by a few small buttes or knolls. The Nez Percé camp was in the creek bottom just where the stream made its last turn to the south. Here, sheltered from the north by small twin buttes, the Indians rested, only the smoke streamers from their campfires revealing their presence to the troops approaching beyond the two buttes.

[2] *Ibid.*, 113.
[3] *Ibid.*, 114.

North of the buttes, the ground was gently rolling for a quarter of a mile or more in each direction, sloping away to the east to the creek. On the north, a gentle slope led to a draw and so to the top of the ridge, while the west was bound by the steep ramparts of the main ridge, with outcrops of rock ledges here and there. Only the great western ridge and the two small buttes presented obstacles to the free movement of troops, and between the foot of the ridge and the buttes was a broad grassy saddle. The whole of this gently rolling ground is now a wheat field.

Captain Perry and his men came down the slope from the north and down the draw. Where it widened, he formed his men in a column of fours, Company F at the head, Company H in the rear, with an interval between. About 200 yards in advance of Company F, Lieutenant Edward R. Theller led an advance patrol of eight men. Although Perry knew he was near the Indian camp, none of his command had caught a glimpse of it yet.

As the head of the column came out on the level ground, Lieutenant Theller and his men rounded the eastern shoulder of the eastern butte and discovered a group of six Indians some 300 yards away, advancing under a flag of truce. To the east and rear of this group, a few scattered riders were sitting on their horses, watching. Behind them were the tipis of the Indian camp, more than one-half a mile away.

Lieutenant Theller immediately deployed his men and sent word to Captain Perry that Indians were in sight. Soon one of Theller's scouts, Ad Chapman, fired twice at the Indians with the flag of truce, but did not hit them. The scattered Indians to the rear then advanced to support their peace envoys, and one of them, with a lucky shot at extreme range, killed Trumpeter Jones of Company F, a serious loss.[4]

Meanwhile, Captain Perry was deploying his forces along

[4] L. V. McWhorter, *Yellow Wolf: His Own Story*, 56.

the northern part of the open ground out of rifle shot from the two buttes. He anchored the left of his line on a small outcrop of rock, placing the eleven volunteers from Grangeville there in a strong, sheltered position. He dismounted Company F and sent the horses to the rear, where they were protected by a swell in the ground. Company H, commanded by Captain J. G. Trimble, came up smartly to his right and deployed but did not dismount. Thus Captain Perry had time to choose a favorable position and to deploy his troops before the fighting began. Here is no hint of ambush or surprise attack. The fighting began with the two shots fired by the scout, Ad Chapman. The twin buttes, too far from Perry's lines for snipers, blocked any attempt at direct frontal assault and forced the Indians to approach from the flanks, which they might have chosen to do in any case.

After their hasty withdrawal from Lake Tolo, the Indian camp on White Bird Creek was a welter of uneasy indecision. Long discussions around the council fires brought no definite plan of action. Some of the more timorous favored immediate withdrawal across the Salmon, where they could play hide-and-seek with the soldiers in the tangle of mountain ridges. Others favored a parley in an attempt to reach a settlement without a war, the plan finally adopted. Meanwhile, many of the men staged a party with the captured whiskey and spent the latter part of the night in drunken slumber.

The morning of the battle found the Indian camp astir by dawn. Scouts had watched Perry's march to Grangeville and had brought the warning. The horse herd was brought in, the war horses caught and tied near the tipis, and the rest held under close guard near the camp. As the soldiers approached, some of the men stripped for battle and placed themselves across the soldiers' line of march to protect the camp against a cavalry charge. They were able to muster about sixty to sixty-five men, many of them still suffering from the effects of the whiskey, several of them elderly and never considered fighters, and about a third of the total armed only with bows and arrows. Nearly fifty of them followed Ollikut to a position just south of the western butte which was hidden from the advancing troops. Fifteen more, with Two Moons as leader, moved around to the east of the buttes, and one of these fired the lucky shot that killed Trumpeter Jones. There is no indication that they had any plan of attack. If the soldiers attacked, the Indians would try to protect the camp.

As the fighting started, Perry had eleven volunteers on the rocky knoll to his left, forty men of Company F deployed on the line (the remainder of the company were holding the horses to the rear), forty mounted men of Company H deployed on the right, and no reserves. The Nez Percés had nearly fifty men on Perry's right, sixteen on his left, and no reserves. Chapman's two shots at the envoys advancing under a flag of truce, Trumpeter Jones's bugle calls from the east butte, and the answering shot which killed him gave notice to both sides that the fight had started.

The Indians did not hesitate in the face of superior numbers. Two Moons led his fifteen mounted Nez Percés up a shallow draw on the east, delivering an attack at a sharp gallop against the volunteers on their rocky knoll. Firing as they charged, they wounded two men with their first shots. The entire group of volunteers then left in a great hurry and some confusion for Grangeville.

On the west, concealed by the butte, Ollikut waited with his men. With him were Wal-lait-its, Red Moccasin Tops, and Strong Eagle, each wearing a red blanket coat, in contrast to their almost naked comrades, and each eager to earn status as a fighting man. When shots were heard to the east, these three dashed forward, the rest of the group following them helter-skelter, bending low on their galloping war horses and shooting as they came.[5] They struck the west end of Trimble's line,

[5] *Ibid.,* 57.

dropping his trumpeter and disorganizing his men. In the excitement of their first fight, the recruits were unable to control their plunging horses or to return an effective fire. With the volunteers running on the left, and the line on the right dissolving into a confused melee of men and horses, Company F gave way in the center and made a rush to the rear for their mounts. Thus, in about five minutes, Perry's command had changed from an organized fighting force to a fleeing rabble. Nineteen men, including Lieutenant Theller, were trapped against a rock wall in a small ravine and wiped out. In all, thirty-four soldiers were killed, two soldiers and two civilians volunteers were wounded. The Nez Percés had two wounded. Sixty-three guns were picked up on the battlefield by the victorious Indians, many of them having been discarded by soldiers mounting restive horses in a hurry.

While mediocre leadership and poorly trained troops contributed to this defeat, the important factor might well have been the loss of both trumpeters at the outset, leaving Captain Perry with no means of controlling his men. It is hard to understand why Trumpeter Jones was riding with the advance patrol when his post of duty was by Captain Perry.

Once the field of battle had been cleared of living soldiers, the Nez Percés, following military custom the world over, despoiled the slain of their arms and ammunition. Contrary to Indian custom, the Nez Percés did not strip or multilate the dead, not even to the extent of taking scalps, nor did they take any scalps during the entire war, but Howard's forces, particularly his scouts both red and white, took many scalps from the Nez Percés.

Both the army reports and newspaper accounts glossed over the facts about the poorly trained recruits, worn out by thirty-six hours of marching and two nights without sleep. Too many people were ready to believe that the Nez Percés were supermen led by military geniuses.

War

While the red men celebrated their victory that night in their camp on White Bird Creek, anxious settlers from Spokane to Salt Lake barricaded themselves in their little villages as the telegraph flashed the dreadful news, worse in some ways than Custer's defeat the year before. The same telegraph that carried the story of the battle to the nation's press hummed with the settlers' frantic appeals for troops and guns to protect them all from bloody massacre.

General Howard, profoundly shocked at the catastrophe, wasted no time in vain regret. His plans had been made with possible war in view; his department was in a state of readiness, with the men alerted and the supplies at hand. His mistake, from the military point of view, had been his underestimation of his opponents, and even this judgment had been based on accurate information. And while Howard did not expect Captain Perry to be defeated, neither did he expect to end the trouble with one blow. Even as Perry prepared to march from Lapwai, orders had gone to military posts at Walla Walla, Stevens, Vancouver, Canby, Townsend, Klamath, and Harney ordering all available men to be rushed to Lapwai. A dependable messenger raced across the hills to Captain Whipple in the Wallowa, urging him to hurry. Artillerymen returning from Alaska were intercepted and directed up the Columbia. Men were shipped from San Francisco. To provide a substantial reserve if the war spread, an infantry regiment entrained at Atlanta, Georgia, for San Francisco, traveling via the new Union Pacific Railway.

While he waited for his forces to assemble, Howard spent his time at Lapwai in drilling the garrison and in planning a campaign. He dared not move against the Indians until he had a definite superiority in numbers, and the hostile band was now reported to contain more than 300 fighting men. This caution on Howard's part should not be mistaken for fear. He had displayed great personal bravery during the Civil War, proving he was no coward, but he refused to take unnecessary risks. The one defeat had convinced him that, man for man, the Nez Percés were at least the equal of his best troops. What they lacked in drill and discipline, they more than made up by their accuracy of aim, an unusual trait in mounted Indians. Against such men, Howard might meet defeat again unless he exercised skill and caution. Another fight like that at White Bird could stir other tribes to revolt. Western garrisons were below normal strength because of the concentration of troops at Chicago to quell the railway strike. It was important that Howard should prevent the trouble from spreading.

By prompt, decisive action, in less than a week, Howard had assembled at Lapwai a force of 400 soldiers and about 100 scouts and packers, all equipped for a campaign. On June 22, just one week after Captain Perry's departure, Howard's column followed the same route toward the Salmon. He moved cautiously with scouts and skirmishers covering the column at all times.

From a camp near Lake Tolo, Howard led a reconnaissance in force to the White Bird battlefield. There he paused to bury the dead, the bodies lying as they had fallen, fully clothed and unmutilated. Howard then moved on south to the river, sending Captain Trimble with a small cavalry force to the mouth of Slate Creek by a roundabout trail.

Meanwhile, the Nez Percés remained in their camp at Horseshoe Bend, a few miles up the Salmon from the mouth of White Bird Creek. Here they were joined by several men who had just returned from the buffalo country, among them Five Wounds and Rainbow, both famous warriors. At the news of Howard's approach, a council of chiefs met to plan a course of action.

Rainbow and Five Wounds advised that they wait on the riverbank for the army to approach, hoping to entice Howard across the river. Once the troops were across to the left or west bank, the Indians could move downstream and cross over to the right or east bank. Then they would have a clear trail across Camas Prairie to the Clearwater River.

The plan worked smoothly. Seeing the Indians almost within rifle range on the opposite bank, Howard hastened to cross with his command, a difficult task with the river still at the flood stage. Then for days the column plodded on through the rain and mud, up and down high, steep ridges, losing several pack mules along the way when they fell into ravines. At length, the quarry's trail led down to the river's edge at Craig's crossing.

Howard attempted to follow. After he had lost a large raft piled with equipment, and several cavalry horses had drowned in the swirling waters, he abandoned the attempt and led his weary command back along the dreadful trail to White Bird Crossing, where he had boats to aid him. When Howard found this smaller river too dangerous for his best cavalry, perhaps he remembered Joseph's plight of a month before when his band and all their herds had faced the full flood of the mighty Snake with Howard's troops at their backs to urge them on.

While General Howard was engaged in this futile pursuit, he had given substantial reinforcements to his enemy by a rather stupid and wholly dishonorable act. Looking Glass and his band were camped on the Clearwater just above Kooskia. They had stayed in the buffalo country until they thought the trouble had been settled. Except for their hunting trip, against the wishes of Agent Montcith, they had followed most of the government regulations. Some of their white neighbors, eager to stir up trouble, carried word to Howard that the band was planning to join the hostile group at the first opportunity. They cited as proof the fact that the

Indians had killed a few of their own cattle and were drying the meat, their only method of preserving it in the summer heat.

Most of the Wallowa band, including some of Joseph's immediate relatives, had moved to the Looking Glass village when the big camp broke up at Lake Tolo. These Indians had stayed away from the fighting from the first. Now a few of the young men slipped away and joined the hostile group. Howard considered this cause enough for a surprise raid on Looking Glass and his camp, so he sent some cavalry under Captain Whipple against the band, with no orders to treat the Indians well or to respect their property.

Whipple's plans for a surprise attack were nullified to some extent when he found the Indian village some ten miles farther away than the settlers had reported it. Instead of being in position to attack at dawn, he did not get his troops in place until after sunrise. While the soldiers were taking their places in the timber near the village, Whipple rode in to ask Looking Glass to surrender. The chief was surprised at the request but showed no sign of hostility. He and Whipple were still talking when a subdued bugle call from the timber aroused the chief's suspicion. As Looking Glass began to rally his men, a volunteer, Washington Holmes, precipitated the attack by firing at one of the Indians.

The waiting troops charged at once, firing promiscuously. Most of the Indians gained the shelter of the trees, but in their haste they abandoned all their food, camp equipment, and horses. Captain Whipple reported that he had killed several Nez Percés in this attack, but the Indians listed their losses as one boy of seventeen, wounded so badly that he died later in the day, and a woman who was drowned with her baby as she tried to swim the river. Two men were wounded.[6]

Captain Whipple's abortive attack on Looking Glass oc-

[6] McWhorter, *Hear Me, My Chiefs!* 269–70.

cured while General Howard was across the Salmon on his futile chase. To protect Howard's supply line and the settlers on Camas Prairie, Whipple brought his forces back to Cottonwood and entrenched his position. He sent two civilian scouts to investigate a rumor that the Indians had recrossed the Salmon. One scout was killed, but the other returned with the news that the whole Nez Percé force was approaching Cottonwood from the west. Whipple sent Lieutenant S. M. Rains with ten men to reconnoiter on July 3. They met a war party led by Five Wounds, Rainbow, and Two Moons, which was planning an attack of some sort on Whipple's camp. The warriors wiped out Rains and his men with one blow and retired well satisfied with their day's work.

On July 4, Captain Perry brought reinforcements and supplies to Cottonwood from Lapwai and, as senior officer, took command of the camp. The following day, a force of seventeen civilian volunteers from Mount Idaho and Grangeville attempted to ride across the prairie to join Perry at Cottonwood. At the same time, the main body of the Nez Percés was escorting the women and children with the camp pack train to the north of Cottonwood. This left a group of some fourteen young Nez Percés patrolling the area between Grangeville and Cottonwood in the path of the volunteers. In the resulting skirmish between these two small groups, two Indians were wounded, one of them fatally. Two white men, D. B. Randall and Ben Evans, were killed and two or three others were wounded. The young Indians lacked the experience and leadership to press the attack on the defeated civilians.

Unhampered by the soldiers, the main body of Nez Percés went on east down Cottonwood Creek and camped at its mouth on the South Fork of the Clearwater on the west bank just above the present town of Stites. Here they were joined by Looking Glass and his band and most of the Wallowa band who had remained in the area after Whipple's attack on them five days before. After this accession, the Nez Percés were at their peak strength, with 191 men of all ages. About 50 of these took no part in any of the fighting. The women and children numbered about 450. That night at the council meeting Looking Glass addressed the chiefs:

"Two days ago my camp was attacked by the soldiers. I tried to surrender every way I could. My horses, lodges and everything I had was taken away from me by the soldiers we had done so much for. Now, my people, as long as I live, I will never make peace with the treacherous Americans. I did everything I knew to preserve their friendship and be friends with the Americans. What more could I have done? It was because I was a good friend of theirs I was attacked. The officer may say it was a mistake. It is a lie. He is a dog and I have been treated worse than a dog by him. He lies if he says he did not know it was my camp. I am ready for war. Come on and let us attack the soldiers at Cottonwood. Many a man dies for his dear native land and we might as well die in battle as any other way."[7]

A day or so later, a small band of Nez Percés led by Olli-kut, Five Wounds, and Rainbow attacked eighty volunteers led by Edward McConville, holding them all night on a small hill since known as Mount Misery because of the whites' unpleasant experience there. While the volunteers shivered in their entrenchments, the Indians culled their horse herd and took forty-three animals, most of them having been taken from Looking Glass a week before. The next day, McConville led his dejected men back to Mount Idaho while the gleeful Nez Percés returned to their camp.

[7] *New Northwest*, December 6, 1878.

Chief Joseph in 1900, photographed in Washington, D.C., by De-Lancey Gill. (Courtesy Smithsonian Institution, B.A.E. Collection)

Whitebird Battlefield. The Indian camp was along the creek to the right of the picture. The long slope which Captain Perry and his men descended is to the left of center. Trumpeter Jones was killed on the

right end of the rock outcrop in the center of the picture. (Courtesy
Phil Shira, Grangeville, Idaho)

Ollikut, brother of Chief Joseph, in 1876.

27: Battle of the Clearwater

IT was pleasant that July morning in the Nez Percé camp. With McConville chased home and no sign of Howard on the back trail to the south and west, vigilance was relaxed. No organized scouting was carried on. Some of the people lounged around the camp or bathed in the river, while a few started racing horses along the river bottom. Just past midday, they were startled by a cannon shot from the valley rim to the northeast and looked up to see Howard and his troops preparing to attack the camp from that direction. About 120 men answered the call of the chiefs, snatching up their guns and ammunition belts while the women and boys brought up the horses.

Brave, daring old Toohoolhoolzote took twenty-four of the best and dashed across the river. He led his men up the steep eastern slope and placed them at the head of a small ravine across the line of Howard's march. The rest of the fighting force formed in two groups, one just to the north and the other to the south of the camp, for the South Fork offered some protection directly to the east and the canyon of Cottonwood Creek furnished an escape route to the west.

Howard found the Nez Percé camp partly by accident. When he returned to Camas Prairie after his futile march across the Salmon River, he was able to concentrate all his forces in one command. With the troops of Whipple, Perry, and Trimble, he now had about 400 soldiers plus another 180 scouts, packers, and teamsters, about three times the strength of the hostile Nez Percés, and was anxious to fight a pitched battle with them.

McConville, on July 9, sent word to General Howard that he had found the hostile camp and asked that the troops advance at once. Howard wasted no time in moving, but, for some reason never satisfactorily explained, he did not strike directly toward McConville and the Indians. Instead, he led his men across the South Fork of the Clearwater just east of Grangeville and proceeded north along the eastern rim of the valley, his progress concealed and seriously impeded by the thick timber. It is evident from his actions that neither Howard nor his guides knew just where to look for the Indian camp. He held his line of march to the north, well back from the valley rim to avoid the many small ravines, and finally came out on more open land where the clumps of trees made fringes on either side of the rolling grasslands.

They found the Indians by chance. Howard's aide, Lieutenant Robert H. Fletcher, rode a quarter of a mile west of the column to a projecting point on the valley rim, just for a look at the country. Evidently Howard's numerous scouts did not operate that far from the main route of the troops. Fletcher came out on an open point which gave him a good view of the valley floor several hundred feet below, where, to his surprise, he saw the Nez Percés racing their horses. He carried this news back to Howard, who ordered up his artillery, a four-inch howitzer and two Gatling guns, and opened fire on the surprised Indians. Howard then reversed the line of march of his troops and hurried south to get around the head of a large ravine which was too deep and steep to cross in a hurry. If he could turn this ravine, he had a rather good approach to the Indian camp down a long, steep slope. This movement was checked by the timely arrival of Toohoolhoolzote and his twenty-four men.

Once Howard's forward units were engaged, he rapidly deployed his entire command, completely enclosing a large area of open ground with the general, the packs, and the extra equipment securely sheltered in a small depression in the middle. The soldiers began digging rifle pits and strengthening their position. They held these lines for thirty hours.

As soon as the Nez Percés were sure that Howard had halted and was on the defensive, many of their fighting men left the camp to aid Toohoolhoolzote's valiant little band. Desultory fighting continued along the line through the long summer evening and into the night.

By that time, the Nez Percés were tiring of the affair. They were not conditioned mentally for a long battle when they could fight or leave as they chose. They had been forced to fight to protect their camp. Now the camp was safe and they had no definite plans of what to do next, nor did they have a common objective. Several of the fighting leaders wanted to organize a charge in an attempt to break Howard's line, while others proposed pulling out since there was no apparent benefit to be gained by further fighting. With less than 100 men on the line against nearly 600, and the Indians in disagreement, little could be accomplished.

On the morning of July 12, Howard advanced his lines to gain control of a small spring, for his command was running short of water. With more and more Nez Percés leaving the firing line to go back to camp, the fifty or so left and were not able to halt the well-organized troop movements and gave way before the advance. Soon they all decided to leave and broke off the fighting. During this battle, the five different bands of hostiles had each been fighting under its own chief, except for the Wallowa band, which followed Ollikut. Joseph took some part in the fighting, but not as a leader. On July 12, he was in charge of the camp to see that all the families got packed and out of the way in time.

Once the Indians quit fighting, Howard's men quickly overran the abandoned camp, capturing a few tipis and several sick and lame horses. The general's report made much of this haul and listed a huge number of casualties among his foes. One of his officers had a clearer view of the affair:

"At the Clearwater, the opposing forces were about equal. If anything, the troops had the advantage in numbers as well as in position. And yet, strictly speaking, the Indians were not defeated. Their loss must have been insignificant and their retreat to Kamiah was masterly, deliberate and unmolested, leaving us with a victory barren of results."[1]

Howard listed his losses as thirteen killed and twenty-three wounded. The Nez Percés counted four killed and six wounded. By this fight, Howard had pushed the Nez Percés away from the settlements, but he had not whipped them. He could not prevent their retreat along the Lolo Trail and he could not calm the settlers.

The Indians, on their part, had to make some long-range plans. In a council to determine their future course, White Bird, Looking Glass, and Toohoolhoolzote all favored flight to the buffalo country. On the plains of Montana and Wyoming, they could join with the Crows and leave the fighting behind. They all considered this a war with Howard, not with the United States, and believed that the fighting would end once they left Howard's territory. Joseph was against this:

"What are we fighting for? Is it our lives? No. It is for this fair land where the bones of our fathers are buried. I do not want to take my women among strangers. I do not want to die in a strange land. Some of you tried to say once, that I was afraid of the whites. Stay here with me now and you will

[1] Brady, *Northwestern Fights and Fighters*, 135.

have plenty of fighting. We will put our women behind us in these mountains and die on our own land fighting for them. I would rather do that than run I know not where."[2]

A counter proposal was made by Chief Looking Glass. When Rainbow and Five Wounds returned from the buffalo country in June, they had brought word that the Crows were talking war. Chief Looking Glass made an impassioned plea that the Nez Percés join forces with the Crows, who would be glad to welcome such an addition to their forces. The council voted to go to the buffalo country and appointed Chief Looking Glass as the leader. On the morning of July 16, the Nez Percés packed their horses and started along the mountainous Lolo Trail. Five young men volunteered to act as the rear guard in case Howard's men followed too closely.

A note of comedy was added at this point. The chiefs decided that one of the young men, No Heart, should talk to Howard across the Clearwater River at Kamiah, proposing a possible surrender of the hostile band. While this discussion was under way, a shot was fired, the whites say by an Indian, the Indians say by a white. This broke off the parley and No Heart slapped his bare buttock in derision as he turned to ride away.[3]

Howard's optimism at the beginning of the parley is shown by his own report. "Joseph may make a complete surrender tomorrow morning. My troops will meet him at the ferry. He and his people will be treated with justice. Their conduct to be completely investigated by a court composed of nine army officers selected by myself Colonel Miller is designated to receive Joseph and his arms."[4]

Shortly after this fiasco, the retreating Nez Percés met

[2] C. E. S. Wood, "Chief Joseph, the Nez Percé," *Century Magazine*, Vol. XXVIII, No. 1 (May, 1884), 138.

[3] McWhorter, *Hear Me, My Chiefs!* 329.

[4] Thomas A. Sutherland, *Howard's Campaign against the Nez Percé Indians*, 1877, 11.

Chief Red Heart and his band, who were on their way home from the buffalo country. They did not want to join the hostile band, but continued toward their homes. Chief Three Feathers and a few of his people left the hostiles to return with them. Howard took the entire party captive. This peaceful group makes up almost the entire bag of prisoners Howard claimed to have captured as a result of the Clearwater battle. Chief Red Heart and his people were stripped of their guns, horses, and baggage. They were herded on foot across the plateau to Fort Lapwai and later were shipped to Fort Vancouver, where they were kept in close confinement until the next spring.

28: Following the Lolo Trail

WHO would care to face a rough mountain trail burdened with wounded men, noncombatants, and excess baggage, and with a determined enemy at his heels? Certainly not the war-wise Nez Percés. They planned a little surprise to delay and discourage General Howard until they could establish a safe lead. From Kamiah, their trail led to the northeast up over the first timbered ridge, down across Lolo Creek, a small tributary of the Clearwater, and up another steep, timbered slope to Weippe Prairie, the camas meadows where the tribe first welcomed Lewis and Clark. A small rear guard was stationed in the timber to discourage close pursuit.

Major Edwin Mason, scouting the trail with a small force of cavalry and a number of scouts from the treaty group of Nez Percés, had a brief skirmish with this guard, losing two of his scouts. He returned at once to Kamiah with his report.

Meanwhile, General Howard was laying plans to block both ends of the Lolo Trail and thus capture the hostile bands. One column of troops was to follow the Indians to prevent their doubling back into the settled portions of Idaho, while a second, under Howard's personal command, hastened to Missoula over the longer but easier Mullan Road. Howard hoped that the hostiles would do no more than keep just out of reach of the pursuing column, thus giving him time to reach the eastern end of Lolo Canyon, on the Montana side, ahead of them.

When Major Mason returned to make his report, a small band of Nez Percés followed him. They hung around the main camp until Howard moved out with his forces on the first leg of the march to Missoula. Then they gathered up about 400 head of horses belonging to their friends in the fighting forces and to the peaceful Indians in the valley. This raid gave the settlers a bad case of jitters, which increased as other stories of stolen stock circulated. It is evident from later reports that several of the white ranchers took advantage of the confusion to run off stock for themselves, hoping that all the blame would fall on the hostile raiders.

The jittery settlers began protesting to the authorities that if Howard took all the troops the countryside would be at the mercy of the savages. They brought enough pressure to bear that Howard was forced to remain another ten days until an infantry regiment from Atlanta could arrive. He utilized the delay to re-equip his troops and to develop a new plan of action. At this time, he particularly cautioned his subordinates against any action which might add allies to the enemy, tacit admission of his own mistakes in June which had increased the opposing forces from 20 to nearly 200 men.

While Howard was soothing the nerves of the farmers and villagers by his benign presence, the Indians proceeded along the difficult Lolo Trail at a good speed. The unusual size of the band and the correspondingly great number of animals made it difficult for them to find suitable camping places and ample pasture. The worst of the trail was passed by forced marches in order to reach good grass before the animals played out. At this time, the band consisted of about 190 men and more than 400 women and children. In addition to a horse for each person to ride and about an equal number of pack animals, they had a remount herd estimated to have contained between 2,000 and 3,000 head.

With Howard delayed at Kamiah, the chiefs felt free to take their time, but even so the crossing was no pleasure trip. The trail had always presented real hardships, even to people accustomed to mountain travel. The column of soldiers, following the route a few days later, considered it one of the worst trails in North America, an overestimation arising chiefly from lack of experience on mountain trails. Here are extracts from an account of their trip:

"The ascent of the heights beyond Kamiah was tedious in the extreme. It was raining hard, and the muddy, slippery trail was almost impassable, filled with rugged rocks and fallen timber. The descent to the Lolo fork [of the Clearwater—not Lolo Creek] was made by slipping, crawling and scrambling over rocks and thick underbrush. At the 'We-Ipe' was an opening in the forest with water and grass. Here was a camp made for the weary, footsore animals and exhausted men, after a sixteen mile march of the greatest severity.

"The trail ahead being obstructed by fallen trees of all sizes and descriptions, uprooted by the winds and matted together in every possible troublesome way, a company of forty 'pioneers' with axes, was organized and sent to open the trail, wherever possible. It is true that the Indians had gone over this trail ahead of the troops but they had jammed their ponies through, over and under the rocks, around, over and under logs and fallen trees and through the densest undergrowth, and left blood to mark their path, with abandoned animals with broken legs or stretched dead on the trail.

"It is remarkable that the average daily march of sixteen miles was made over the Lolo trail, when we realize the necessity of climbing ridge after ridge, in the wildest wilderness, the only possible passageway filled with timber, small and large, crossed and crisscrossed. The following, from the record of

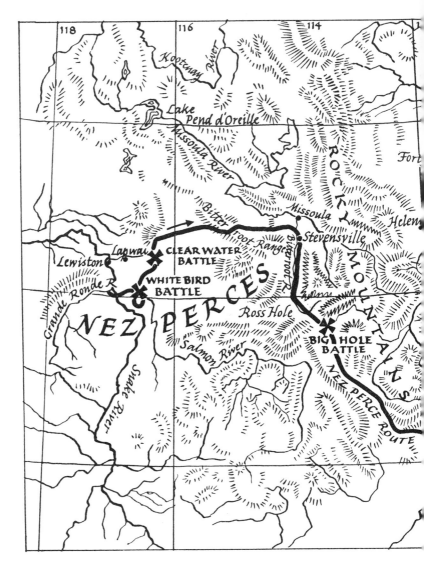

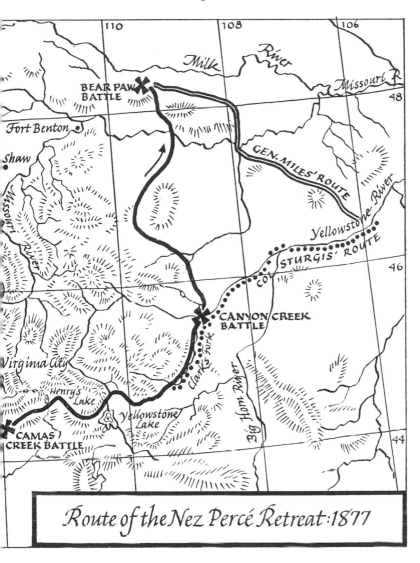

110 108 106

Milk *River*

Missouri R.

48

BEAR PAW
BATTLE

Fort Benton

Shaw

GEN. MILES' ROUTE

Yellowstone River

Missouri River

Yellowstone River

46

STURGIS' ROUTE

CANYON CREEK
BATTLE

Clark's Fork

Virginia City

Henry's Lake

Yellowstone Lake

Big Horn River

44

CAMAS
CREEK BATTLE

Route of the Nez Percé Retreat: 1877

August 2nd, will serve to show the nature of these daily marches:

" 'The column left camp at seven A.M. Artillery at the head of the column. The trail led through the woods of the same general character, a "slow" trail, owing to the mountainous country and fallen timber. The summit of the hills was covered with rough granite boulders, making a path quite difficult. Our men travel it well, and are in good order. We march sixteen miles and encamp on a slope of a mountain. Poor grazing; the only feed consists of wild dwarf lupine and wire-grass. Several mules were exhausted, and some packs of bacon were abandoned along the way. Dead and broken-down Indian ponies very numerous along the trail. Camp made about four P.M.' "[1]

The daily marches of the Nez Percés must have been somewhat similar. After five days of such travel, they reached Lolo Hot Springs, the famous "Traveler's Rest" of Lewis and Clark. Here they halted for a time, believing the worst of their troubles over. Their enemy, Howard, was far to the rear and could be kept there. Ahead was familiar country, filled with friendly people whom they had known for years. It seemed as though they regarded the conflict as a private affair between Howard and themselves, with all other men, both red and white, as onlookers. To some extent, they held this opinion until the final battle.

In such a frame of mind, they headed down Lolo Canyon for the Bitterroot Valley on July 27. Here they found their route blocked by Captain Charles C. Rawn, who had taken all his forces from the work of building Fort Missoula in order to head off the Indians. Supplementing his 30 soldiers were about 200 volunteers from Missoula and the Bitterroot Valley. They had erected a line of fortifications, since known as

[1] Brady, *Northwestern Fights and Fighters,* 20-21.

Fort Fizzle, across the narrow way, needing only to hold their lines to insure ultimate victory.

The Indians seemed not in the least disturbed by the obstruction. They made no effort to attack, but sent three of the chiefs, Looking Glass, White Bird, and Joseph, ahead under a flag of truce to talk with Captain Rawn. They said they had no quarrel with anyone except Howard. If Rawn would grant them free passage through the valley with their belongings, they in turn would promise to harm no one. They would proceed as they had in previous years on their hunting trips. Each chief would be personally responsible for all members of his own band.

Under ordinary conditions, such a proposal from a band of Indians on the warpath would have been regarded as a trick, but most of these Indians were well known to the volunteers. They had often camped at Missoula or Stevensville for a week at a time, visiting, trading, and horse racing, with the whites always welcome in their camp. Just the year before, Looking Glass had had his eyes treated by a leading doctor in Missoula. So satisfactory had been the Indians' conduct in the past that the volunteers immediately voted to accept their proposal. If they could protect their valley by a treaty, it would be foolish to force a fight with its useless bloodshed, at the same time exposing their homes to danger in case the Indians were not completely wiped out. Captain Rawn, acting under positive orders from General Howard, could not accept such terms. He wanted to carry out his orders, holding the Nez Percés in the canyon by negotiations or by force until Howard could attack them from the rear.

After a prolonged wrangle, the volunteers broke the deadlock by picking up their things and going home.[2] The desertion left Rawn with sixty men, his regulars and some thirty

[2] *Report of the Secretary of War, 1877,* 500.

Missoula volunteers who seemed anxious for excitement. It has not been definitely established whether Rawn agreed to the terms of the Indians or not. Some of the men present thought that he had agreed not to attack the Indians providing they made a detour along the mountainside around the end of his intrenchments, as though they had tricked him, and that he kept the news from the more belligerent volunteers for fear they might commit some rash act which would nullify the treaty without stopping the Indians. Rawn drowned his disappointment in whiskey, while the motley horde of hostiles rode past the south end of his line in full view of the soldiers. A few scattered shots were fired, but evidently with no harmful intent. Rawn then withdrew to Fort Missoula with his men, while the Nez Percé chiefs directed their line of march south up the valley and went into camp near Carlton, where another big council was held.

These frequent halts to discuss plans show how absurd it is to consider Joseph the commander of the Nez Percés. He could advise and persuade, but he could not command except by special vote of the council. In this meeting, as in several of the previous ones, his advice was disregarded and his plan voted down.

The council debated the best route to follow in crossing the mountains. The shortest and easiest, up the Big Blackfoot River, across Lewis or Cadotte Pass and down the Sun River, was blocked by Fort Shaw, and the line of march was exposed to an attack by the volunteers at Helena. A more southern route down the Jefferson River to Three Forks and across Bozeman Pass to the Yellowstone, a route much used in recent years by the Nez Percés, was blocked by Fort Ellis and exposed to attack by the forces from Virginia City. The chiefs knew that it would be necessary to detour both the forts and the populous mining camps if they wished to insure a peaceful passage.

White Bird and Red Owl proposed to avoid the dangers by a swing to the north. They could cross the rivers west of Missoula, either by stealth or by a new treaty, and head north across the Flathead country. From the northern end of Flathead Lake, an easy trail led up across Marias Pass to the plains country along the present line of the Great Northern Railway, just south of what is now Glacier National Park.

Some old-timers hold that the Nez Percés abandoned the northern route through fear of an attack by the Flatheads under Chief Charlo. It is extremely doubtful if fifty Nez Percés would have hesitated to face the entire Flathead tribe, and there is evidence to indicate that the Flatheads feared them. Charlo was careful to explain in some detail how impossible it would be for sedentary Indians like themselves to oppose such terrible fighters. They had no guns, no ammunition, no training, and would require white protection if the hostiles invaded the Flathead country. To be sure, Chief Charlo talked big to some of his white friends, describing how he had refused to shake hands with the killers and had threatened them with dire vengeance if they should dare to harm Charlo's friends. He even proposed to join with the whites in raiding the Nez Percé horse herds, but he was too smart to try it without their help. A contemporary was unkind enough to suggest that Charlo was much more interested in horse stealing than in fighting or helping the whites.[3] Only a year before, a pinto racer owned by Poker Joe, a Nez Percé, had badly beaten all the best horses the Flatheads could bring to race against him, and Charlo wished to recoup his losses.

The real opposition to the northern route came from the other chiefs within the council. Looking Glass and Five Wounds wanted to go south of the Bitterroot, through the Ross Hole country, and on to the headwaters of the Jefferson.

[3] Paul C. Phillips, "Battle of the Big Hole," *Frontier*, Vol. X, No. 1 (November, 1929), 13.

Then, instead of turning east to Three Forks and Bozeman on the old trail, they should make a big swing to the south, following the great arc of the Continental Divide to Yellowstone National Park. From the park it would be a simple matter to reach the Stinking Water, now the Shoshone River of Wyoming, and the country of their friends, the Mountain Crows. The road was open, the grass was good, and there were few whites. If further flight was necessary after they reached the Crow country, the broad prairies stretched away to Canada.

For about 100 years, there had been a rather strong intertribal friendship between the Crows and the Nez Percés. Crow tradition states that their first horses came from the Nez Percés, and trade was well established between the two by 1800. To this older relation had been added a new one by the treaty of 1855, when the Nez Percés and Blackfeet had agreed to divide the buffalo country peaceably. Since then, hunting parties from Idaho had hunted in the great triangle between the Missouri and Yellowstone rivers and the Crazy Mountains. Crows living to the south of the Yellowstone were accustomed to cross the river to hunt the same area. The resulting close contact strengthened the friendship of the two tribes, and the Crows secured some help against their aggressive enemies, the Sioux, who were being forced westward by the increasing pressure of the farmers on their eastern borders.

In the fighting that resulted, the Sioux had the advantage because of their greater numbers, and the Crows suffered severely. As early as 1865, they had sought an alliance with their friends from the west who had been so effective against the Blackfeet. The Crows sent word to the Nez Percés that they were almost exhausted and needed help. No formal alliance was made at this time, but small bands of Nez Percés fought the Sioux many times during the next decade, probably in conjunction with the Crows. In 1874, the offer of an alliance was renewed, and may have been accepted by a portion of the nontreaty Nez Percés, for there are several references to the bond between the two tribes in 1877.

When the Sioux prepared for their last great stand against the whites, they invited many of their enemies to join in the common cause. It is indicative of Nez Percé prestige on the Plains that they were invited to this council in eastern Montana. Eagle from the Light, Looking Glass, and Joseph were all on the Yellowstone in the spring of 1875.[4]

The refusal of the Nez Percé envoys to join in the plans of the Sioux brought them immediate loss. When they returned to Idaho that fall, they reported that the Sioux had stolen several hundred head of their horses,[5] news which pleased Monteith.

Crow scouts served the next year, 1876, with the various columns of troops that scattered the hostile bands after the battle on the Little Bighorn. This service earned them new enmity from the Sioux, and Looking Glass believed that the Nez Percé warriors would be welcome reinforcements to the Crows and would be invited to settle permanently with them.

During all this discussion, Joseph refused to support either side. He was obsessed with one idea, the desire to return to Wallowa. He still favored surrendering on the best terms they could get from Howard, if it would mean a return to their homes.

Looking Glass at length offered the winning argument: "Did you, or did you not, with the other chiefs, elect me for leader through this country, because I knew it and the people, and did you not promise me that I should have the whole command to do as I pleased?"

Joseph replied: "You are right, Looking Glass. We did elect you head man of the camp. Go ahead and do the best."[6]

[4] Monteith to Smith, March 1, 1875, Lapwai Agency files.
[5] Monteith to Smith, September, 11, 1875, Lapwai Agency files.
[6] *New Northwest*, January 10, 1879.

After the southern route had been adopted, the band moved south a few miles to Stevensville, where they stopped to replenish their supplies of flour, sugar, coffee, and tobacco. The merchants welcomed the trade, selling them all of such articles they desired, at exorbitant prices, which the Indians paid from their store of gold dust, coin, and currency. On the advice of the chiefs, the whiskey was locked up during the stay, the townspeople readily agreeing to the precaution. Ammunition and guns were not offered for sale. In a few cases, the Indians confiscated small amounts of ammunition from men riding too close to the camp, but they must have paid for it, as there is no suggestion that any robbery had been committed.

How jealous the chiefs were of the good reputation of their bands and how strictly they enforced the terms of their agreement are evident from their strict policing of the town. One of the braves became quarrelsome in a store, probably because of the excessive prices. At his first angry words, his chief, Looking Glass, took him by the collar, marched him out to the street, and sent him back to camp under guard. The whites made no complaints of stock's having been stolen or killed, nor of any settlers' having been molested.

Some ranch houses, temporarily abandoned by their owners, were pillaged, possibly by whites willing to take advantage of the situation. Only one house is known to have been entered by the Indians. Some of the unruly young men under Toohoolhoolzote plundered the house of Myron Lockwood of two hundred pounds of flour, thirty or forty pounds of coffee, one file, two or three shirts, and some other small articles. When Looking Glass heard of this, he made the men put Lockwood's brand on seven of their horses, which were left at the ranch in payment. Lockwood's side of the story is interesting. He did not return to the ranch for a long time, being wounded at the battle of the Big Hole and taken from there to the hospital in Deer Lodge. From there he wrote:

Following the Lolo Trail

"I learn that the *Missoulian* has stated hereto-fore that the Nez Percés, in compensation for my loss of property at their hands, turned into my fields a large number of ponies, upon which they placed my brand. The foundation for this exists in the fact that out of sheer deviltry the red rascals turned into a growing wheat field of mine, and branded with my brand a couple of worn-out worthless cayuses, sore backed, spavined and scarcely able to walk. And while thanking you I deny the white deviltry that inspired the *Missoulian's* mention."[7]

Was Lockwood striking back at the band that had wounded him, or was he being "ribbed" by his friends in the Bitterroot, or was the *New Northwest* possibly egging him on to give them a good opening at their enemy, the *Missoulian?* Certainly he could not have seen the horses he described so vividly. The story as published by the *Missoulian* was obtained from settlers in the valley at the time and agreed substantially with that told by the Indians after the war.

Army officers and easy-chair critics have criticized the storekeepers of Stevensville for selling goods to the Indians and the settlers for trading horses with them. When one stops to consider that these same Indians could easily have taken all the goods and horses in question, without payment, such criticism loses its force. After all, who would go out of his way to pick a scrap with such fighters when they were behaving at least as well as regular troops?

At this time, the Nez Percés received an unexpected and substantial reinforcement. Poker Joe or Lean Elk, chief over six lodges, was spending the summer in the valley instead of returning to Lapwai as Looking Glass had done. An intelligent half-blood, well known for his race horses and his wily schemes, he and his fresh men with their fresh horses greatly strengthened the fugitives.

[7] Lockwood to editor, September 10, 1877, *New Northwest*, September 14, 1877.

After they left Stevensville, the Indians moved steadily up the Bitterroot Valley, traveling about fifteen miles a day. They climbed the Continental Divide and dropped down to the Big Hole River, where they planned to camp a few days to rest their mounts, cut tipi poles, and prepare for the long trail to the Crow country. What few whites they saw from time to time they allowed to pass unmolested, for the Indians believed that they had no enemy but Howard, still miles to the rear. This failure to consider all whites as potential enemies, and the resulting lack of vigilance, led them to the brink of disaster.

Up the Bitterroot Valley, well ahead of Howard, came a new foe. At the news of the approach of the hostiles, Colonel John Gibbon, stationed at Fort Shaw on the Sun River, assembled all the men available at his post, as well as those available at Fort Benton on the upper Missouri and Fort Ellis on the Gallatin near Bozeman. His own forces he led across Cadotte's Pass and down the valley of the Big Blackfoot. At Missoula, his effectives totaled 163 men, including Captain Rawn and his detachment. To these were added 35 volunteers. Along the trail of the Indians, they hurried by forced marches, gaining steadily on the unsuspecting red men. By using farm wagons, hired in the valley, to transport his men, Gibbon was able to cover thirty-five miles a day without exhausting his forces.

29: All Whites Are Enemies

G RAY dawn in the valley of the Big Hole found the red men slumbering peacefully in their lodges, scattered in a long line on the south bank of the stream. Clumps of willows bordered the water course, while beyond the camp grew a few scattered pines. A few thin streamers of smoke rose from the banked fires in the chill morning air. A lone rider, starting out to tend the horse herd, stopped in surprise at the long line of soldiers advancing on the sleeping camp. The shot that stretched him lifeless on the wet grass was the signal for a hail of death, spouting from 150 rifles, that pierced the sheltering tipis. Then, with a wild whoop, Colonel Gibbon and his men charged across the stream and into the camp, shooting everything that moved.

Startled warriors leaped from their blankets and dashed for the willow thickets or the small depressions, some even without their guns. Dazed older people and small, frightened children, slower to realize the danger, were shot down as they stood or were killed in their blankets. Blazing rifles at close range burned the clothes and flesh of the screaming victims who could neither run nor fight. Babies had their skulls crushed by rifle butt or soldier's boot.[1]

[1] C. E. S. Wood, "Chief Joseph, the Nez Percé," *Century Magazine*, Vol. XXVIII, No. 1 (May, 1884), 139.

With victory seemingly won, the soldiers turned to plundering and burning the lodges, but the coverings were drenched with dew and would not ignite. The eastern half of the camp had escaped the initial attack, for the leader of the left wing of the troops, Lieutenant James H. Bradley, was killed almost at once, and his men drifted to the right to join the main body instead of holding to their goal. A few of the Indians here had awakened early, perhaps sensing the approach of the enemy. This group, spared from the first attack, now formed a skirmish line and advanced against the exultant soldiers. As their movement grew in strength, they were supported by scattered fire from many of the warriors who had fled but were now returning.[2] Soon the deadly fire of the red marksmen had forced the soldiers out of the camp, across the creek to the north, and up the slope to the first spur of timber, where Gibbon took up a strong defensive position on a wide knoll.

Through the hot August day, the troops huddled behind their slight natural defenses or crouched in hastily dug rifle pits, bravely beating off all attacks. They were entirely surrounded by the Indian snipers under the leadership of the aged White Bird, who fought courageously that day. Meanwhile, under the leadership of Joseph, the women and old men struck the camp, packed their horses, and moved off down the valley.

That afternoon, a small detachment of soldiers approached the battlefield with a howitzer. Six of the warriors attacked them, killing one and driving off the rest. They also took a pack horse loaded with 3,500 rounds of ammunition. The howitzer was of no value to them, however, because they did not know how to use it, so they removed the wheels and damaged the firing mechanism and left it by the trail.

Later that afternoon, the Indians tried to burn out their

[2] McWhorter, *Hear Me, My Chiefs!* 380.

foes by firing the dry grass, but the wind shifted before the flames quite reached the soldiers. Gibbon planned to have his men dash through the smoke and fire, rather than waiting to be burned, but this action was not necessary.

Evening found Gibbon in serious straits. He had lost twenty-nine men killed. Forty more, including himself, were wounded. He was hemmed in by a force of determined warriors under competent leaders and was short of food, water, and ammunition. Only the timely arrival of General Howard with the cavalry caused the Nez Percés to break off the fighting. In this battle, with the advantage of a well-planned surprise attack and superior forces, Colonel Gibbon had failed to defeat these western warriors.

General Howard and Colonel Gibbon agreed that the Indians had lost eighty-nine in the fighting at the Big Hole, but their report makes no effort to classify the dead. Years later, Yellow Wolf gave the names of twelve of the fighting men. He said: "Only twelve of the fighting men were lost in that battle. But our best were left there."[3] Among them were Rainbow and Five Wounds, the experienced war leaders, and Red Moccasin Tops and Wal-lait-its, the two young men who had made the first Salmon River raid. The loss of these four, and several more of nearly equal caliber, was severely felt in the days to come. The rest of the casualty list was made up of noncombatants—the old, the sick, the crippled, the women and children.

The Nez Percés were shocked at this slaughter of noncombatants. They had carried on their war, except for the second Salmon River raid, according to the army code of Civil War days. Worse than this to them was the fact that General Howard gave permission to his Bannock scouts to dig up and mutilate the Nez Percé dead. Howard does record, for his own credit, that the sight of the mutilated bodies lying

[3] McWhorter, *Yellow Wolf*, 159.

around disturbed him, so he later ordered them reburied by his men.[4]

Howard's conduct here earned him the contempt and hatred of his enemies such as was not felt against any of their other foes. They had expected nothing different from the Bannocks. At the same time, the Nez Percé attitude toward all whites underwent a marked change. No longer did they look on Howard and his men as their only enemies. From now on, all whites must be considered unfriendly. No longer did they spare everyone not a soldier. Suspicious characters who could be scouts or messengers might be shot down without warning. Horses and cattle were taken from ranches along the way. Stage stations, camping parties, and prospectors all suffered. But even now the Nez Percés did not harm captured women, nor did they scalp the dead, and most of the hostile acts against civilians were committed by young men who were temporarily freed from the restraints of their chiefs. This unusual humanitarian attitude on the part of hostile Indians attracted a good deal of attention throughout the country, and this explanation was later printed in a western newspaper:

"As to their religious belief, he [Joseph] said that all of the good Indians of their tribe held to communion with the spirits of their deceased friends. That these spirits frequently came to them in the still hours of the night and conversed with them, and gave them directions what to do and how to live. That this change in their mode of warfare, whereby they had shown such kind and humane treatment to the prisoners, had been in accordance with the directions of their spirit friends. That these spirits told them to always do what was right toward everyone; that they must stand up for what was right, and if they should be killed while doing so it would be all right with them. As the Indians expressed it 'It would make no difference.' "[5]

[4] Howard, *Nez Percé Joseph*, 210.

From the Big Hole battlefield, the band followed the Continental Divide to the south, keeping in the rough country to hinder their pursuers. At times, it was thought that they were heading west toward their homes by way of the old Nez Percé Trail, but each time they swung back to the southeast. This casting back and forth seems to have been the result of indecision rather than the working out of a definite plan. Finally, they crossed the Divide into the valley of the upper Snake and turned eastward, definitely headed for the Yellowstone Park region, where the first of the national parks had been established five years earlier.

General Howard then detached a portion of his cavalry and sent it under the command of Lieutenant George Bacon to cut across the arc of the Divide on the Montana side, up Centennial Valley, past Red Rock and Henry lakes to Targhee Pass. By this shorter route, Bacon should reach the pass ahead of the Indians and was to entrench himself there, holding the hostiles at bay until the main force under Howard could arrive. Howard planned to follow the broad trail marked by the thousands of hoofs, keeping within a day's march of the fugitives, and thus prevent their turning back.

Howard's dogged pursuit wore on the nerves of the entire band. Something had to be done to annoy him, to retard his march. To a horseman, the severest blow, short of losing his life, is to lose his horse. If Howard could be set afoot with no cavalry and no pack train, he would be quite helpless for a time. Accordingly, the chiefs planned a night raid on the army horse herd.

Since this is the one occasion in the entire war in which the council planned an attack which was later carried out, a detailed study of the operation should give some insight concerning Indian strategy and methods.[6]

[5] *Bismarck Tri-Weekly Tribune,* November 21, 1877.
[6] McWhorter, *Hear Me, My Chiefs!* 417–21.

At this time, Lean Elk was in charge of the camp and the marching. Looking Glass had lost his position of leadership and much of his prestige in the surprise attack at the Big Hole. Lean Elk kept his camp about a day's march ahead of Howard, so at Camas Creek the troops slept on the campgrounds used by the Nez Percés the day before. This gave some weight to a dream by Black Hair in which he saw the Nez Percé warriors return to their old camp and bring away Howard's horses.

A council of the chiefs and fighting men decided to make a night attack and a raid on Howard's horses. The attacking group was composed of twenty-eight volunteers led by Ollikut, Two Moons, Wottolen, and Peopeo Tholekt. Chief Joseph had no important part in planning the raid and did not participate in it. This underlines Joseph's later statement that Ollikut was the leader of the young men of the Wallowa band.

The Indians approached the sleeping camp in three small groups. Some of them dismounted and crept ahead to cut loose the closely picketed cavalry horses. Before their work was completed, one of the men, Otskai, who often did "crazy things," shot off his rifle and alarmed the soldiers. For this grievous breach of orders, he was not punished, only laughed at, a result indicative of the absence of military discipline of any kind among the Nez Percés.

At the sound of Otskai's shot, the Nez Percés charged the camp, shooting and yelling. They stampeded all the pack animals, but luckily Howard had ordered all the cavalry mounts closely picketed that night and the Indians did not have time to cut them loose.

After several hectic minutes, the soldiers were mounted and in hot pursuit of the raiders, still visible four or five miles away. The fresh cavalry mounts rapidly cut down the distance between the two groups. At length, the Indians formed a skirmish line to protect their booty and awaited the attack. When the soldiers in turn formed a skirmish line, they were neatly flanked by a few of the Nez Percés. After some fighting, the troops retreated with ten of the mules. They lost one man killed and eight wounded.

Capture of the pack string was less than the Indians had expected from their night's work, but it effectively stopped Howard for a time. While the Indians pushed on to Henry Lake and across Targhee Pass to the Madison Basin unhindered, Howard went into camp at the lake, days behind them, wondering what had happened to Lieutenant Bacon's command, which was to cut off the Indian retreat.

Lieutenant Bacon had waited two or three days at the pass with no sign of the Indians. He finally concluded that they must have swung off in some other direction, so he took the back trail to find Howard and was now approaching along the old trail many miles to the rear. Thus there was no hindrance to the Nez Percé march at Targhee Pass. Again one of Howard's plans had miscarried, through no fault of his own, although he might have suffered severe censure had Lieutenant Bacon and his small force been compelled to face the full fury of the Nez Percés.

At Henry Lake, the doctor insisted that the troops be given a rest, for they were almost exhausted. Meanwhile, General Howard drove in a "stout wagon [that] was not made for comfortable riding" down the Madison River and across the ridge to Virginia City, some seventy miles away, to obtain supplies and send some telegrams. This gave the Nez Percés the extra days they needed to get through the rough, strange terrain between West Yellowstone and Stinking Water Valley.

In Yellowstone Park, the Indians captured the George Cowan party from Helena. All the supplies and camp equipment were taken and their fine light wagon was broken to pieces.[7] The varnished spokes from the wheels went for whip

[7] J. W. Redington, "Scouting in Montana in the 1870's," *Frontier*, Vol. XIII, No. 1 (November, 1932), 58.

handles. The chiefs were anxious to turn the captives loose before they could come to harm, but a party of young men rode after Cowan and one of them shot him down.

Lean Elk learned of the departure of the young men and hurried after them, fearing they might commit just such a deed. He arrived in time to prevent any mutilation and Cowan was left for dead by the trail. In some way, he managed to live until he reached Howard's forces, and in time he recovered from his wounds. The rest of the Cowan party went unharmed, although it took some planning on the part of the chiefs to insure the safe escape of the women.[8]

The Nez Percés captured a prospector, John Shively, who served as a guide to the band on the promise that he would be released unharmed later. He was treated well and has left some interesting details of the camp life and mode of travel of the band:

"They had bread, no meat, scouse, camas and tea of shrubs. They were going to the Crow country but did not know the route.... Every lodge drives its own horses in front of it when traveling, each lodge keeping its own bands separate.... About one-sixth of the horses have sore backs or are disabled. . . . They keep no scouts ahead."[9]

Shively said he could notice no particular chief in command. All matters were decided in council by several chiefs. Joseph was very pleasant to him, always meeting him with a nod and a smile. Shively made his escape shortly, none the worse for his experience.

[8] *New Northwest*, February 7, 1879.
[9] *New Northwest*, September 14, 1877.

30: Hide-and-Seek in the Mountains

WHILE the main body of the Nez Percés was struggling through the rough country east of Yellowstone Park, Chief Looking Glass rode on ahead to confer with the Crow leaders. He wanted to enlist their help, or at least secure permission to live in their country for a time. This placed the Crows in a rather difficult position since they were allied to both parties in the quarrel. The Mountain Crows favored neutrality, not daring to antagonize the whites and not willing to fight their friends. One of their leaders, Le Forge, the "White Crow," promised his aid in keeping the Crows from joining the whites in the war.[1] If the soldiers demanded scouts, the Crows would have to furnish them, but they would not fight.

Shortly after this, a call did come for Crow scouts. Many of the Mountain Crows, including Le Forge, had important business elsewhere, and the warriors who did serve were careful to avoid actual combat. Since the officers did not know of the Crow–Nez Percé friendship, these scouts acquired an undeserved reputation for cowardice. They were good scouts, however, and had no compunctions about picking up any stray Nez Percé horses they could find.

When Looking Glass returned with his discouraging re-

[1] Thomas B. Marquis, *Memoirs of a White Crow Indian*, 128–29.

port, the Nez Percés realized that their only possible refuge was to the north. In their path was a very mountainous country new to them, for they had always kept to the north of the Yellowstone River. Through these mountains, they kept many scouts ahead, picking the best trail over the high ridges. The wide-ranging scouts killed many prospectors as they moved east, bringing fresh accusations of atrocious conduct from the whites. Since most of the men killed were acting as scouts and messengers for the armies to the front and rear of the Nez Percés, they were fair game. By cutting off these men and preventing communication between Howard and the fresh troops to the east under Colonel Samuel Sturgis, the Indians thwarted Howard's plans again.

Colonel Sturgis had come up from the Tongue River cantonments to meet the Indians as they emerged from the mountains. Since all the whites familiar with that region agreed that no one could cross the mountains from south to north with horses, the Indians were expected to come out along either the Clark's Fork of the Yellowstone (not to be confused with the much larger Clark's Fork of the Columbia in western Montana) or the Stinking Water, now the Shoshone, in northern Wyoming.

Sturgis, in his camp near Hart Mountain, was right across the path of the Nez Percés if they were heading for Canada, but he was too far north to prevent their going east along the Stinking Water. With the hostiles estimated at 400 warriors, triple their actual number, Sturgis did not dare split his command and place half on each route, since neither detachment would be strong enough to withstand the enemy. He had to keep his troops intact and guard the most probable route.

His problem was simplified by orders from Howard, who sent word that the Nez Percés would probably cross the Stinking Water about 100 miles southeast of the Crow Agency.[2]

[2] *Report of the Secretary of War, 1877,* 510.

Hide-and-Seek in the Mountains

Colonel Nelson A. Miles, then at Fort Keogh, had sent Sturgis an order to please move farther south.[3] The prospectors and scouts all assured Sturgis that the Indians could not reach the Clark's Fork without coming across the high country to the south because there was no break in the south wall of the valley passable to horses.[4] If he moved camp a few miles, he would be in position to cut off the hostiles from either route. They assured him that the distance was short and that his wagons could make the trip.

Since all these people were in agreement, Sturgis acted on their advice and moved ahead to find the country a tangled mass of ridges and ravines, scarcely passable for his cavalry. His patrols, working to the west of the main column in the direction from which the Indians must come, had picked up traces of them the day before. A party of three prospectors, scouting for Sturgis, had been surprised in camp and two of them killed outright. The third, left for dead, survived long enough to tell the story of the attack and was certain that the Indians were Nez Percés. The same day, a second patrol discovered a large herd of Indian horses a few miles north of the prospector's camp under the care of boys who apparently expected no danger. Convinced now that he could trap the hostiles before they could reach the open country, Sturgis moved with all his forces toward the Indians.

From a study of the orders to him and the reports of his scouts, it is clear that Sturgis had not been tricked by the Nez Percés into leaving his camp at Hart Mountain. It is doubtful that the boys with the horse herd were decoys to lead the troops into rough country. The same purpose could have been accomplished more surely and with less risk by a party of warriors. Sturgis had acted as best he could according to his orders and his information.

[3] *Ibid.*, 510.
[4] *Ibid.*, 510.

Meanwhile, the Nez Percé scouts had discovered a trail to the north where no trail had ever been known to the whites. When they saw Sturgis leave his camp to move south, they recognized their opportunity and took advantage of it. First they wanted to leave a tangled trail to prevent Sturgis from following too rapidly. This was a difficult feat with such a large number of horses, but they accomplished it in the following manner. They started southwest, holding the direction steadily across an open basin for some distance, then milling their horses over a large area. From the maze of tracks, they headed sharply to the north and gained a steep ridge, timbered heavily on the slope but with a grassy crest. Instead of following the easy trail offered by the crest, they kept well down in the timber for several miles.[5] This finally brought them to the break in the mountain wall, a steep, narrow, heavily timbered chasm with no visible outlet. Down this they slid to the canyon floor far below, with the towering cliffs on either side scarcely twenty feet apart. After three or four miles, the gorge opened abruptly into the valley of the Clark's Fork, not far from Sturgis' former camping place. Down the broad valley to the north the Indians hurried, heading for the Yellowstone crossing and the plains beyond.

Sturgis picked up the Indian trail after a time and followed it, astonished to find it marked with wagon tracks. Down in the fearful gorge, he found the body of a cavalry horse, convincing him that Howard was on the trail ahead. Another hour of marching brought him to the canyon mouth, and to his great astonishment he found himself at his old camp, with Howard's men resting nearby.

While the leg-weary soldiers of both camps snatched a little rest, the commanding officers held a council of war. Howard's disappointment sharpened his criticisms of his junior

[5] "Journal of S. A. Fisher, Chief of Scouts," *Montana Historical Society Contributions*, Vol. II (1896), 277.

officer and filled Sturgis with a burning desire to redeem himself by overtaking the fugitives before they could reach the Missouri. Dawn found his command, reinforced by the pick of Howard's men, plodding along the trail in a cold drizzle. Near midnight, after a forced march of sixty miles, they camped near the Yellowstone crossing. The next morning they forded the river and rested a few minutes while the warm sunshine thawed out their tired limbs, but sprang to their saddles again when a scout brought word that the Indians were just a few miles down the river.[6]

The Nez Percés had pushed forward steadily, crossing the Yellowstone at the old ford near Laurel and following down the north bank. Here they captured a stage coach after the passengers had made a hasty dive into a willow thicket. From this coach they derived a great deal of amusement, riding in it by turns with the horses at a full gallop. A short distance down the river, they swung to the northwest up the bed of Canyon Creek, still driving the coach. The creek had carved a passage through the rimrock from the prairie above, furnishing an easy trail up from the river bottom.

Their brief period of fun was rudely disturbed by a skirmish line of soldiers and scouts charging madly toward them across the open country to the west, trying to cut them off from the canyon mouth a short distance ahead. A band of River Crows, less friendly than their mountain brethren, joined in the charge, but they did not head for the canyon with the troops:

"At the sight of twenty-five hundred head of hostile horses, the Crows went wild, charged one corner of the rear of the herd and cut out three hundred horses, which they stampeded over the hill and rushed back to their reservation. Horses were all they were after, so they did not stop to help the whites in the impending battle."[7]

[6] Brady, *Northwestern Fights and Fighters*, 214–16.
[7] Redington, "Scouting in Montana in the 1870's," *Frontier*, Vol. XIII, No. 1 (November, 1932), 59.

Meanwhile, some of the Nez Perce advance guard had reached the shelter of the rocks on each side of the canyon mouth and beat off the charge with a brisk rifle fire, while the rest of the warriors deployed between the advancing troops and the line of march, holding the whites at bay while the women and children drove the horse herd and the pack train to safety.

As the Indians continued their retreat up the canyon, a running fight followed for several miles, with little loss on either side. One of Howard's scouts, in the thick of the battle and on the field later, said that he saw no dead Indians, although he did notice the bodies of four soldiers. This would indicate few casualties for the red men, in spite of Sturgis' claims, since the burial squads would have taken care of the soldiers first.

Howard had little confidence that Sturgis would catch the Indians after his failure at Hart Mountain. He had already sent a call to Fort Keogh for fresh men under Colonel Nelson A. Miles to take up the chase. Miles was rated as a more energetic officer than Sturgis and had a body of seasoned troops at hand. The distance from his post to the mouth of the Musselshell on the Missouri was less than from Canyon Creek to the Missouri. If Miles marched quickly, he might reach the river ahead of the weary Indians, particularly if the pursuing force under Howard should slow down. Howard had discovered early in the campaign that the Indians slackened their pace as soon as they had a safe lead. Now he planned to keep two days march to the rear of the Nez Percés, his scouts in constant contact with their movements.

The plan worked quite well. The Nez Percés slowed their march across the Judith Basin and on down to the Missouri, nursing their wounded and conserving their horses. Large numbers of worn-out mounts had to be abandoned for Howard's scouts to catch later, all of them quite lame. This was accomplished by making a cut on one foot of the animal before turning it loose, thus rendering it of no value to the pursuers for some time.[8]

Here in the Judith Basin, the scouts found what price the River Crows had paid for the 300 horses captured by them at Canyon Creek. One of their lesser chiefs, Dumb Bull, and his band had been wiped out by the Nez Percés as the Crows were hunting for their winter meat.[9]

Since crossing the Yellowstone, the Nez Percés were again in familiar country. No need now for days of anxious scouting to find the trail. They headed for the Cow Island Crossing on the Missouri, well below Fort Benton and the head of navigation during the low water of late summer. The crossing here would offer no difficulties to the Indians.

Cow Island was a rather important point during late summer and early fall. Here the goods for Fort Benton, Helena, and other up river points were unloaded, to be transported the remainder of the distance in Mackinaw boats. Here also were unloaded the year's supplies for the Canadian Northwest Mounted Police, which were hauled the rest of the way by bull train, the road leading up Cow Creek ravine to the plains above.[10]

The steamer *Benton* had just finished unloading and had gone out of sight downstream before the Nez Percés arrived. The tons of stores, piled high along the riverbanks, were guarded by a sergeant and twelve men, who had erected a small earthwork against just such an emergency. Four civilians, probably clerks of the various trading companies, were also present. The entire group prudently retired behind their barricade, where they were subjected to a perfunctory attack by a portion of the braves while the band plundered the stores.[11]

---

[8] *Ibid.*, 67.   [9] *Ibid.*, 62.   [10] *Ibid.*, 63.

[11] Henry Romeyn, "Capture of Chief Joseph and the Nez Percé Indians," *Montana Historical Society Contributions*, Vol. II (1896), 285.

To the Indians it must have been great fun opening boxes and choosing what they wanted after months of privations. Michael Foley, who worked for Colonel Clendennin, sent a dispatch to his boss at Fort Benton:

> Rifle Pit, at Cow Island
> September 23, 1877, 10 A.M.
>
> Colonel:
> Chief Joseph is here, and says he will surrender for two hundred bags of sugar. I told him to surrender without the sugar. He took the sugar and will not surrender. What will I do?
>
> MICHAEL FOLEY.[12]

After the Nez Percés had secured what goods they wanted, they proceeded up Cow Creek, leaving the remainder of the stores almost unharmed. Soon a party of thirty-six volunteers and a few soldiers arrived from Fort Benton under the command of Major Guido Ilges and Lieutenant E. E. Hardin. They followed the retreating band a short distance and engaged them in a brief skirmish, but displayed good judgment in turning back before the affair became serious. During these activities, a few Indians slipped back and fired the stores.

Three men then took a Mackinaw boat and started down the river, hoping to overtake the *Benton,* which would have to go very slowly in the shoal water. If they failed in this, they might meet the *Silver City,* then at Grand Island, or the *Big Horn,* which was coming up the river a few days behind the *Benton.*[13]

Colonel Miles had wasted no time at Fort Keogh after he

---

[12] *New Northwest,* October 12, 1877.
[13] *New Northwest,* October 5, 1877.

received word from General Howard. Something of a "glory chaser" like Custer, he welcomed the chance for active service. The messenger arrived at sundown. That night Miles had his men ferried across the Yellowstone and early the next morning was off in pursuit of the Indians and a general's star. If he, singlehanded (not counting his soldiers), should succeed where Howard, Gibbon, and Sturgis had failed, he might expect quick promotion, with his wife's two influential uncles, Senator John Sherman and General William T. Sherman, to aid him. In this instance, Miles was aided by fortune, partly because he was able to organize his men and march at once.

He reached the mouth of the Musselshell just in time to hail the *Benton* as it swept down the river. When the captain reported that he had seen no sign of the Nez Percés, Miles felt sure that they had not reached the river yet and that he could move up the south bank in time to intercept them. The steamer went on down the river a couple of miles to take on a load of fuel at the next woodyard. Soon it was again on its way while the troops watched it from the bluff. At this moment, the three men arrived from Cow Island in the Mackinaw boat, bringing news of the Indian attack and departure.

Miles might be forgiven a moment of exasperation as he stood there, his prey almost within his grasp, his path blocked by the rolling waters of the dangerous Missouri. Already that day, the troops had watched helplessly as one of the scouts and his horse were sucked under, the man unable to swim clear of the exhausted animal because of the ammunition in his belt. Without boats of some kind to assist in ferrying the troops across the river, Miles knew that the Indians could reach Canada and safety before they could be headed. And there, still in sight but well out of reach, was the steamer. A signal to her and she would turn back to serve as a ferry, saving days of delay, but how could he signal? No horseman, hindered by ravines, gulleys, cut banks, and thickets, could hope to overtake the boat now booming along in the full sweep of the current.

One of the lieutenants, probably J. W. Biddle, had an inspiration. If shells from the twelve-pound fieldpiece could be fired to explode against the bluff near the steamer, the captain would know that something was wrong and would return to investigate. Miles was quick to see the value of the suggestion (and to take the credit for it later) and ordered the gun to be fired. Soon the shells were bursting far downstream where the smoke of the steamer still showed above the cottonwoods. After two or three shots, the steamer turned back, and in a few hours had placed the entire command on the north bank of the river, a most efficient ferry service in the wilds of the buffalo country. By such a close margin was Miles successful, as though the very fates were loading the dice against the red warriors.

31: "From Where the Sun Now Stands"

RISING from the grassy plains north of the Missouri is a small isolated mountain mass known to all the tribes of the region as the Bear Paws. Their southern slopes drop away to the badlands, the "breaks" of the Missouri, but to the north the open range stretches from their flanking ridges to far beyond the Canadian border, scarcely broken by the shallow trough dug by the Milk River. Here, in the former days, ranged hundreds of deer and antelope, thousands of buffalo. Several clear mountain streams, rising in the timbered heights, flow northward to mingle with the alkaline waters of the Milk.

On one of these streams, the Nez Percés camped while they secured a supply of meat and buffalo robes for the winter. With Howard and his men far to the rear, they chose the camping place for comfort rather than for defense, pitching their lodges in a small hollow near the creek, the gently sloping ground offering easy approach to horsemen on all sides except the south, where the hill was more abrupt. Located thus, some twenty or thirty feet below the surface of the surrounding prairie, the camp was sheltered somewhat from the keen northern winds with their promise of early snow. The creek supplied mountain water so valued by the Indians, and the scrub growth along its banks furnished fuel for the cooking fires.

From day to day, the piles of buffalo robes and meat grew steadily as the hunters levied toll on the shaggy herds. Unstinted meals of fresh meat, supplemented by luxuries from the Cow Island stores, and many days of rest proved godsends to the wanderers, particularly to the wounded and the small children. The horses gained weight and strength on the nutritious buffalo grass, their tender hoofs growing tough once more. Everyone welcomed a chance to relax after months of steady flight. Lulled into a sense of false security, they again neglected to scout the neighboring country, and just as at the Big Hole a fresh army crept close for a surprise attack.

All day that twenty-ninth of September, 1877, a cold autumn storm had driven in from the northwest, the wet snow covering the higher ground but melting to a drizzling rain at the lower levels.[1] By morning the rain had stopped, but the chill wind still whistled through the dead grass on the knolls, swirled around the lodges in the little hollow by the creek, and drove the gray cloud masses across the sky. Gone were the pleasant days of rest. Now the fugitive band must pack and move across the border to safety. The camp was astir early, filled with the bustle of preparation. While some of the Indians adjusted and lashed the loads, others were busy in the herd, catching the animals to be used that day. Among these were Joseph and his twelve-year-old daughter.[2]

About 100 horses stood ready under their packs, when off to the south appeared a line of horsemen, galloping furiously for the camp. Noncombatants took charge of the packed animals, starting at once along the trail to the north, while 50 or 60 braves guarded them.[3] The rest of the men, led by White

[1] Romeyn, "Capture of Chief Joseph and the Nez Percé Indians," *Montana Historical Society Contributions*, Vol. II (1896), 286.

[2] C. E. S. Wood, "Chief Joseph, the Nez-Percé," *Century Magazine*, Vol. XXVIII, No. 1 (May, 1884), 141.

[3] Romeyn, "Capture of Chief Joseph and the Nez Percé Indians," *Montana Historical Society Contributions*, Vol. II (1896), 287.

Cut Bank at Bearpaw Battleground (Courtesy Montana Historical Society)

Site of the Battle of the Bears Paw on Snake Creek. (Courtesy Montana Historical Society)

Bird, grabbed their rifles and crouched just below the brow of the hill south of the tipis to await the shock of the charge.

Miles was intent on winning a dashing, spectacular victory with his first charge. Forming his line with the Second Cavalry on the right, the Seventh on the left, and the mounted Fifth Infantry, delayed in crossing a ravine when the pack train blocked the narrow trail, filling in the center a little behind the rest, he charged the camp across four miles of prairie, probably in his excitement underestimating the distance. With nearly 600 men—cavalry, infantry, scouts, and Cheyennes— he expected to crumple the Nez Percé lines like so much paper, his mounted forces driving in from three sides and cutting off all escape.

To oppose this formidable force, White Bird could muster about 120 men. Joseph was still with the horse herd, unaware of the danger. As the charging forces neared the crest of the hill, a deadly fire from the blazing Winchesters emptied many a saddle, stretching most of the officers dead or wounded on the field and effectually halting the advance. Whoever raised his voice in command became at once the target of a score of rifles. With a line of blue-clad dead to mark the limit of the advance, the surviving soldiers hastily sought shelter, but they did not waver or fall back. The rash charge across the open prairie against a hidden foe had accomplished nothing and had accounted for most of the losses in the attacking force during the entire five-day battle.

The Second Cavalry on the right wing suffered less than the others. They were out too far to strike the waiting line, and swept by the camp to fall on the horse herd, capturing most of the animals at once. Just as they had come in sight over the hill by the camp, Joseph realized his danger.

"My little daughter, twelve years of age, was with me. I gave her a rope, and told her to catch a horse and join the others who were cut off from the camp. . . .

313

"I thought of my wife and children who were now surrounded by soldiers, and I resolved to go to them or die. With a prayer in my mouth for the Great Spirit Chief who rules above, I dashed unarmed through the line of soldiers. It seemed to me that there were guns on every side, before and behind me. My clothes were cut to pieces and my horse was wounded, but I was not hurt. As I reached the door of my lodge, my wife handed me my rifle saying: 'Here's your gun. Fight.' "[4]

After the Second Cavalry had chased the pack train with its guard about five miles, the warriors turned and fought them off. The troops then returned with the captured horses and helped complete the lines of investment. Some of the warriors from the escaping group followed them back and managed to slip through their lines to the camp.[5] Joseph was rather bitter in his censure of the others, calling them deserters.[6]

About three o'clock that afternoon, Miles sent three companies of soldiers to cut the Indians off from the creek so that they would have to surrender for lack of water. They were beaten back after some hot fighting among the lodges, leaving several wounded behind. The Nez Percés did not harm them further, but carried them water from time to time.[7] A few survived the battle. Miles now decided it would be necessary to besiege the camp, since direct assault had proved so costly. Both sides then dug in, constructing elaborate rifle pits and sniping at each other.

Shortly after daybreak the next morning, the threatening storm swept down from the north, a wall of dirty gray blotting

[4] Chief Joseph, "An Indian's View of Indian Affairs," *North American Review*, Vol. CCLXIX (April, 1879), 428.

[5] Romeyn, "Capture of Chief Joseph and the Nez Percé Indians," *Montana Historical Society Contributions*, Vol. II (1896), 287.

[6] *Bismarck Tri-Weekly Tribune*, November 21, 1877.

[7] Romeyn, "Capture of Chief Joseph and the Nez Percé Indians," *Montana Historical Society Contributions*, Vol. II (1896), 287.

out the landscape with a curtain of driving snow.[8] The troops shivered miserably in their canvas tents, envying the Nez Percés their warm lodges designed for just such conditions and pitched in a more sheltered spot. During two days of storm, the fighting was confined to occasional potshooting. Even the guards were less vigilant. The warriors might have broken through the cordon of soldiers and escaped if they had been willing to abandon their families and the wounded. Joseph said later: "We were unwilling to do this. We had never heard of a wounded Indian recovering while in the hands of white men."[9] He remembered how Howard's scouts had scalped and killed every one of the aged and wounded who had been abandoned along the trail when it became impossible to carry them any farther.

As the siege dragged on, Miles became more and more nervous. Any day might bring Sitting Bull and his reputed 2,000 warriors sweeping down from his refuge just across the Canadian border to turn the tide of battle. One afternoon in particular, the general anxiously watched an approaching mass that, through the falling snow, resembled a large body of mounted Indians. Much to his relief, it proved to be a herd of buffalo running before the storm, the patches of snow that clung to their shaggy coats resembling Indian trappings.[10]

Miles feared reinforcements for his own troops almost as much as he feared allies for the Nez Percés. Any hour might bring Sturgis, his equal in rank and as anxious for promotion. Even worse, Howard might arrive and take command of all the troops because of his superior rank and thus get the lion's share of the credit for the capture. To forestall such a calamity, Miles began negotiating with Joseph, whom he regarded

---

[8] *Ibid.*, 287.

[9] Chief Joseph, "An Indian's View of Indian Affairs," *North American Review*, Vol. CCLXIX (April, 1879), 429.

[10] General Nelson Appleton Miles, *Personal Recollections*, 274.

as head chief of the hostiles. He pointed out the advantages of surrendering without further fighting, but Joseph remained dubious. Finally, Miles enticed Joseph into his camp under a flag of truce and then took him prisoner, hoping in this way to force the Nez Percés to capitulate. Is it not interesting that all the recorded violations of the flag of truce in this war between savage and civilized were committed by the latter?

One of Joseph's followers soon came to find out what was wrong. He was allowed to see his chief for a moment, but Miles would not allow them any private conversation. Meanwhile, the Nez Percés checkmated the hostage scheme by securing a captive of their own. Again violating the flag of truce, Lieutenant Lovell Jerome was attempting to spy on conditions in the Indian camp. They decided to detain him until their own chief was returned unharmed. The exchange of the two men brought a renewal of active fighting.[11]

Joseph refused to surrender because of the harsh terms asked of him. He offered to make peace if Miles would allow the Nez Percés to march unhindered toward Canada or Idaho. Of course, Miles had no authority to grant such a request. According to army precedents in dealing with Indians, he held out for unconditional surrender. When it seemed that a stalemate had been reached, two factors gave Miles a decided advantage in the conflict.

By the night of October 1, the twelve-pounder had been brought up. At first it proved ineffective because it could not be depressed enough to bear on the hostiles in the hollow. The artillerymen got around this difficulty by digging a deep hole for the tailpiece, elevating the muzzle to a high angle, and using the cannon as a mortar, much like the trench mortars in more recent wars. A very light charge of powder would then

[11] Chief Joseph, "An Indian's View of Indian Affairs," *North American Review*, Vol. CCLXIX (April, 1879), 428.

drop a bombshell almost vertically into the camp in the hollow, making the rifle pits hazardous locations. The shells were greatly feared by the Indians.[12]

Howard's arrival helped show the Nez Percés the futility of further resistance. Soon hundreds of new soldiers could be brought up to join the besieging forces, and more fighting would bring annihilation. With Howard were some of the treaty Nez Percés, George and Captain John in particular, and a white man who knew the Nez Percé language. The presence of these men greatly facilitated the conversations, and with two to check each speech there was little danger of accidental or deliberate mistranslation. Also, Howard had more authority than Miles in the matter of granting concessions. He promised the Indians that they would be returned to Lapwai in the spring if they would lay down their arms at once. They could not hope to make the trip that fall with their horses worn out and so many wounded to care for. Already the crest of the Bitterroots was piled high with snow.

Howard reached the battleground on October 4. The following morning, Captain John was very busy carrying messages from one camp to the other. While the officers were discussing matters in the general's tent, Joseph and the few remaining Nez Percé chiefs were conducting their last war council, Joseph trying to convince the rest that surrender was the only possible course. In the presence of Captain John, he made his final speech to his comrades, a speech which was also intended as an answer to General Howard.

By this time, the storm had abated and the clouds were breaking away. The little group of officers stood in the cheery sunshine as they awaited the return of their messenger. Shortly after two o'clock he rode slowly up the hill and dismounted near them.

"Then old Captain John brought this reply (and his lips

12 Miles, *Personal Recollections*, 274.

quivered and his eyes filled with tears as he delivered the words of his chief):

" 'Tell General Howard I know his heart. What he told me before, I have in my heart. I am tired of fighting. Our chiefs are killed. Looking Glass is dead. Toohoolhoolzote is dead. The old men are all dead. It is the young men who say yes and no. He who led on the young men is dead. It is cold and we have no blankets. The little children are freezing to death. My people, some of them, have run away to the hills and have no blankets, no food; no one knows where they are— perhaps freezing to death. I want to have time to look for my children and see how many I can find. Maybe I shall find them among the dead. Hear me, my chiefs. I am tired; my heart is sick and sad. From where the sun now stands I will fight no more forever.' "[13]

Two hours later, Joseph rode slowly up the hill, accompanied by five of his warriors on foot. When he reached the group of waiting officers, he dismounted and, with an impulsive gesture, offered his rifle to Howard in token of surrender. Howard stepped back and indicated with his hand that Miles should receive it. The chief was then put under guard.

From then until after dusk, the captives straggled in from the hollow. White Bird, the only important chief besides Joseph still alive, did not come. In the darkness he slipped through the relaxed guard lines and headed for Canada, accompanied by fourteen men and a number of women. He had planned his escape that morning and had induced Joseph to surrender first, saying that he, White Bird, would follow after he had finished supervising the surrender of the rest of the Indians.[14] Howard later placed much emphasis on the escape

---

[13] *Report of the Secretary of War, 1877*, 632. Note that a later version of the story has Chief Joseph delivering the speech directly to General Howard rather than to the tribal council.

[14] *Report of the Secretary of War, 1878*, 180.

of White Bird, insisting that his treachery made void the terms granted the rest of the prisoners. This was most unfair. After Joseph was under guard in Howard's camp, he could not be held responsible for the actions of Indians at a distance, especially the followers of another chief. Joseph was obligated only for his own men. It was up to Howard to guard the rest of the captives or to make an agreement with their chief, White Bird.

Howard asked some of the friendly Sioux to run down all the small groups of Nez Percés hiding in the hills, but the Sioux would not.[15] A few of the strays were captured later, but most of them either joined White Bird in Canada or were slaughtered by their old enemies, the bloodthirsty Gros Ventres and Assiniboins. In all, 100 were reported to have escaped.

The captives numbered about 418, consisting of 87 men, 184 women, and 147 children. Of Joseph's children, only the baby girl born during the Whitebird Canyon fight remained. About half of the men and many of the women were wounded. The Indians surrendered 1,100 horses, 100 saddles, more than 100 guns, and various other articles.

It had taken General Howard four months to halt the great trek of the Indians, and the Nez Percé War had proved to be costly for the government. Army reports indicate that the extra cost (above normal expenses) to the three military divisions participating in the pursuit—the Pacific, the Missouri, and the Platte—had been $931,329.02. Official casualty lists showed that 127 soldiers and approximately 50 civilians were killed; 147 soldiers were wounded; and that approximately 151 Indians were killed and about 88 wounded. Was half the Wallowa worth the price?

[15] *Report of the Secretary of War, 1877,* 31.

32: Flatboating on the Yellowstone

THE captives were taken at once to Fort Keogh, expecting to pass the winter there and to return to Idaho in the spring. Soon an order from General Phil Sheridan, Miles's superior officer, instructed that all the Nez Percés should be sent to Fort Lincoln at Bismarck, Dakota Territory, because it would be cheaper to feed them there. Miles vainly protested against this breach of faith. He had become a staunch friend of Joseph, rating him above all other Indians he had ever known in personality, character, and intelligence. Miles was convinced that the best solution, as well as the most honorable one, was to return the captives to their own country in Idaho as had been promised.

However easy it might have been to order the prisoners transported through 800 miles of wilderness infested by hostile Indians, the task itself presented many difficulties. Few of the 400 were able-bodied adults capable of marching overland. Special provisions had to be made for the wounded, the sick, and the children if they were to survive the journey. Steamboats were out of the question at that time of year because of the low water and the two very bad rapids farther down the Yellowstone.

The army officers decided to use a fleet of fourteen flatboats moored near the fort. These had been built near Livingston and had been floated down to the fort loaded with vegetables, butter, and eggs from the Gallatin Valley for the soldiers' mess.[1] The boats were about thirty feet long, eight feet wide, and could accommodate from twenty to twenty-five persons apiece. In each boat were placed a number of the aged, the sick, the wounded, some able-bodied women to look after them, two or three grown boys to help with the oars, and some of the smaller children. The able-bodied men and some of the women marched overland with the wagon train under military escort. One man was considered sufficient to steer each flatboat, supervise the rations, and guard his score of prisoners.

Earlier in the season, the boat trip would have been quite a pleasant outing for the Indians, who had been accustomed to nothing larger than canoes. Now the chill fall air warned them that they must make all speed if they wished to avoid being caught in the ice, yet the dangerous character of the river allowed them to run only during the daylight hours. Each night they tied up the boat, preferably at an island where there would be less danger of an attack by the Sioux. Most of the Indians slept on the shore, leaving plenty of room for those too ill to endure the transfer each night and morning. By this arrangement, the trip was easier on all concerned and several more passengers could be carried on each boat.

Rations of dried pork, brown sugar, hardtack, rice, beans, flour, and baking powder for the trip were issued to each boat by the army commissary at Fort Keogh. In addition, each boat had a large sack of green coffee to be roasted and ground as it was needed. For fresh meat, the men shot an occasional deer, while the boys hunted beaver, ducks, and sage hens. It is an excellent testimonial to the Nez Percé character that the single white man in one of the boats did not hesitate to lend his gun to the hunters and that the boys were allowed to make bows

[1] *New Northwest*, October 5, 1877.

and arrows. Luckily we have the firsthand account of Fred G. Bond, one of the flatboatmen on the trip:

"Just at the streak of dawn the Indians now my people began to move arround. Coffee Hardtack with a piece of boiled salt pork was the food for our breakfast. The evening befor I had them place stones filled between with sand to build a fire on the bottom of the boat to cook at any time and keep coffee hot for the weather was cool showing that winter was near. After breakfast everything that we had no use for was thown into the river and the coals and chared ends of fire wood was covered with sand all moccasin tracks were beaten out with a dead leafless brush and to all appearance you hardly knew there been a camp there. This was done to blind some roveing hostiles from following us. I had all the heavy baggage piled in the stern of the boat thus relieving her bow and causing more surface at the stern for water preasure giving the boat more speed. That summer Montana could boast of a bumping crop of grasshoppers thousands had fell in the river that now formed a rope like mass for miles and miles following in the swiftist channel of the river. Shades of Night [all of these names for the Indians were given to them by the boatman] who was now at her post of duty pointed out this endless chain of grasshoppers and I nodded my head yes so. She took up her chant, swing her arms the way she wished me to stear and my people was platting and cleaning their hair drinking coffee and was jolley. Good bye to our neighbors the rest of the flat bottomed fleet. Everything was done for speed. In a long stretch of the river the young Indians plyed the now muffled side sweeps, not a rag was allowed to drag over the side of the boat, even if one of the children reached over the side of the boat its mother rage at them and like to-day speed was king. There was times that Shades of Night hugged so close to some cutbank her following the swiftist of the river we all have to duck down to dodge under some bent over trees or be swept overboard. . . . Each day at mid sun I tied up for an hour giving my people time to relieve their limbs moving around on mother earth. The boy's shaped bows and arrows from the young groth of ash to shoot the bank beaver that was plentyfull. . . .

"I tied up one eving at this table sage brush lands and told Washington to take the young Indians with him and kill some sage hens for meat. They returned with five sage hens they had killed with their bows and arrows. . . . We was now down the river far enough to catch shovel nose spirgeon so I made a fish hook out of wire from a camp kettle and with a ten foot line of luck string I caught a 3 foot fish, this started them wild for fishing. Then we shot Wolf Rapids. These rapids are longer than Buffalo Rapids and arc wild and dangerous but they contain more water because the river is more narrow and deep with the help of Powder River flow most all the rocks are covered but there is no main channel that I know of. The early day steamboats came up the rapids by towline fastened to the shore and a windlass on the steamboat. . . .

"Shades of Night complained that the skunks was trying to get our grub on the boat at night so we had to pole the boat out in deeper water at night or loose some of our rations. . . . We were also now in the land of the Bull Berry and they were fully ripe. A Bull Berry is red and tastes some what like a cramberry. Stewed with sugar they are good food for travelers. My People knew of this food and they geathered pounds of it sad for our sugar ration. If we happened to tie up for our mid sun rest near a berry patch Washington had to cut a whip to herd them aboard again. . . .

"The weather was extreamly fine with cool frosty nights. After tieing up for the nights and our feast was over I would explain to my people about our head chief at Washington, D. C. . . . We seat there and talk till the moon would throw its silvery rays on the frozen river mist on the drift wood.

All then would be hushed when Washington gave a prayer and at times the beavers at play would scent Shades of Night and dive giving the water a slap with their paddle like tail that caused a report like that of a pistol. . . ."

When the boat reached Fort Buford far ahead of the rest of the flotilla it was detained. "[The colonel there] said I had no business to run away from the rest of the flotilla and he put me under garrison arrest until he heard from Fort A. Lincoln. . . .

"They assigned me to a companys quarters with beding and company rations for there was no room in the guard house. . . . The Officer of the day told me to keep inside the lines of the garrison it was all right. I asked a passing corporal the way to haybag quarters. He was a married man and he lived in haybag row. A Haybag is a married or single white woman who does laundry sews and makes bread, cakes and all kinds of goodies for the soldiers to buy at all times. They was then furnished quarters and fuel by the government free. So he took me to his wife's quarters and I bought all the white bread and cakes they had along the intire row. . . . With the help of some white children I got all my titbits down to my people who had a good fire and coffee made."

About the time the last of the flotilla arrived from up the river, word came from Fort Lincoln that all the boats should leave at once before the river froze. It was now early November.

"Everything was ready except rations. They was rushed aboard while I was waiting for my clearance papers I sent Viola and her mother to haybag row to buy up all the bread, cakes and pies they had. In my rations I received twenty-five pounds of spuds to be eaten raw to kill the scurvey if it appeared also one gallon of vinegar. This was a great help for medican. . . . Once more we was drifting on that vast muddy river that would put weak coffee to shame by its color. . . . A smokeless fire was now burning on our pebble stove with three gallons of pure Rio for my people to drink eat and be merry. On we drove till day turn to twilight then I drove our craft upon a gravely beach. . . .

"Day after day we sailed, drifted and pushed ice packs from our bow. . . . Once in a while deer or antelope would fall before the never failing shot of Washington and the twang of the youth Indian bow with steel pointed arrows would furnish beaver tail for replenish our feast, for beaver tail is good food if cooked proper."

At the Mandan villages, the party was in serious danger. The Indians feared that the Nez Percés might be the advance guard of a hostile raiding force, and 300 Mandans crowded to the shore, ready to start a fight with the captives.

"Two middle aged Indians kept crouding in the river towards the boat. I halted them but still they pressed towards the boat then I thought of what Billy Edwards the light weight champ of years ago had taught me at Woodhaven, L. I. A good upper cut to the point of chin the result would be a knock out blow, so I stept quickly towards those two and gave each of them a good upper cut. They each fell in the river knocked out. . . . Then I backed to the boat and stood there with folded arms. I heard a small moan behind me and knew it was Shades of Night ready to sink her eight inches of sharp steel to the hilt on the first one who toutch our boat, then I seen two young bucks trying to work their way with a bull boat to our stern. . . . I plunged into deeper water and shoved their bull boat out into swifter water and they was carried further down stream. . . . I did not wish bloodshed. What would certainly happen if any Mandan reached our boat. . . . I heard a deep snarl from Washington who held ready our only gun and the young Nez Percé with bow and arrows."

Finally, a government employee, Mr. Samuels, arrived and the boat was allowed to procced down the river.

"We push off safely except the small Mandan boys pelted us with rocks on our way till I got my gun. That bluff them away."[2]

In a few days, the boat reached Fort Lincoln. Because of the wild tales told them at Fort Buford, many of the Nez Percés expected to see the whole band of prisoners executed.

"I made the Fort landing all right and threw to them my bow line. My boat swong down stream and I made them fasten a stern line. A landing plank was put in place by some soldiers. A young officer who had a company of armed men lined up demanded me to hussel those Indians a shore lively. I asked him if he was the commanding officer and he said no, that he was the officer of the day and had no time to fool around. So I told him cold I had orders to deliver these people and boat to the commanding officer only. He was hot and so was I for I could see he was from West Point, N. Y. and needed a souse in the river to relieve him of some of the West Point starch. He sent an orderly for the commanding officer who soon came and proved to be a western man. I explained to him all about my scared people and how they had traveled with me some 600 miles by water giveing me no trouble. If he would withdraw the company of soldiers and get an ambulance we have no trouble to land them."[3]

On November 17, 1877, the *Bismarck Tri-Weekly Tribune* gave the following account of the arrival of the Nez Percé captives:

"Saturday forenoon Major Bates and two companies of the First Infantry, arrived in mackinaws with two hundred Nez Percés, comprising the wounded, women and children. They were quartered at Fort A. Lincoln. They were eight days coming from Fort Buford with a comparatively easy

---

[2] Contrast this eyewitness account with the garbled version in Miles, *Personal Recollections*, 279.

[3] Fred G. Bond, *Flatboating on the Yellowstone*, 8–18.

voyage. The balance of the captives, 240, with the Seventh Cavalry are expected in this evening or tomorrow. The wagon train sent out here to meet the overland portion of the Nez Percés and Joseph will not be needed as there will be no escort back for the wagons from Buford. They will all come on to Bismarck.

"Gen. Miles [although he was often called "General" at this time, Miles was not promoted to brigadier until 1880] and Lieut. Baldwin arrived in an ambulance, Saturday afternoon, from Fort Stevenson. ... the citizens' reception of Gen. Miles, this evening at the Sheridan House, is a foregone conclusion with the following program: . . ."

At the banquet, Colonel Miles was chosen to give the toast to Chief Joseph, who was the guest of honor at a luncheon in the Sheridan House the next day. Bond described Joseph's arrival thus:

"The little city was by now on the buzz getting ready to give a grand ball and supper in honor of Chief Joseph. The ladies at the fort joined in. There was no printed tickets. The tickets was a $10.00 gold coin, ladies free and oppen to all. A runner came in from the West and reported that Gen. Miles and his command had camped the night befor in the Painted Woods. The NPRR agent had wired on the now single wire to Fargo, N. D. 200 miles away for a full train of passenger cars to take the Nez Percé prisoners to the Indian Territory, so my people was to feel the speed of the Iron Horse of one hundred ponies. ... The next day Washington and I had just got seated to breakfast in the resteraunt when the Irish waitress and the cook rushed out of the Resteraunt saying they comming they comming we joined the anxious crowd and shore enough at the head of 4th street comming down its slope was the Gen. Miles command. These troops now formed a hollow squar around the entire command protecting all flanks. The band was playing star spangled banner. Gen Miles with Chief

Joseph on his left was in advance. The appearance of all was heart rending very sad. At the corner of main and 4th street the stampeed commenced. Women children even men rushed the hollow squar with all kinds of cooked food. I seen our resteraunt waitress beating her way through the hollow squar with one half of a boiled ham. They beat the guards back to the center line and the wagons. The command had to halt till each Nez Percé prisoner and even the over land Guard was furnished with food of good kind. . . . I grasped Washington hand and said See. His answer was they are white people not soldiers. Satisfied the women and children drew back and the command passed to the fort. We went in to finish breakfast but Washington was too sad to eat and the Irish waitress said The Divils to put those poor people under soldiers guard."[4]

In his account, Bond confused the great banquet and ball given for Colonel Miles on November 19, 1877, with the dinner given Joseph and his two aides the afternoon of November 21, the day after Miles left for St. Paul. Joseph's invitation, which is unique in the history of our Indian wars, was printed in the *Bismarck Tri-Weekly Tribune*:

> Bismarck, D. T., Nov. 21, 1877.
> To Joseph, Head Chief of the Nez Percés.
> Sir:—Desiring to show you our kind feelings and the admiration we have for your bravery and humanity, as exhibited in your recent conflict with the forces of the United States, we most cordially invite you to dine with us at the Sheridan House, in this city. The dinner to be given at 1½ P. M. to-day.

The invitation was accepted.

"Joseph and the other chiefs named, about twelve o'clock, held a reception in the Sheridan Parlors, and was presented to a number of the ladies of the house. They were told that

[4] *Ibid.*, 18–20.

328

this respect was on account of their humanity to our soldier prisoners.

"The dinner was heartily enjoyed; the first square meal since they left home last June. Yellow Wolf wanted to know if he could have what he asked for. Willey answered, 'Yes.' Yellow Wolf replied 'Salmon.' It came; they were indeed tickled. Joseph said, 'Well! Well! this reminds me of my own country.' "[5]

Two days later, with rations of hardtack and beef, the Indians were put on the train for the trip to Fort Leavenworth via St. Paul.

[5] *Bismarck Tri-Weekly Tribune*, November 21, 1877.

ALTHOUGH the terms of surrender granted Joseph had specified that he and his people should be returned to Idaho the following spring, the Secretary of War did not consider the government bound in any way by the promise of General Howard. Over the protests of both Howard and Miles, General Sherman ordered the captives to be sent to Indian Territory. There they would be safe from reprisal at the hands of the still-angry settlers, they could not join any of the other discontented bands in the Northwest, and they could be forced into a more civilized way of living. Sherman believed that once the Nez Percés went back to Lapwai they would renew their demands for the Wallowa country and would refuse to become farmers on the reservation. In Indian Territory, farming would be their only means of making a living and they would be in a poorer position to make demands concerning Wallowa and all the stock left there.

Sherman's fears of new Indian troubles in the Northwest were well grounded. During the summer of 1878, General Howard was busy crushing various rebellious bands, punishing them for raids and depredations. He estimated that at times the hostile forces in his district numbered 800 warriors,[1] four times the greatest strength of the hostile Nez Percés in

[1] *Report of the Secretary of War, 1878*, 128, 210.

330

1877. One can hardly blame the generals for not wanting such a force to secure a leader of Joseph's reputation. They did not realize that the real fighting leaders of the Nez Percés had been killed at Big Hole and Bear Paw. Much of the subsequent opposition to Joseph's return was based on the fear that he would furnish leadership and a rallying point for all the restless Indians.

Even though there were sound reasons for keeping the Nez Percé captives in exile for a time, there is little justification for the treatment given them at Fort Leavenworth. Conditions were not so bad during the colder weather when the lack of sanitation had little effect on the health of the camp. The prisoners were reasonably well fed and had little to do. About Christmas time, Joseph sent a letter to White Bird in care of Major Walsh of the Canadian Northwest Police, in which he said they were being well treated and were amusing themselves by dancing every day.[2]

Warm spring weather brought a drastic change. When the War Department turned the captives over to the Indian Bureau, the agent reported on the Indian camp thus:

"The camping place selected by the commandant for these Indians was in the Missouri River bottom, about two miles above the fort, between a lagoon and the river, the worst possible place that could have been selected and the sanitary conditions of the Indians proved it. The physician in charge said that 'One half could be said to be sick, and all were affected by the poisonous malaria of the camp.' After the arrival of Joseph and his band in Indian Territory, the bad effects of their location at Fort Leavenworth manifested itself in the prostration by sickness at one time of 260 out of 410, and within a few months they had lost by death more than one quarter of the entire number."[3]

[2] *New Northwest*, February 1, 1878.
[3] *Report of the Commissioner of Indian Affairs, 1878, xxxiii.*

331

Other factors than the climate and the poor camping place added to the death rate. The captured band contained a large proportion of old people. The long chase had weakened many of these old ones and the little children. At the time of the surrender, about forty men and some of the women were disabled by wounds. Even allowing for all these factors, there were many deaths that might be charged to neglect.

Once the Nez Percés had become somewhat acclimated and had recovered from their hardships, their story is one of peaceful progress. Each agent who had charge of them commented on their intelligence and industry. In their self-reliance and their interest in churches and schools, they were an agreeable contrast to many of the other tribes. While each year brought an improvement in their conditions, they were not satisfied with their new home and each year petitioned to be returned to their homeland.

The government had not returned any of the horses, saddles, and guns taken from the captives at the time of their surrender, but instead furnished 100 head of cattle as soon as the Nez Percés were settled in Indian Territory.[4] Their ability in handling stock excited the admiration of the agent in charge. In 1880 he wrote: "The Nez Percés appear to be natural herders, and show more judgment in the management of their stock than any Indians I ever saw."[5] Horses were harder to get than cattle, yet three years later they owned 189 horses, 10 mules, and 183 cattle.[6]

In addition, they were raising their own vegetables and much of their grain. They secured a cash income from the manufacture and sale of bows, arrows, moccasins, gloves, and the like.[7] These articles sold readily because of their fine work-

---

[4] *Report of the Commissioner of Indian Affairs, 1879–1880*, 85.
[5] *Ibid.*, 85.
[6] *Report of the Commissioner of Indian Affairs, 1882–1883*, 79.
[7] *Report of the Commissioner of Indian Affairs, 1883–1884*, 89.

manship and the romantic interest surrounding the workers.

In spite of their improved farms and their prosperous state, though far less prosperous than it had been before the war, they longed for their homeland with an intensity that can be understood only by those who have been raised in some beautiful spot which they have later been forced to leave. As the sea, or the desert, or the prairie calls to some people, so did the mountains of the Wallowa call to these poor exiles. They missed their friends, their salmon fishing, their hunting, their camas digging, their summer encampments, but most of all, they missed the smell of mountain air, the taste of mountain water, and the inspiration of mountain peaks. How ignorant a man the commissioner must have been who wrote: "They will have to be sent to Indian Territory; and this will be no hardship to them, as the difference in the temperature between that latitude and their old home is inconsiderable."[8] As though the difference in temperature was all that could matter to an Indian!

All this time, General Miles remained a staunch friend to Joseph. He was constantly recommending that the band be sent back to Idaho, or even to the Wallowa. Public interest in the affair grew after the publication of "Chief Joseph's Own Story" in 1879. This was followed by Howard's "Reply" and later by his book, *Nez Percé Joseph, His Pursuit and Capture*, in 1881. At length, public sentiment reached such a pitch that some of the widows and orphans were permitted to return. Twenty-nine of them reached Lapwai in the summer of 1882.

This concession convinced the others that they too would be sent back soon. They ceased improving their farms and showed no interest in putting up hay for the winter until the agent arranged that the neighboring cattlemen would buy all the hay in case the Indians left before it was used. In 1885, all the rest of the band were sent back to the Northwest, 188 of

[8] *Report of the Commissioner of Indian Affairs, 1877*, 13.

them going to the reservation at Lapwai, the remaining 150, including Joseph, being sent to the Colville Reservation in Washington, more than 200 miles away and on the reservation of another tribe.

The method used in determining how the band should be divided was a rather peculiar one. In 1882, the agent at Lapwai reported to his superiors that the Indians belonging to the Presbyterian church on the reservation had voted to accept the return of thirteen widows, thirteen children (presumably of the widows), and five orphans.[9] It seems rather unusual that the United States government should need permission of an Indian church, dominated by a white missionary, to move its wards from one reservation to another, particularly when the church members constituted a minority in their own locality.

The record for 1885 is not so clear. In the report of the Indian commissioner we find:

"The reason for sending these Indians to two separate agencies was partly on account of their desires in the matter, but principally on account of indictments said to be pending in Idaho against Chief Joseph and some of his immediate followers, for murders committed by them before their removal to Indian Territory in 1878, and numerous threats were made that, in the event of their return to Idaho, extreme measures would be taken by the citizens to avenge wrongs alleged to have been perpetrated by these people over eight years ago."[10]

Such a strong statement does not seem warranted by any of the expressions of the citizens in 1885, although it undoubtably was true of conditions in 1878. Miss Kate McBeth, then a mission worker at Kamiah, indicated in her book that the division was made between Christians (meaning Presbyterians) and the others.[11] That most of the Indians were actually

---

[9] Warner to Trowbridge, October 16, 1882, Lapwai Agency files.
[10] *Report of the Commissioner of Indian Affairs, 1885*, lvii.
[11] McBeth, *Nez Percés Since Lewis and Clark*, 88.

attending church regularly and were well behaved during their stay in the Indian Territory is attested by the various agents in charge of them, so the test was more than living a good life and accepting Christian teachings.

A later report from Nespelem indicates that when land allotments were made at Lapwai under the Severalty Act of 1887, Joseph and his followers could have had farms assigned to them if they had so desired, but they refused. They preferred staying where they were, raising some livestock, and living much as they had before the war, to settling in houses and becoming farmers in a community of unfriendly neighbors. More important, possibly, they still believed they had a good chance to return to the Wallowa. They no longer hoped to have all the whites removed to make room for the Indians, but there was talk of buying farms for the Indians at government expense so they could return to their old home, where they would be much better off than on the poorer farms now available near Lapwai. However, nothing was ever done in the matter.

It is rather difficult to explain why Joseph should have been regarded so highly by all the whites who knew him, excepting only those who lived near his old home. Certainly many of the people who talked so bitterly against him had never even seen him, much less suffered in the least at his hands. Perhaps it is a case of all the racial hatreds and antagonisms of many years, including those of the war, being focused by chance on one of the individuals least to blame, just as, on the other hand, all the admiration for Nez Percé skill, bravery, and character were focused on one man who by chance survived. Strangely enough, the man in both cases was the same, Chief Joseph, giving us a full-fledged Joseph legend in two parts. In one, he is presented as a deep-dyed villain, cruel and treacherous, a lustful murderer, and in the other as the superlative military leader whose genius was responsible for all the

Nez Percé success, a man of noble character, great kindness, and all the other virtues you might care to mention. The truth, of course, lies somewhere between the two, with Joseph's admirers having the weight of historical evidence in their favor, the villainies being supported only by local folklore.

A sad feature of the war is that it did not end the friction between red man and white in Idaho. Again and again, the settlers clamored loudly for troops to annihilate bands of peaceful Indians gathered at the root grounds for some tribal celebration. The whites still demanded possession of all the Indian pasture lands and even their improved farms. They wanted to withdraw the fishing rights guaranteed the Indians by the treaties[12] They obstructed and hindered the agents in many ways, including the sending of anonymous vile charges to the Indian Bureau or forging an Indian's signature to a fraudulent complaint. They still wanted one law for the whites and another for the red men, but they wanted the right to try the red men in the prejudiced local court. In 1883, the agent at Lapwai wrote concerning the last proposal: "An Indian would not receive justice in a jury trial in four cases out of five."[13]

The same group of men who were so opposed to Indians in general were very anxious that Joseph should not be allowed to return to the reservation, for he was by now the most powerful leader in the tribe and he would rally the Indians against white aggression. He would be more of an obstacle to the whites than before the war, for now he had friends in high government circles who would be ready to listen to his side in any complaint before deciding it.

Reservation chiefs and leading Nez Percé church members united with the whites and their missionaries on this one item, all of them acting from self-interest. Joseph at Lapwai

[12] *Report of the Commissioner of Indian Affairs, 1887–1888, 85.*
[13] *Report of the Commissioner of Indian Affairs, 1882–1883, 56.*

would reduce the power of each to a considerable extent, even though he did not strive for the tribal leadership. These groups combined to spread stories of Indian crimes, attributing them all to Joseph.

Seemingly, the stories became more violent against the chief as his reputation increased in the East, making his return more probable. If the citizens of Idaho once admitted the truth concerning Joseph and the causes of the war, how could they justify their own actions in the matter? It was shortly after the publication of "Chief Joseph's Own Story" had aroused such interest and sympathy for the exiled chief that Arthur Chapman, professing to be Joseph's friend, began circulating the entirely false tale that Joseph had killed Mrs. Manuel with his own hands during those bloody days along the Salmon River.[14] All reliable witnesses who were acquainted with the events of that week were absolutely certain that Joseph was many miles from the spot at the time the woman was killed by men from White Bird's band and by some of the wild young men of the tribe, but even to this day the false story is given credence in some circles.

A rather ironical development of the affair was that the Indians of Joseph's own band, and Joseph himself, the least guilty of all the nontreaty group as far as the Salmon murders were concerned, were thus reviled and threatened with violence while the actual culprits and their chief, who probably was not present during the killings, were overlooked. White Bird, who had run off to Canada after the surrender, and several of his men were allowed to drift back to Lapwai without arousing any protest.

[14] Howard, *Nez Percé Joseph*, 101.

34: Aftermath

IN one important respect, the Nez Percé War of 1877 had simplified the Nez Percé problem because it had eliminated the antitreaty faction. Those who had not been killed in the war or exiled to the Indian Territory drifted back to the reservation a few at a time since there was no other place for them to go. Once they had submitted to the agent, every effort was made to break them of their old ways and of the bad habits acquired from their wild life. The first step was always the most difficult, for when they first appeared on the reservation they liked to ride around in their war regalia, boasting of their past deeds and of their freedom from farm work. Like veterans the world over, those who talked the loudest were almost always those who had the least to talk of and were inclined to get into minor difficulties, leading some of the older boys with them.

Monteith was able to handle these problem cases with little difficulty and no violence. He realized that the best method was to strip them of their glamour, so he forced them to wear ordinary coats instead of blankets and to cut their long hair.[1] This simple change in costume robbed them in one stroke of most of their romantic appeal. They found it hard to strut

[1] *Report of the Commissioner of Indian Affairs, 1878, 53.*

under such a handicap and soon settled down to ordinary work.

During this period, punishment was inflicted promptly on offenders against the peace of the reservation, and they could not evade the officials by a flight to one of the nontreaty villages, as they had done before the war. By far the most common breach of the peace was getting drunk. Although the government regulations forbade the selling of liquor to Indians, there were many ways of evading the rules. A common one was for a white man married to an Indian woman to keep open house for his wife's relatives and their friends. In addition, the half-bloods, who had full standing on the reservation as members of the tribe, were treated as whites in the saloons of the neighboring towns, although this equality did not apply anywhere else. Even under such circumstances, the low number of cases of drunkenness registered at the agency indicates that the Nez Percés, in sobriety, compared favorably with the whites of the region.

The commissioner's report for 1878 contains an account of the punishment meted out to drunken Indians:

"Such cases as have come to my notice have been summarily dealt with. My mode of punishment has been to confine the guilty party in the guard house at Fort Lapwai for thirty days with a request that he be kept at hard labor during that time, and take one horse to pay for his board. The horse is sold and the proceeds is paid into the hands of the commanding officer of the company which furnished the rations. This mode has proven to be a success. The loss of the horse is the heaviest part of the punishment."[2]

This form of punishment was used until the troops were withdrawn in 1885. The agent claimed that the Indians near the post showed a decided improvement in their morals as soon as the troops had gone and that there was less need of the guardhouse. After that the Indians were fined by the

[2] *Ibid.*, 54.

agent, the amount ranging from five dollars for fighting to thirty dollars for unlawful cohabitation.[3] On the basis of court records alone, one would conclude that the Nez Percés were, on the average, of higher moral standards and social conduct than the average white community.

Yearly reports of the agents showed a steady increase in the material prosperity of the tribe. Each year, more land was placed under cultivation, more houses were built, more children were in school. All these and many other less important items indicate that the tribe were making steady progress toward the goal set for them.

Friction between red man and white continued, many minor difficulties being reported each year. The Indians complained of white men's pasturing their stock on the reservation, of timber's being stolen, of the illegal sale of liquor. The whites objected to the Indians' hunting in the Wallowa each summer. Summer encampments were always a source of annoyance to the settlers in the vicinity. Stock disputes of all sorts were quite common. On the whole, however, the complaints gradually decreased in number and importance.

Besides recording the steady improvement of the tribe, the agents' reports followed a set pattern in one other way. Each new man, on taking over his duties, emphasized the poor condition of all the buildings and improvements on the reservation, and went on at great length to tell of the many changes for the better under his efficient management, until one wonders if this was a required formula and a part of the Indian Bureau ritual.

Until 1880, the head chief and the twelve subchiefs were paid yearly salaries, presumably to keep their charges under control and to punish them for minor offenses. The system had numerous defects, but it could not be changed until the period stipulated in the treaty had elapsed. When 1880 brought an

[3] Lapwai Agency Cash Record Book, April, 1893–December 31, 1895.

end to the payments under the treaty, the agent succeeded in organizing an agency police to take care of the work formerly assigned to the chiefs. The police were picked men and rendered very good service. Offenders arrested by them were tried by a court of three wise men of the tribe rather than by a council of chiefs. This system was so satisfactory that it was used until the Indians came under the local courts after the disbanding of the tribe in 1895.

In this matter of breaking the power of the chiefs and in many other ways, the agents worked closely with the local church, even after the mission board had lost all official control over the appointments. A good way for an agent to get into much trouble in Washington was to oppose any of the church practices even when he knew they were against the best interests of the tribe. It was less dangerous for him to defy state and county officials or the local businessmen of the community than to oppose the missionaries in anything.

The Presbyterian missionaries continued in an unbroken line from the return of Henry Spalding to the reservation in 1872 to take up the work so rudely interrupted by the Whitman massacre twenty-five years before. He found that a large number of the Indians still remembered him and that a large portion of the tribe was again interested in religious instruction, with much of the same spirit they had shown during the first years of the early mission. In the two years remaining before his death, he preached a great deal and baptized a large number of converts. After his death in 1874, Sue McBeth took over the work.

Miss Sue McBeth had been sent to Lapwai in 1873 by the mission board to serve as a teacher in the agency school. John Monteith was very much disappointed with her work there. She was about forty years old at the time and partly crippled as the result of some sort of paralytic stroke. Her physical disability prevented her from handling her schoolwork properly, but Monteith realized that it would be impolitic to discharge her. He finally relieved her of all her school duties and provided her with a house at Kamiah, where she was given the task of training several promising young Nez Percé men for the ministry. The new work could be conducted in the living room of her home, unhindered by her physical disability.

In this new work, Sue McBeth's remarkable mind and spirit were soon able to show their worth, and after being a misfit grade teacher she became the spiritual guide and counsellor for a large portion of the Nez Percé tribe. Her pupils filled the pulpits in the local churches and even traveled to other reservations throughout the West to preach to their red brethren.

The Catholic mission at Slickapoo, a few miles above Lapwai, protested that it was unfair for the agent to use government funds to educate young men for the Presbyterian ministry when the Catholics were denied permission to erect even a schoolhouse on their own land and at their expense. Because of this protest, Miss McBeth was dropped from the agency payroll, but she was able to continue her work with the help of funds from the mission board. Soon afterward she moved to Lapwai, where, through the benefactions of a wealthy Pittsburgh woman, a house was deeded to her as her personal property. Here she was joined in 1879 by her younger sister, Kate McBeth.

The two sisters were sincere in their efforts to bring out the best in Nez Percé character and to make useful citizens of the tribesmen. They thought this could best be done by doing away with all the old life and the old ways. With this in mind, they fought against Indian customs, Indian dress, Indian trinkets, Indian horses, and particularly those spirited, colorful steeds known as war horses. Of course, they opposed horse racing, gambling, and drinking, and they always fought against the power of the chiefs, a power that had grown since the chiefs had been placed in charge of the distribution of the treaty goods and could punish their enemies by withholding their share of goods each year.

"She [Sue McBeth] fully believed that there could be no Christian citizenship in any tribe, until the tribal relations were broken up, and that the churches could not long exist that were not established on the purity of the home. The two objects to be attained were clearly before her. The first, the power of the chiefs over the people must be broken, and the man must feel his individuality instead of feeling he was part of a band. Second, the moral tone of the people must be raised."[4]

This meant in practice that a man should transfer his loyalty from his band and his chief to his church and his missionary teacher, for Miss McBeth believed she should dominate the Indians even more completely than the chiefs had done. While she was willing to forgive them for many of their lapses, she maintained that the breaking of the Seventh Commandment should be reason enough for the expulsion of a church member or the exclusion of a prospective member. She did not explain why this one commandment should be so much more important than all the rest, nor why she was so horrified by the sight of an Indian with any portion of his body uncovered.

She and her sister were willing to help the women in learning to care for their families, to keep house, to cook, and to make clothes, no matter how sinful they might be, but if they had broken the Seventh Commandment she would not allow them to learn to read the Bible: "A book must not be put into the hands of a dishonorable woman, thereby giving her influence, or power, among her people for harm." To this Kate

4 McBeth, *Nez Percés Since Lewis and Clark*, 88.

McBeth added her own comment: "The desire of the people to know and read was so great, she knew she could draw the line tight, and still have good schools."[5]

Through the efforts of these two women, the Nez Percés built up a good church system and made excellent progress in settling down as ordinary farmer folk. The missionary work had the effect of again dividing the tribe, however, because the teachers tried to prevent all association between the church crowd and the "heathen" group. They taught the church members that such contact was "sinful" and tried to keep the groups separate even at celebrations and holiday gatherings.

Throughout the period from 1867 to 1895, the Catholic mission was working steadily for its converts. Without government help, even against rather open opposition on the part of the various agents, the work prospered. The priests did find the Nez Percés harder to convert than the Coeur d'Alênes or the Flatheads, but they kept trying. At no time did the Catholic church have as many members as the reservation Presbyterian churches, but as late as 1895, eighty-five pupils were enrolled in the church school at Slickapoo.[6]

Today a resident Jesuit priest still cares for a small congregation at the old mission and helps with the large orphanage for both white and Indian children which has been built nearby.

At Lapwai, a niece of the McBeths, Miss Mazie Crawford, lived for many years in the house which she inherited from her aunts and carried on the work which they began. She wielded a great deal of influence in the church, acting as guide, protector, and friend of the many Indian families. Both she and Kate McBeth have written accounts of the mission work.

[5] *Ibid.*, 103.
[6] James H. Hawley, *History of Idaho*, 832.

344

Nez Percé mother and daughters in holiday dress display cornhusk bags they have made.

Nez Percé girl and finery, Kamiah, 1891.

Nez Percés Elizabeth Penney and two friends playing with dolls at Kamiah, 1892. (Courtesy Idaho Historical Society)

Old woman weaving cornhusk bag, photographed by Major Lee Moorhouse, ca. 1900. (Courtesy Smithsonian Institution, B.A.E. Collection)

35: Lands in Severalty

WITH the first rush of settlers to the western lands, Congress had attempted to solve the Indian question by the establishment of reservations in the more remote areas on land supposedly of little value to the whites. The continued advance of the farmers and miners led them to encroach on all the reservation areas, and in each case the story followed the broad outlines of that of the Nez Percés. Since the reservations, as they had been handled, had failed to solve the Indian problem, it became necessary to adopt a new plan, preferably one that would prevent the Indians from retarding the development of the country in which they lived.

The chief objections to the reservation plan, on the part of the whites, were that it blocked off large areas of land that should have been available for exploitation; it gave the Indians more than their share of the natural resources of a section; it prevented the local government from levying taxes on the Indians; and it kept the Indians outside the jurisdiction of the local courts, subject to a different code of laws.

If the reservations were abolished and the Indians were given full citizenship, all these objections would be removed at once. To achieve this end, Congress passed what is usually known as the Severalty Act of 1887. The act acquired its name from the chief provision that Indians would henceforth hold their lands in severalty instead of in common. Each family head would have a deed to his own holdings, which would then be subject to the usual laws of the community in which he lived. In order to prevent fraud and the wholesale exploitations of the new landowners, the act provided that the process should be a gradual one, usually requiring that a period of twenty-five years elapse before the Indians could sell or mortgage their lands. Also, no tribe should be subject to the provisions of the act until it appeared that it would benefit by the change.

Under the act, each Indian more than eighteen years of age, and each orphan of any age, was entitled to eighty acres of land. Each minor child was given forty acres. Any land remaining in the reservation after the allotments had been made was to be sold to the national government, the money being distributed to the members of the tribe.

By presidential order, the act was applied to the Nez Percés in 1889, but because of various complications the alloting was not finished until 1895. A great deal of care had to be exercised to see that all legitimate claims were allowed and all fraudulent ones rejected. The most knotty problems here were created by the various mixed marriages and by many intertribal marriages. Some of the Indians on the reservation properly belonged to the Cayuse, Umatilla, Yakima, Palouse, Couer d'Alène, Flathead, Shoshoni, or Delaware tribes. It might be that the person from the other tribe was now married to a Nez Percé and was accepted as a member of the tribe. Added complications resulted if these persons had been married before and had brought children from the earlier marriages with them. And last but not least, a child might claim an allotment under one name one day and be loaned to a neighbor long enough to get a second allotment a month later.

The government officials saw that the affair called for

the services of persons more skilled in Indian ways than the ordinary government clerks. To handle the work at Lapwai, they appointed Alice Fletcher, of the ethnological department of Harvard University. She had done a great deal of work with Indian tribes and had been in charge of the special report on Indian education and civilization which the government had printed in 1888.

At Lapwai, Miss Fletcher did a very thorough and careful piece of work. The land-allotment ledger compiled by her is an accurate genealogical record of the Nez Percé tribe for most of the nineteenth century and preserves a great many details which might otherwise have been lost. Here is recorded the name of each Nez Percé entitled to share in the tribal lands, and to identify him beyond question, Miss Fletcher put in the names of his brothers, sisters, father, mother, and usually some of the aunts and uncles and grandparents.

When the allotment of lands had been completed in 1895, the surplus lands were sold for nearly $300,000, giving each family a substantial amount of cash, most of which was spent quickly on articles of real worth—better houses, furniture, farm machinery, farm horses, spring wagons, good clothes, and the like. In this expenditure, the natural shrewdness of the Indians was a great help, but much credit should also be given to the McBeths for their influence.

It had been rather hard to convince the Nez Percés that the excess lands should be sold. It was good grazing land and the tribe wanted to keep it for communal pasture, but pressure on the part of the government and the businessmen finally pushed through the sale. While in some ways it would have been beneficial to the tribe to retain the excess lands, on the whole it seems that they were wise to sell, since their action eliminated one of the chief sources of quarrels between Indian and white over stock and pasture. Also, the Indians probably got more actual good from the cash than they could have expected to receive from the grasslands after the herds of the white men had pastured on them each year.

While the admission of Indians to full citizenship subjected them to the local courts, it also gave them the right to vote in the elections, to the annoyance of many of the local people. Led by their teachers, the Indians proved the deciding factor in voting the county dry under local option.

Many of the Nez Percés have developed into substantial citizens and to this day continue to farm their lands. Some who do not care to work so much land have leased most of their farms to white men, usually at the rate of $1.50 per acre per year. With this cash income, a little garden patch, a house of his own, and a few odd jobs, the Indian manages quite well.

The young people have acquired white ways completely. They do well in the local schools, and occasionally one of them continues through the state university. During the last of the nineteenth century, many of the young men sought adventure by joining the cavalry, making very fine soldiers. By now their choices of jobs and a way of life do not follow any set pattern, but are as varied as those of their white comrades.

The adjustment of the tribe to conditions since the breakup of the reservation in 1895 offers an interesting topic for investigation. Unless a decided effort is made to preserve some of the fine old customs and traditions of the tribe, these may be lost, with the consequent permanent cultural loss to the local community. The people of central Idaho have reason to be proud of this fine tribe and should take interest in preserving something of their colorful past.

Bibliographical Essay on Materials Used

B ECAUSE of the extreme adaptability of the Nez Percés
to new conditions and ways of living, there is little left in
their culture that does not reflect the white influence. Probably
the best museum collection of the tribe is that gathered by the
McBeth sisters after the Nez Percé War and presented to the
Peabody Museum at Harvard University. The best collection
of the twined flat wallets, popularly known as corn husk bags
and a Nez Percé specialty, is owned by Mrs. J. W. Dunning
of Spokane.

Much of the published material on the Nez Percés occurs
as supplementary material in various books on related subjects, so there are few titles in the catalogs under the tribal
name. Incomplete bibliographies will be mentioned in con-
nection with the books in which they occur.

Manuscript Material

An important body of unpublished material used in this work
came from the files of the Indian agency at Lapwai, Idaho, now
in possession of the Idaho Historical Library at Boise, including
six volumes of letter-press copies of the agency correspondence
from January 1, 1871, to December 31, 1876; and from January

1, 1880, to December 31, 1882. In addition, the agency still has the original land-allotment records.

The Indian Bureau archives supplied a typescript of the complete stenographic reports of the treaty council at Walla Walla in 1855. The original diary of Robert Newell for 1868 is in the possession of the Newell family at Lewiston, Idaho.

The Father Joset Papers, in the archives of the Jesuit College of Mount St. Michaels, Spokane, Washington, are letters which contain interesting supplementary material. W. V. Rinehart's manuscript, "Oregon Cavalry," is in the Bancroft Library, the University of California.

Printed Journals, Diaries, and Reminiscences

The most important of this group are *The Original Journals of the Lewis and Clark Expedition, 1804–1806,* edited by Reuben Gold Thwaites (8 vols., New York, 1904–1906). Other early accounts are those by Alexander Ross, *Adventures of the First Settlers on the Oregon or Columbia River,* Vol. VII in Reuben Gold Thwaites (ed.), *Early Western Travels* (32 vols., Cleveland, 1905–1906), and *The Fur Hunters of the Far West* (2 vols., London, 1855) by the same author, a clerk in the various fur companies. His accounts are paralleled somewhat by Ross Cox, *Adventures on the Columbia River* (2 vols., London, 1831), whose work is less dependable than Ross's. Two additional works on the fur trade complete this group. Frederick Merk (ed.), *Fur Trade and Empire* (Cambridge, Massachusetts, 1931) is a reprint of George Simpson's Journal. Supplementing this is a journal by Archibald McDonald, *Peace River, a Canoe Voyage from Hudson's Bay to the Pacific by the late Sir George Simpson, (Governor, Hon. Hudson's Bay Company) in 1828* (Ottawa, 1872).

On the missionary period, George Catlin, *Letters and Notes on the Manners, Customs, and Condition of the North American*

Indians (2 vols., New York, 1842), gives portraits of two of the Nez Percés. John Kirk Townsend, *Narrative of a Journey Across the Rocky Mountains to the Columbia River and a Visit to the Sandwich Islands* (Philadelphia, 1839), mentions Nez Percés at the rendezvous. Samuel Parker, *Journal of an Exploring Tour Beyond the Rocky Mountains under the Direction of the A.B.C. F.M. Performed in the Years 1835, '36 and '37* (Ithaca, New York, 1838), contains much firsthand information. In the series by Archer Butler Hulbert and Dorothy Printup Hulbert, *Overland to the Pacific* (6 vols., Denver, 1935–37), the most useful were Vol. 4, *The Call of the Columbia;* Vol. 5, *The Oregon Crusade;* and Vol. 6, *Marcus Whitman, Crusader.* Joel Palmer, *Journal of Travels over the Rocky Mountains, 1845–1846,* Vol. XXX in Thwaites (ed.), *Early Western Travels,* also comes in the mission period. A diary of Origen Thomson, *Across the Plains in 1852* (Greensburg, Indiana, 1896), describes trading for horses in the Blue Mountains.

Lawrence Kip, *The Indian Council in the Valley of the Walla Walla, 1855* (printed, not published, San Francisco, 1855), and his *Army Life on the Pacific, a Journal of the Expedition Against the Northern Indians, the Tribes of the Coeur d'Alênes, Spokanes, and Pelouzes, in the Summer of 1858* (Redfield, New York, 1859) are valuable, well-written accounts.

Since this account of the Nez Percés stresses the Indian side of the picture and the Indian activities, various works dealing only with detailed accounts of the whites in the Nez Percé War have been omitted. So many of the reminiscences were written so long after the events that they are unreliable for details. One work of much value in studying the battles was Cyrus Townsend Brady, *Northwestern Fights and Fighters* (New York, 1909), which contains many firsthand accounts written by army officers. Another good account is Thomas A. Sutherland, *Howard's Campaign against the Nez Percé Indians, 1877* (Portland, Oregon, 1878), by a newspaper correspondent with the troops. Two excellent volumes, giving much of the story from the Indian point of view are Lucullus Virgil McWhorter, *Yellow Wolf: His Own*

Story (Caldwell, Idaho, 1940), and *Hear Me, My Chiefs! Nez Percé Legend and History* (Caldwell, 1952). A large volume of little value is General Nelson Appleton Miles, *Personal Recollections* (Chicago and New York, 1896). Last of the list, and the most entertaining, is Fred G. Bond, *Flatboating on the Yellowstone* (New York, 1925), by a man who had charge of a boatload of captives in the fall of 1877.

Government Reports and Documents

The most important reports for the Nez Percés are found in the annual *Report of the Commissioner of Indian Affairs,* published in separate volumes yearly since 1854. Before that time, they appeared in the executive documents of Congress. Very little on the Nez Percés appeared before 1854. Reports of Anson Dart, Indian superintendent of Oregon, are found in 32 Cong., 1 sess., *House Exec. Doc. 2; 32* Cong., 2 sess., *House Exec. Doc. 1;* and 36 Cong., 1 sess., *Sen. Exec. Doc. 2,* Pt. 1.

Texts of laws and treaties are taken from Charles J. Kappler (ed.), *Indian Affairs, Laws and Treaties* (4 vols., 1904–1909). Vol. II contains Stevens' treaties. J. Ross Browne, *Report,* dealing with the early Indian troubles and the Whitman massacre is in 35 Cong., 1 sess., *Sen. Exec. Doc. 40.* The War Department *Topographical Memoir, Department of the Pacific,* is 35 Cong., 2 sess., *House Exec. Doc. 114.* A great deal of the material on Isaac Stevens is in the *Pacific Railway Survey Reports,* Vol. XII.

The best account of the military operations of 1877 and some material on the captives in 1878 are found in the two volumes of the annual *Report of the Secretary of War* for the two years. The extra cost of the war is in 45 Cong., 2 sess., *Sen. Exec. Doc. 14.*

Other government publications include the *Special Report* of the Indian Commissioner issued in 1867 and a military report by H. Clay Wood, *The Treaty Status of Young Joseph and His Band of Nez Percé Indians under the Treaties between the United States and the Nez Percé Tribe of Indians, and the Indian Title to the Land* (Portland, Oregon, 1876).

Bibliographical Essay on Materials Used

Publications by state governments include *Oregon Adjutant-General's Report, 1866* (Salem, Oregon, 1866), which is important for the treaty council of 1863, and the State Historical Society of Idaho, *Fifteenth Biennial Report* (Boise, 1936), containing letters and telegrams to the governor during the war scare.

Newspapers

The complete files of the weekly *Teller* of Lewiston, Idaho, for the period of the Nez Percé War are in the city hall at Lewiston. For the Montana campaign, the *New Northwest*, of Deer Lodge, Montana, another weekly, proved valuable. The accounts of the banquets for Miles and Joseph at Bismarck, North Dakota, are from the *Bismarck Tri-Weekly Tribune*.

General and Special Books

A well-illustrated collection of short articles, not too accurate in small details, is Robert G. Bailey, *River of No Return* (Lewiston, Idaho, 1936). S. A. Clarke, *Pioneer Days of Oregon History* (2 vols., Portland, Oregon, 1902), has good material. William H. Gray, *History of Oregon* (New York, 1870), was used only for a description of Narcissa Whitman. James H. Hawley, *History of Idaho* (4 vols., Chicago, 1920), is useful for local statistics.

The only important anthropological work is Herbert J. Spinden, *The Nez Percé Indians* (Lancaster, Pennsylvania, 1908). This also contains a good selected bibliography. The work of James A. Teit, *Salishan Tribes of the Western Plateau*, in Bureau of American Ethnology *45th Annual Report*, is helpful because he makes so many comparisons of his tribes with the neighboring Nez Percés. Samples of Nez Percé language and folklore are given by Archie Phinney, himself a Nez Percé, in *Nez Percé Texts* (New York, 1930), but most of the printed material in their language consists of translations of the Bible.

A useful book to supplement the *Journals of Lewis and Clark* is Olin Dunbar Wheeler, *Trail of Lewis and Clark* (2 vols., New York and London, 1926). Two western books by Washington Irving, *Astoria, or Anecdotes of an Enterprise beyond the Rocky Mountains* (Paris, 1836), and *The Adventures of Captain Bonneville, U. S. A., in the Rocky Mountains and Far West* (New York, 1849), and Hiram Martin Chittenden, *The American Fur Trade of the Far West* (2 vols., New York, 1935), furnish much material on the period 1811–35. Another good book in this group is Bernard DeVoto, *Across the Wide Missouri* (Cambridge, Massachusetts, 1947).

On the early missionary period, E. M. Drury, *Henry Harmon Spalding* (Caldwell, Idaho, 1936), is the best. Supplementary volumes are Cornelius James Brosnan, *Jason Lee, Prophet of New Oregon* (New York, 1932); Elizabeth Spalding Warren, *Memoirs of the West: The Spaldings* (Portland, Oregon, 1917); A. J. Allen, *Ten Years in Oregon: Travels of Dr. E. White and Lady West of the Rocky Mountains* (Ithaca, New York, 1850); Miles Cannon, *Waiilatpu, Its Rise and Fall, 1836–1847* (Boise, 1915); William Isaac Marshall, *The Acquisition of Oregon and the Long Suppressed Evidence about Marcus Whitman* (2 vols., Seattle, 1911).

Material concerning the mountain men came in part from Mrs. Frances Fuller Victor, *River of the West* (San Francisco, 1870), and Alpheus Hoyt Favour, *Old Bill Williams, Mountain Man* (Chapel Hill, North Carolina, 1936). Items on the crossing of the Blue Mountains came from Simeon Ide, *A Biographical Sketch of the Life of William B. Ide* (Claremont, New Hampshire, 1880).

For the Indian troubles of 1847–58, the following proved helpful: Mrs. Frances Fuller Victor, *Early Indian Wars of Oregon* (Salem, Oregon, 1894); Hazard Stevens, *Life of Isaac Ingalls Stevens* (2 vols., New York, 1900); and Benjamin Franklin Manring, *The Conquest of the Coeur d'Alênes, Spokanes and Palouses* (Spokane, 1912).

The most important single work on the war is General Oliver O. Howard, *Nez Percé Joseph: An Account of His Ancestors,*

Bibliographical Essay on Materials Used

His Lands, His Confederates, His Enemies, His Murders, His War, His Pursuit and Capture (Boston, 1881). It differs somewhat from his official report, probably because it was written in self-defense after the publication of "Chief Joseph's Own Story." A recent fictionized biography of Chief Joseph, Chester Anders Fee, *Chief Joseph: The Biography of a Great Indian* (New York, 1936), has some good material, but there is no way of distinguishing his authentic material from the "doctored" or from that which is purely the product of the imagination. This book also contains an uncritical bibliography of material. Helen Addison Howard and George D. McGrath, *War Chief Joseph* (Caldwell, Idaho, 1941), gives practically a blow-by-blow account of the war from the white man's point of view. It contains a comprehensive, well-selected bibliography. Two smaller works on the war are Will Cave, *Nez Percé Indian War of 1877* (Missoula, Montana, 1926), and A. J. Noyes, *In the Land of the Chinook* (Helena, Montana, 1917), which has pictures of the Bear Paw battlefield and a good account of the fighting there. Thomas B. Marquis, *Memoirs of a White Crow Indian* (New York, 1921), has material on the Nez Percé–Crow relations.

Finally, we have two accounts dealing with the mission work of the later period: Kate McBeth, *Nez Percés Since Lewis and Clark* (New York, 1908), and Mary M. Crawford, *Nez Percés Since Spalding* (Berkeley, California, 1936).

Periodical Articles

Items from various periodicals are listed below. In most cases the title indicates quite well the subject matter.

"Captain Bonneville to the Secretary of War, September 26, 1835," in *Washington Historical Quarterly*, Vol. XVIII, No. 3 (July, 1927). "An Indian's View of Indian Affairs," often called "Chief Joseph's Own Story," in *North American Review*, Vol. CCLXIX (April, 1879). Paul C. Phillips, "Battle of the Big Hole," in *Frontier*, Vol. X, No. 1 (November, 1926), a collection of letters dated in 1877. J. W. Redington, "Scouting in

Montana in the 1870's," in *Frontier*, Vol XIII, No. 1 (November, 1932), material originally written in 1877 and revised somewhat for publication. "Bishop Rosati's Letter to Belgium, December 31, 1831," in *American Catholic Historical Society of Philadelphia Yearbook, 1888*, Vol. II, 188–89. "Journal of S. A. Fisher, Chief of Scouts," in *Montana Historical Society Contributions*, Vol. II (1896). Captain Henry Romeyn, "Capture of Chief Joseph and the Nez Percé Indians," in *Montana Historical Society Contributions*, Vol. II (1896). "The Whitman Journal," in *Oregon Historical Quarterly*, Vol. XXVIII, No. 2 (June, 1937). "Narcissa Whitman Diary, 1836," in *Transactions of the Oregon Pioneer Association, 1890*.

The most important of these is Charles Erskine Scott Wood, "Chief Joseph, the Nez-Percé," in *Century Magazine*, Vol. XXVIII, No. 1 (May, 1884). Father Mengarini, "The Rocky Mountains," in *Woodstock Letters*, Vol. XVII, No. 3, gives a valuable comment on the Indian hunters from the St. Lawrence. Articles by Francis Haines in this field are "McKenzie's Winter Camp, 1812–13," *Oregon Historical Quarterly*, Vol. XXXVII, No. 4 (December, 1936); "The Nez Percé Delegation to St. Louis in 1831," *Pacific Historical Review*, Vol. VI, No. 1 (March, 1937); "Northward Spread of Horses to the Plains Indians," *American Anthropologist*, Vol. XL, No. 3 (July, 1938); "The Western Limits of the Buffalo Range," *Pacific Northwest Quarterly*, Vol. XXXI (October, 1940); "Nez Percé and Shoshoni Influence on Northwest History," *Greater America, Essays in Honor of Herbert Eugene Bolton* (Berkeley, California, 1945); "Tom Hill: Delaware Scout," *California Historical Society Quarterly*, Vol. XXV, No. 2 (June, 1946); "Problems of Indian Policy," *Pacific Northwest Quarterly*, Vol. XLI, No. 3 (July, 1950).

Index

Index

Index